AEROFILMS GUIDE

CW00342234

CRICKET GROUNDS

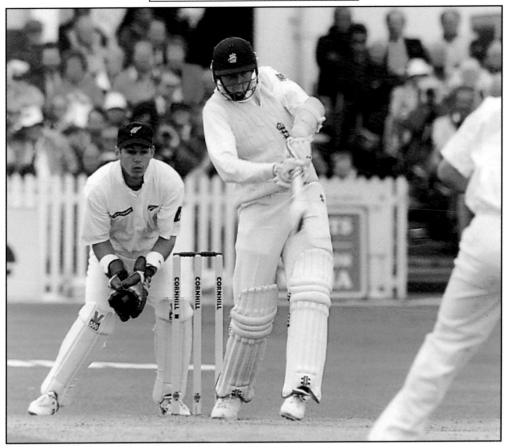

Edited by William A. Powell

DIAL
HOUSE

CONTENTS

About the Author	3
Editor's Note	4
Marylebone Cricket Club	6
Derbyshire CCC	8
Durham CCC	14
Essex CCC	28
Glamorgan CCC	36
Gloucestershire CCC	50
Hampshire CCC	56
Kent CCC	62
Lancashire CCC	70
Leicestershire CCC	80
Middlesex CCC	82
Northamptonshire CCC	86
Nottinghamshire CCC	90
Somerset CCC	96
Surrey CCC	102
Sussex CCC	106
Warwickshire CCC	114
Worcestershire CCC	116
Yorkshire CCC	120
Cambridge University	132
Oxford University	134
Minor Counties Cricket Association	136
Friends of Arundel Castle	140
England NCA XI	142
Scottish Cricket Union	146
Aerofilms Limited	Inside back cover

Dedicated to
My Parents — Jamila and Peter

Aerial photography © Aerofilms
Text © Ian Allan Ltd 1995
Cricket action photography © Empics

First published in 1995

ISBN 07110 2357 3

Published by Dial House

An imprint of Ian Allan Ltd,
Terminal House, Station Approach,
Shepperton, Surrey TW17 8AS.

Printed by Ian Allan Printing Ltd, Coombelands
House, Coombelands Lane, Addlestone,
Weybridge, Surrey KT15 1HY.

Front cover: Lancashire and England's Mike
Atherton (right) and Brian Lara, the West Indies'
record-breaking batsman (left). *Empics*. Aerial
view of Lord's. *Aerofilms*. Lord's from the Mound
Stand. *Patrick Eagar*.

Back cover: Yorkshire and England's Darren
Gough. *Empics*. Kent CCC's ground at
Canterbury (left) and Nottinghamshire CCC's
Trent Bridge (right). *Aerofilms*.

Title page: Mike Atherton. *Empics*

Right: Darren Gough. *Empics*

About the Author

William Powell was born in Lahore in 1964 and has had a life-long interest in cricket. He has represented King's Langley CC, where he was a committee member at 16, Watford Town CC, The Cricket Society XI, and the Gentlemen of Hertfordshire. During family summer holidays he has also represented Budleigh Salterton CC, Rye CC and has played cricket abroad in Australia, Pakistan, and South Africa.

An avid collector of cricket books and memorabilia since the age of 13, he was the Official Scorer to the Pakistan Test team in 1987 and was appointed by the Test & County Cricket Board to act as Official Scorer to the Sri Lankan tourists in 1988. He is a member of MCC, Middlesex CCC, and Surrey CCC (together with a number of other counties), The Cricket Society, The Cricket Writers' Club, and The Association of Cricket Statisticians and Historians. He is a corporate member of The Chartered Institute of Building and is an active member of the Hertfordshire Centre and Eastern Region of the Institute. Other books by the author include *The Wisden Guide To Cricket Grounds* (1989 and 1992), *Association of Cricket Statisticians Cricket Grounds of Middlesex* (1990), *The South Africans in England 1894–1994*, *Cricket in Sound and Vision* (1994), and *Cricket Grounds Then and Now* (1994).

Bibliography

The Wisden Guide to Cricket Grounds, W.A. Powell with A.J.Bannister and P.W.G. Powell, 1989.
The Wisden Guide to Cricket Grounds, W.A. Powell, 1992.
Cricket Grounds Then and Now, W.A. Powell, 1994.
Wisden Cricketers' Almanack 1864-1994.
Wisden Cricket Monthly, The Cricketer and *The Cricketer Quarterly.*

Editor's Notes

This *Aerofilms Guide to Cricket Grounds* provides the first comprehensive pictorial survey of all the grounds currently used for first-class cricket. As well as both vertical and oblique aerial photographs, this guide includes information on the facilities available at each ground.

Each cricket ground has a character of its own; some have changed little over the years while others, particularly those used for international matches, have been substantially modernised in recent times. This has been the result of the need to provide better facilities for larger crowds, and, above all, to comply with legislation on safety in sports grounds.

The grounds included number 72 separate locations in all, varying from Lord's Cricket Ground, which can accommodate some 28,000 spectators with facilities of every type, to the simplest local recreation ground used for cricket (and various other sports), with a modest pavilion, a simple scoreboard and space for little more than 2,000 spectators on temporary seating. Many of the larger venues will be familiar to cricket-goers and television viewers but many others, including small private clubs, local authority recreation grounds, university and public school grounds, will be unfamiliar to many fans. This *Aerofilms Guide* provides a new look at both the familiar and the unfamiliar grounds.

William Powell
Hemel Hempstead
January 1995

Acknowledgements

The compilation of a book on a subject as diverse as cricket grounds must rely on the wholehearted support and assistance of many persons concerned with the administration of the game. I therefore acknowledge with much gratitude the co-operation over several years received from the chief executives, secretaries and administrative staff at all the cricket grounds included in this book. I also thank Simon Forty, Peter Waller and Nick Grant of Ian Allan Publishing, Mike Willis of Aerofilms Limited, and Kevin Alcock of Empics for their assistance.

I acknowledge the sources of the illustrations which include:
Aerofilms Limited, Canterbury Printers, Bramley Books, Empics and Patrick Eagar.

Using This Book

Aerial Photographs & Ground Facilities

All the aerial photographs featured in this book were taken by Aerofilms during the 1994 season. Every attempt has been made to include as much information as possible on the annotations to the photographs, bearing in mind the size of the publication. When defining seating areas, the description 'covered seating' has been used for those areas where open seating is banked above covered seating – as often found at the Test Match venues. Executive Suites and similar restricted covered areas have also been defined as covered seating. Toilets situated in separate buildings have not been defined on the aerial photographs. However, additional toilets are to be found within most of the areas of tiered seating and in other permanent buildings. Similarly, the refreshment and restaurant facilities are usually to be found in the existing permanent buildings or at out grounds in temporary accommodation specially provided on match days. The areas available to the general public and to members are clearly defined at all the county grounds, but at local club grounds, and other venues used only occasionally, arrangements may vary from match to match and from year to year. Special arrangements apply at the six Test Match venues and at any other grounds where reserved numbered seat tickets and car park tickets are sold in advance.

Key to Crowd Records

(GC) Gillette Cup
(NWBT) National Westminster Bank Trophy
(BHC) Benson & Hedges Cup
(JPL) John Player Sunday League
(RAL) Refuge Assurance Sunday League
(AELL) Axa Equity & Law Sunday League
(SL) TCCB Sunday League
(BBC) Buckley's Brewery Challenge
(Tour) Tour Match

Notes on Where to Stay and How to Get There

If you are planning a longer stay or require further details on where to eat *en route*, or on local facilities and places of interest, contact the local Tourist Information Centre for the town you are visiting. If you plan to use public transport or your own – whether by bus, car, rail or air – refer to your local Bus Station, AA or RAC Office, British Rail Travel Centre or travel agent for specific details.

Grounds Used by the Various Counties

The lists of Other Grounds includes those grounds that have been used for matches since 1969. The Second XI Grounds listed are in addition to the 'regular' grounds which are also used for Second XI matches.

Tickets for Major Games

To make sure of your seat at any Cornhill Insurance Test Match or Texaco Trophy One-Day International contact the following ticket offices:

Birmingham (Edgbaston)	0121 446 5506
Leeds (Bass Headingley)	0113 278 7394
London (Lord's)	0171 289 8979*
London (The Foster's Oval)	0171 582 7764
Manchester (Old Trafford)	0161 848 7021
Nottingham (Trent Bridge)	0115 981 7005
Ticketmaster	0171 413 1413

* Contact this Ticket Office or Finalists concerned direct for Benson & Hedges Cup or National Westminster Bank Trophy Final tickets.

Premium Telephone Numbers

Note that at the time of writing all premium telephone numbers (0891/0898) quoted charge at the following rates: 39p/min off peak and 49p/min at all other times.

LORD'S (LONDON)

Address: Marylebone Cricket Club, Lord's Cricket Ground, St John's Wood Road, St John's Wood, London NW8 8QN.

Telephone Number for Prospects of Play: 0171 286 8011.

Entrances: St John's Wood Road – via Grace Gates (Players, Officials, Members, Vehicles); St John's Wood Road – via Bicentenary Gate (Employees); St John's Wood Road – via East Gate (Public); Wellington Road – via North Gate (Members, Vehicles); Wellington Road (Members, Public); Grove End Road (Players, Officials, Vehicles, Employees).

Members' Enclosure: Pavilion (Members Only), Sir George Allen Stand (Members Only, upper level), Warner Stand, Mound Stand (Debenture Holders Only, upper level), Tavern Stand.

Public Enclosure: Grandstand, Compton Stand, Edrich Stand, Mound Stand (Lower).

Covered Stands: All Members' and Public enclosures part covered.

Open Stands: All Members' and Public enclosures part open.

Disabled Areas: Special sections in front of Warner Stand and between Sir George Allen Stand and the Pavilion.

Car Parking Facilities: No street parking, except for a few meters and on Sundays. Car parking available for Members only, entrance from Cavendish Road and Wellington Road. During major matches car parking is arranged by MCC for Members on local school grounds. Public car parking in central London car parks or near Regent's Park Zoo which is now metered.

Ground Dimensions: 166m x 133m.

Ground Capacity: 28,000.

Best Crowd: First-Class Match: 137,915 England v Australia 1953 (5 Days).

Anticipated Developments: New MCC Indoor Cricket School under construction winter 1994/95.

↑ North direction (approx.)

Entrances
E1 Grace Gates St John's Wood Road
E2 Bicentenary Gate
E3 East Gate
E4 Wellington Gate
E5 North Gate

P Pavilion
SB Scoreboard
CP Car Parking
T Toilets
CS MCC Club Shops
M MCC Cricket Museum
CO MCC Club Office
N1 Pavilion End
N2 Nursery End
T St John's Wood Underground
C Central London/West End

Stands
S1 Warner Stand
S2 Grandstand
S3 Compton Stand
S4 Edrich Stand
S5 Mound Stand
S6 Tavern Stand
S7 Sir George Allen Stand (including Middlesex Room)

1 Memorial Garden
2 Harris Garden
3 MCC Indoor Cricket School
4 Nursery Ground
5 ICC Office
6 Middlesex CCC Office/Shop
7 TCCB/NCA Offices

Streets
8 A41 Finchley Road
9 St John's Wood Road
10 Grove End Road

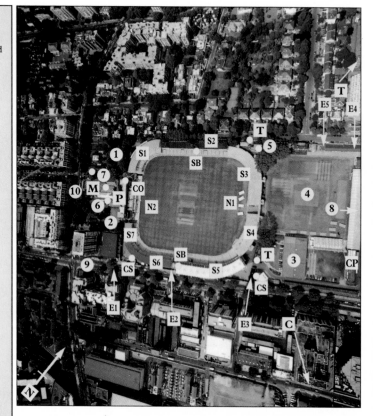

Right Above: South Africa's Kepler Wessels celebrates his century against England at Lord's in the First Cornhill Test of the 1994 series, Jonty Rhodes looks on.

HOW TO GET THERE
Rail: St John's Wood Underground (Jubilee Line) 0.5 mile.
Bus: LRT 6, 8, 13, 16, 16A, 46, 74, 82, 113, 159, 274 pass the ground. Also London Country Coaches 719, 757, 768, 797 from Home Counties pass near ground. (0171 222 1234).
Car: The ground is situated opposite St John's Wood Church bounded by Wellington Road, Wellington Place, St John's Wood Road and Grove End Road.
From north: M1 to motorway terminal roundabout at Brent Cross, then follow A406 North Circular Road, East, then branch right and follow signs West End, take A41 signposted Swiss Cottage and follow Finchley Road to St John's Wood, follow signs Lord's Cricket Ground and A5205 for St John's Wood Road and Grace Gates entrance.
From east: From Holloway district follow signs A503 West End, then at Camden Town follow signs A4201 Regent's Park, enter Regent's Park at Gloucester Gate and use outer circle signposted London Zoo. After passing London Regent's Park Mosque, take immediate right into Hanover Gate and at T-junction take right into A41 Park Road for St John's Wood, keep left for A5205 St John's Wood Road at roundabout for Lord's Cricket Ground.
From west: A40(M) or M41 follow signs Central London, then follow signs A4206 Paddington in Bishop's Bridge Road, enter one-way system signposted Euston and join A5 Edgware Road, then take right into A5205 St John's Wood Road.
From south: From Hyde Park Corner follow signs Ring Road, Oxford into Park Lane A4202, then at Marble Arch follow signs Oxford Circus into Oxford Street A40, then at second traffic lights take A41 Portman Street, follow through Portman Square and Gloucester Place, follow signs A41 Aylesbury and the North, at St John's Wood roundabout take left into A5205 St John's Wood Road for Lord's Cricket Ground.

WHERE TO STAY
AND OTHER INFORMATION
Tourist Information: 0181 760 5630.
Weather: 0898 500401.
Local Hotels: The Hilton International Regent's Park Hotel (0171 722 7722) opposite ground plus many other hotels in central or north-west London.
Local Radio Stations: Greater London Radio (94.9 MHz FM/1488 KHz MW), Capital Radio/Capital Gold (95.8 MHz FM/1548 KHz MW) LBC (97.3 MHz FM/1152 KHz MW).
Local Newspaper: Evening Standard

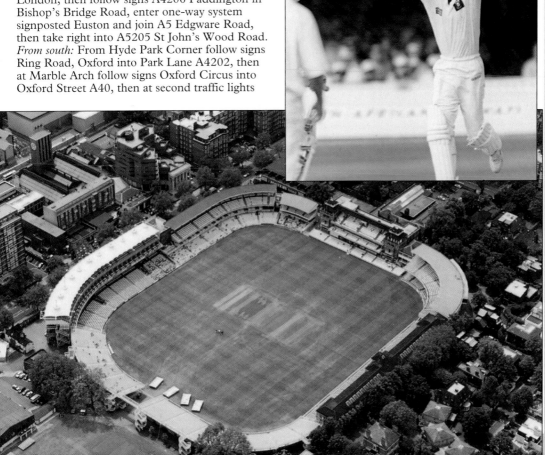

DERBY

Address: County Cricket Ground, Nottingham Road, Derby, Derbyshire DE2 6DA.
Telephone Number for Prospects of Play: 01332 383211.
Entrances: Main Entrance – via Pentagon Roundabout (Players, Officials, Members, Public, Vehicles).
Members' Enclosure: Lund Pavilion, Steetley Stand, Butterley Stand, together with part of the Grandstand seating area.
Public Enclosure: Rest of the ground.
Covered Stands: Lund Pavilion (part), Grandstand (part) and inside Derbyshire County Cricket Supporters' Club Headquarters/Tea Bar area.
Open Stands: Steetley Stand, Butterley Stand, Grandstand (part), temporary seating surrounding the playing area.
Disabled Areas: Next to boundary fence near the South Stand with space for 6–8 cars together

with ample space outside the perimeter of the playing area. Access to the Grandstand is difficult as only steps are available.
Car Parking Facilities: Ample car parking for Members, Public to the south and north-west of the playing area via main entrance off Pentagon Roundabout.
Ground Dimensions: 152m x 167m.
Ground Capacity: 9,500.
Best Crowds: First-Class Match: 14,500 v Australians 1948. Limited-Overs Match: 7,500 v Essex (RAL) 1990.

HOW TO GET THERE
Rail: Derby Midland (BR) 1.25 miles.
Bus: Trent Buses 29 from BR Derby Midland to ground, Derby City 42, 43, 44, 45, 46, 47 from BR Station to Bus Station, thence numerous services pass near ground. (01332 754433).

↑ North direction (approx.)

Entrances
E1 Pentagon Roundabout

P Lund Pavilion
SB Scoreboard
CP Car Parking
T Toilets
CS Club Shop
N1 Grandstand End
N2 Scoreboard End
R BR Derby (direction)
C City Centre (direction)

Stands
S1 Steetley Stand
S2 Butterley Stand
S3 Grandstand

CO Derbyshire CCC Club
    Offices/Indoor Cricket School

Streets
1 A38 Pentagon Roundabout
2 A6 Sir Frank Whittle Way

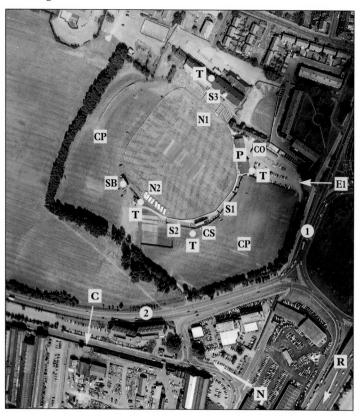

Top Right: Striding back to his mark, Staffordshire born all-rounder Dominic Cork won the Gold Award in the 1994 Benson & Hedges Cup 2nd Round victory over Lancashire at Derby with a swashbuckling 63 not out.

Car: *From north:* M1 Junction 28 follow signs A38 Derby or A6 to Pentagon Roundabout, ground on north side of roundabout.
From east: M1 Junction 25, follow signs A52, then A61 Derby to Pentagon Roundabout.
From south: M1 Junction 24 follow signs A6 Derby, then A52 Ring Road to Spondon, then A61 to Pentagon Roundabout.
From west: A52, A38 and A5111 to Ring Road, then A61 to Pentagon Roundabout.

WHERE TO STAY
AND OTHER INFORMATION
Tourist Information: 01332 255802
Weather: 0898 500411
Local Hotels: Midland Hotel (01332 45894), Clarenden Hotel (01332 365235), Post House Hotel, Sandiacre (0115 939 7800).
Local Radio Stations: BBC Radio Derby (104.5 MHz FM/1116 KHz MW), Radio Trent (96.2 MHz FM/999 KHz MW).
Local Newspapers: Derby Evening Telegraph, Derbyshire Times, Derby Trader.

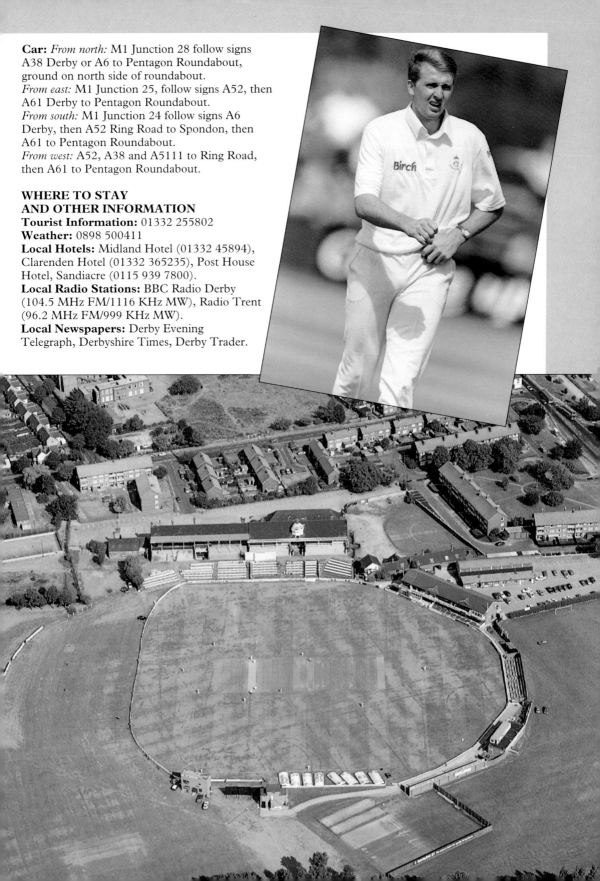

CHESTERFIELD

Address: Chesterfield Cricket Club, The Pavilion, Queen's Park, Boythorpe Avenue, Chesterfield, Derbyshire.

Telephone Number for Prospects of Play: 01246 273090.

Entrances: Boythorpe Avenue (Players, Officials, Members, Public, Vehicles), Park Road (Members, Public), Boythorpe Road (Members, Public).

Members' Enclosure: Pavilion and defined Members' Enclosure situated either side of the pavilion.

Public Enclosure: Rest of the ground.

Covered Stands: Pavilion (part).

Open Stands: Temporary raised seating surrounding the playing area.

Disabled Areas: Next to boundary fence at Pavilion End with space for approximately 6–8 cars, also around the perimeter of the playing area on the former cycle track.

Car Parking Facilities: Car parking available within the ground for Players, Officials, Members only to the west of the playing area adjoining the sports centre. Ample car parking in streets surrounding ground or in nearby town centre car parks a short walk away.

Ground Dimensions: 127m x 117m.

Ground Capacity: 7,500.

Best Crowd: First-Class Match: 14,000 v Yorkshire 1948. Limited-Overs Match: 7,500 v Sussex (GC) 1969.

HOW TO GET THERE

Rail: Chesterfield (BR) 0.75 mile.

Bus: Chesterfield Transport 1 from BR Chesterfield to within 0.25 mile of ground, also Trent Buses and South Yorkshire Traction services from surrounding areas to Chesterfield Bus Station thence 200m walk to ground. (01246 76666).

↑ North direction (approx.)

Entrances
E1 Boythorpe Road
E2 Park Road
E3 Boythorpe Avenue

P Pavilion
SB Scoreboard
CP Car Parking
T Toilets
CS Club Shop
N1 Lake End
N2 Pavilion End
R BR Chesterfield (direction)
C City Centre (direction)

Streets
1 Boythorpe Road
2 Park Road
3 Boythorpe Avenue
4 A617
5 A632

Above Right: South African middle order batsman Daryll Cullinan on his way to 94 against England during the Third Cornhill Test at The Foster's Oval in 1994. He is Derbyshire's overseas player for the 1995 season.

Car: *From north:* M1 Junction 30 then follow signs A619 Chesterfield, then follow signs A619 Buxton and A632 Queen's Park.
From east: A632 or A617 signposted Chesterfield, then as north.
From south: M1 Junction 29, then A617 to Chesterfield, then as north.
From west: A619 or A632 signposted Chesterfield, then as north.

WHERE TO STAY
AND OTHER INFORMATION
Tourist Information: 0114 256 9392.
Weather: 0898 500411.
Local Hotels: Chesterfield Hotel (01246 71141), Portland Hotel (01246 34504).
Local Radio Stations: BBC Radio Sheffield (104.1 MHz FM/1035 KHz MW), BBC Radio Derby (104.5 MHz FM/1116 KHz MW), Radio Hallam (103.4 MHz FM/1548 KHz MW), Radio Trent (96.2 MHz FM/999 KHz MW).
Local Newspapers: Derby Evening Telegraph, Derbyshire Times, Chesterfield Gazette, Chesterfield Star, Sheffield Star.

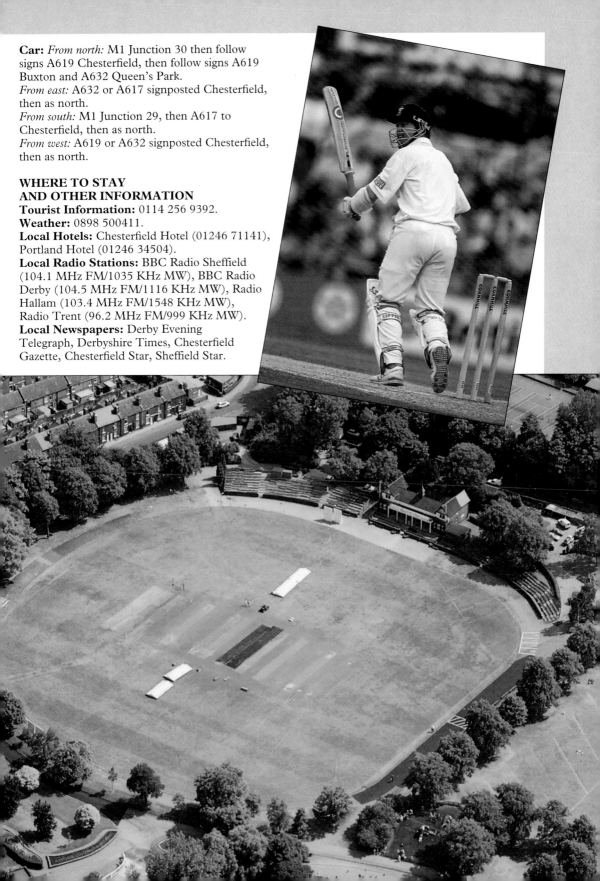

Address: Ilkeston Rutland Cricket Club, The Pavilion, Rutland Recreation Ground, Oakwell Drive, Ilkeston, Derbyshire.

Telephone Number for Prospects of Play: 0115 944 0440 ext 353.

Entrances: West End Drive (Players, Officials, Members, Public, Vehicles), Oakwell Drive (Members, Public).

Members' Enclosure: Pavilion, Pavilion terrace and defined Members' Enclosure.

Public Enclosure: Rest of the ground.

Covered Stands: Pavilion.

Open Stands: East Side Terrace enclosure together with temporary ground level seating surrounding the playing area.

Disabled Areas: No special area although easy access is possible to all parts of the ground for disabled spectators, with the possible exception of the Pavilion terrace. Car parking is available within the ground at the Scoreboard End.

Car Parking Facilities: Ample car parking available to the west of the playing area together with nearby street parking surrounding the ground and town centre car parks a short walk away. Eighty-five cars can be parked in a position to view the cricket at the Scoreboard End of the ground.

Ground Dimensions: 163m x 133m.

Ground Capacity: 7,000.

Best Crowd: First-Class Match: 10,000 v Nottinghamshire 1948. Limited-Overs Match: 8,000 v Somerset (GC) 1977.

HOW TO GET THERE

Rail: Langley Mill (BR) 4 miles, Nottingham Midland (BR) 9 miles.

Bus: Barton Buses 4, 18, 51 from Nottingham Broadmarsh Centre, close to BR Nottingham Midland Station. (0115 925 4881).

Car: Ground situated in town centre off A6007

↑ North direction (approx.)

Entrances
E1 West End Drive
E2 Oakwell Drive

P Pavilion
SB Scoreboard
CP Car Parking
T Toilets
N1 Pavilion End
N2 Scoreboard End
C Town Centre (direction)

Streets
1 West Park Road
2 A6007 Oakwell Drive
3 A609

Above Right: Devon Malcolm seen bowling versus Lancashire in the Benson & Hedges Cup 2nd Round at Derby. He achieved his best bowling performance of 9 for 57 against South Africa at The Foster's Oval during the Third Cornhill Test in 1994.

at rear of fire station.
From north: M1 Junction 26, then A610 and A6096 signposted Ilkeston.
From east: A609, then as north.
From south: M1 Junction 25, then A52 to Stapleford, then A609 signposted Ilkeston, then as north.
From west: A609 or A6096, then as north.

WHERE TO STAY
AND OTHER INFORMATION
Tourist Information: 01332 255802.
Weather: 0898 500411.
Local Hotels: Rutland Arms Hotel, Bath Street (0115 932 3259), Post House Hotel, Sandiacre (0115 939 7800).
Local Radio Stations: BBC Radio Derby (104.5 MHz FM/1116 KHz MW), BBC Radio Nottingham (95.5 MHz FM/1584 KHz MW), Radio Trent (96.2 MHz FM/999 KHz MW).
Local Newspapers: Derby Evening Telegraph, Nottingham Evening Post, Ilkeston Advertiser.

CHESTER-LE-STREET (RIVERSIDE)

Address: County Cricket Ground, Riverside Complex, Ropery Lane, Chester-le-Street, County Durham DH3 3QR.
Telephone Number for Prospects of Play: 0191 387 1717.
Entrances: Ropery Lane (Players, Officials, Members, Public, Vehicles).
Members' Enclosure: Pavilion and defined Members' Enclosure.
Public Enclosure: Rest of the ground.
Covered Stands: Pavilion and other stands (under construction winter 1994/95).
Open Stands: Rest of ground and other stands (under construction winter 1994/95).
Disabled Areas: No special area, request suitable position. Parking by prior arrangement.
Car Parking Facilities: Ample car parking adjoining Riverside Complex for Players, Officials, Members, Public.
Ground Dimensions: 155m x 145m.

Ground Capacity: 15,000.
Best Crowd: First-Class Match: Initial match to be played in 1995. Limited-Overs Match: Initial match to be played in 1995.
Anticipated Developments: New stands and ground under construction, to be ready for 1995 season.

HOW TO GET THERE
Rail: Chester-le-Street (BR) 1 mile.
Bus: X1, X2, X46, X69, 722, 723, 724, 737 Go-Ahead Northern/Tees & District/United/OK Travel/Primrose Coaches/Gardiners through Chester-le-Street 1 mile from ground. (0191 386 4411 ext 2337).
Car: *From north, or east:* A1(M) to Chester-le-Street junction, then follow Shields Road and Park Road North and Central following signs A167 Durham, then at Ropery Lane roundabout turn left off into Riverside Sports Complex for

---

⬆ North direction (approx.)

Entrances
E1 Ropery Lane

P Pavilion
SB Scoreboard
CP Car Parking
T Toilets
CS Club Shop
N1 Ropery Lane End
N2 River End
R BR Chester-le-Street (direction)
C Town Centre (direction)

Stands
1 Stands being constructed during winter 1994/95 for 1995 season

2 CO Durham CCC Club Offices
3 River Wear

Streets
4 Ropery Lane
5 A167
6 A1(M) (direction)

Above Right: An exciting prospect for the 1995 season, Manoj Prabhakar, Durham's new overseas all-rounder seen bowling against England during the England Tour of India in 1992/93.

County Ground and car parks.
From west: A693 or A167 signposted Chester-le-Street, from town centre take Ropery Lane for ground.
From south: A167 from Durham or A1(M) to Chester-le-Street junction, then as north.

WHERE TO STAY AND OTHER INFORMATION

Tourist Information: 0191 384 3720.
Weather: 0898 500418.
Local Hotels: Lumley Castle Hotel (0191 389 1111), Lambton Arms Hotel (0191 388 3265), The Lampton Worm (0191 388 3386), plus several guesthouses in Chester-le-Street.
Local Radio Stations: BBC Radio Newcastle (96.0 MHz FM/1458 KHz MW), BBC Radio Cleveland (95.0 MHz FM/1548 KHz MW), TFM Radio (96.6 MHz FM/1170 KHz MW).
Local Newspapers: Northern Echo, Evening Gazette.

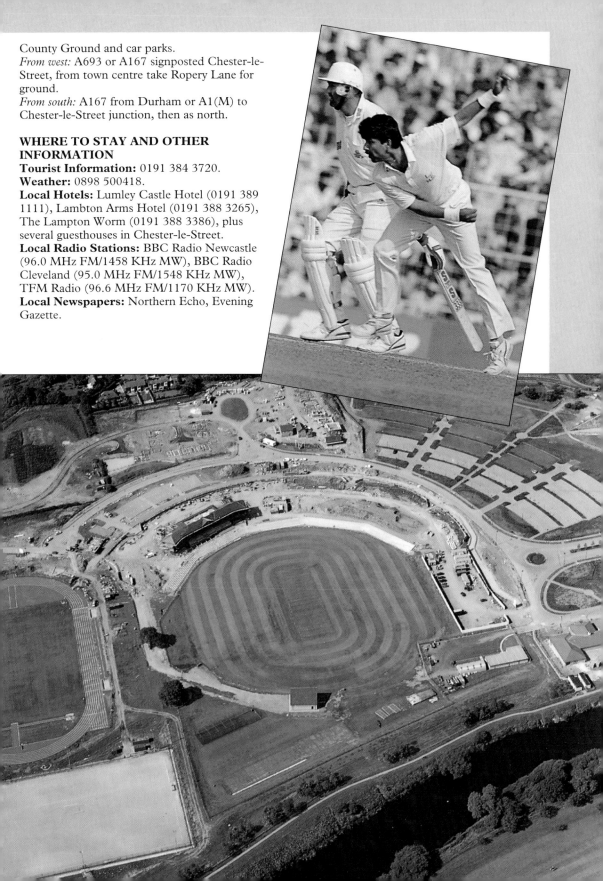

CHESTER-LE-STREET (ROPERY LANE)

Address: Chester-le-Street Cricket Club, The Pavilion, Ropery Lane, Chester-le-Street, County Durham.

Telephone Number for Prospects of Play: 0191 388 3684.

Entrances: Hawthorn Terrace (Players, Officials, Members), Ropery Lane (Members, Public), Eardulph Park – via Chester-le-Street RC Mixed and Infant School (Members, Public, Vehicles).

Members' Enclosure: Pavilion, Pavilion terrace and defined Members' Enclosure.

Public Enclosure: Rest of the ground.

Covered Stands: Pavilion, Clubhouse.

Open Stands: Temporary raised seating areas and ground level seating round the playing area and on the banking surrounding the playing area.

Disabled Areas: No special area, request suitable position. Parking by prior arrangement.

Car Parking Facilities: Available on adjoining school playing field for 1,000+ cars, entered from Eardulph Park, and in town centre car parks. No car parking is available within the ground.

Ground Dimensions: 110m x 109m.

Ground Capacity: 5,000.

Best Crowd: First-Class Match: 4,000 v Pakistanis 1992. Limited-Overs Match: 5,000 v Surrey (GC) 1972.

HOW TO GET THERE

Rail: Chester-le-Street (BR) 0.25 mile.

Bus: X1, X2, X46, X69, 722, 723, 724, 737 Go-Ahead Northern/Tees & District/United/OK Travel/Primrose Coaches/Gardiners through Chester-le-Street 0.25 mile from ground. (0191 386 4411 ext 2337).

Car: *From north or east:* A1(M) to Chester-le-Street junction, then follow Shields Road and Park Road North and Central following signs A167 Durham, then at Ropery Lane roundabout turn right into Ropery Lane for ground and car parks.

↑ North direction (approx.)

Entrances
E1 Hawthorn Terrace
E2 Ropery Lane
E3 Ropery Lane
E4 Car Park

P Pavilion
SB Scoreboard
CP Car Parking
T Toilets
N1 Ropery Lane End
N2 Church End
R BR Chester-le-Street (direction)
C Town Centre (direction)

Streets
1 Ropery Lane
2 Hawthorn Terrace
3 A167
4 A1(M) (direction)

Above Right: Sunderland born, left-arm medium pace bowler, Simon Brown who took a career best 7 for 70 for Durham versus the Australians at Durham University in 1993.

From west: A693 or A167 signposted Chester-le-Street, from town centre take Ropery Lane for ground.
From south: A167 from Durham or A1(M) to Chester-le-Street junction, then as north.

WHERE TO STAY
AND OTHER INFORMATION
Tourist Information: 0191 384 3720.
Weather: 0898 500418.
Local Hotels: Lumley Castle Hotel (0191 389 1111), Lambton Arms Hotel (0191 388 3265), The Lampton Worm (0191 388 3386), or several guesthouses in Chester-le-Street.
Local Radio Stations: BBC Radio Newcastle (96.0 MHz FM/1458 KHz MW), BBC Radio Cleveland (95.0 MHz FM/1548 KHz MW), TFM Radio (96.6 MHz FM/1170 KHz MW).
Local Newspapers: Northern Echo, Evening Gazette.

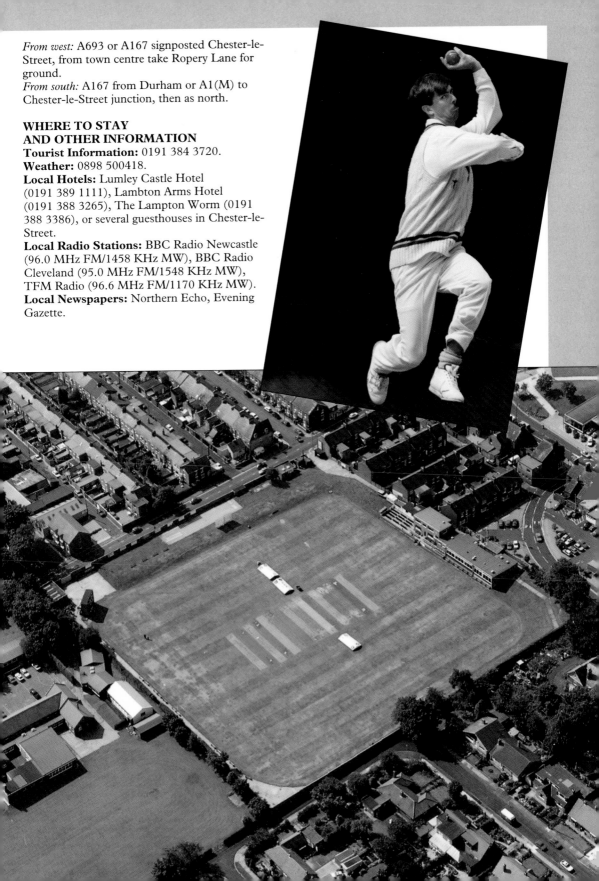

DARLINGTON

Address: Darlington Cricket and Athletic Club, Feethams Cricket Ground, South Terrace, Darlington, County Durham DL1 5JD.
Telephone Number for Prospects of Play: 01325 466415.
Entrances: South Terrace (Players, Officials, Vehicles), South Terrace – via Main Gate (Members, Public, Vehicles), Darlington Football Club Ground – via car park (Members, Public).
Members' Enclosure: Pavilion, Pavilion terrace, South Terrace enclosure and defined Members' Enclosure, including temporary raised seating.
Public Enclosure: Rest of the ground.
Covered Stands: Pavilion, Tea Bar.
Open Stands: Pavilion terrace, South Terrace enclosure, East Side Benches, temporary raised and ground level seating surrounding the playing area.
Disabled Areas: Special area to the left of the Pavilion.
Car Parking Facilities: Limited car parking within the ground to the rear of the Pavilion for 120 cars and at the football ground end for 400+ cars.

Otherwise town centre car parks or street parking to south-west of town centre, a short walk away.
Ground dimensions: 124m x 133m.
Best Crowd: First-Class Match: 5,000 v South Africans 1901/West Indians 1923. Limited-Overs Match: 5,000 v Middlesex (NWBT) 1987.

HOW TO GET THERE
Rail: Darlington (BR) 0.25 mile.
Bus: Darlington Transport Company bus 2 links BR Darlington with ground, also Darlington Transport Company and United buses 1, 1A, 3A, 3B, 4, 4A, 5, 6, 6A, 7, 11A, X13, X14, X35, X50, X51, X70, 68, 68A, 722, 723 link Darlington Bus Station with surrounding areas, Bus Station 0.25 mile from ground.
(01325 488777 or 468771).
Car: *From north:* A1(M) then take A167 signposted Darlington and town centre, then follow signs Northallerton for Victoria Road, then at roundabout take left into South Terrace for Feethams Ground.

↑ North direction (approx.)

Entrances
E1 South Terrace
E2 South Terrace (Main Gates)
E3 Car Park from Darlington FC

P Pavilion
SB Scoreboard
CP Car Parking
T Toilets
CS Club Shop
CO Durham CCC Club Office
N1 South Terrace End
N2 Football Ground End
R BR Darlington (direction)
C Town Centre (direction)

Stands
S1 South Terrace

1 Darlington FC Ground
2 River Skerne

Streets
3 South Terrace

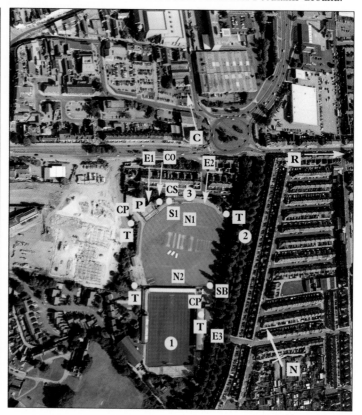

Above Right: Former Middlesex opening batsman Michael Roseberry is Durham's new skipper for this season. Born at Houghton-le-Spring and schooled at Durham he will be amongst locals.

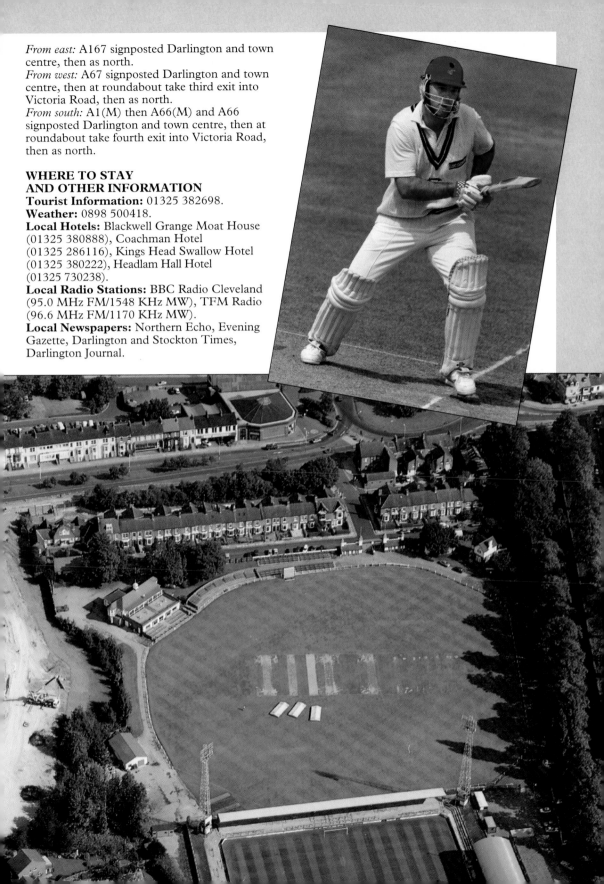

From east: A167 signposted Darlington and town centre, then as north.
From west: A67 signposted Darlington and town centre, then at roundabout take third exit into Victoria Road, then as north.
From south: A1(M) then A66(M) and A66 signposted Darlington and town centre, then at roundabout take fourth exit into Victoria Road, then as north.

WHERE TO STAY
AND OTHER INFORMATION
Tourist Information: 01325 382698.
Weather: 0898 500418.
Local Hotels: Blackwell Grange Moat House (01325 380888), Coachman Hotel (01325 286116), Kings Head Swallow Hotel (01325 380222), Headlam Hall Hotel (01325 730238).
Local Radio Stations: BBC Radio Cleveland (95.0 MHz FM/1548 KHz MW), TFM Radio (96.6 MHz FM/1170 KHz MW).
Local Newspapers: Northern Echo, Evening Gazette, Darlington and Stockton Times, Darlington Journal.

DURHAM UNIVERSITY

Address: Durham University Cricket Club, The Pavilion, The Racecourse Ground, Green Lane, Durham City, County Durham.

Telephone Number for Prospects of Play: 0191 374 3404.

Entrances: Green Lane (Players, Officials, Members, Public, Vehicles), Towpath (Members, Public).

Members' Enclosure: Pavilion and defined Members' Enclosure on the bank alongside the River Wear to the north of the playing area.

Public Enclosure: Rest of the ground.

Covered Stands: Pavilion, Squash club.

Open Stands: Temporary raised seating areas and ground level seating surrounding the playing area and on banking to the south of the playing area.

Disabled Areas: Car parking area and special position in ground available near Pavilion by prior arrangement.

Car Parking Facilities: Car parking available adjoining the ground for 2,000+ cars, entrance off Green Lane; otherwise town centre car parks within a short walk of ground.

Ground Dimensions: 148m x 118m.

Ground Capacity: 8,500.

Best Crowd: First-Class Match: 10,500 v Australians 1993. Limited-Overs Match: 6,000 v Lancashire (SL) 1992.

HOW TO GET THERE

Rail: Durham (BR) 1.25 mile.

Bus: 20, 41, 57 United/Gardiners/OK Travel buses pass 0.25 mile from ground. No 20 links BR Durham Station with Old Elvet leading to Green Lane and ground. (0191 386 4411 ext 2337).

Car: *From north:* A1(M) to Durham City Junction (north), then follow A690 for Durham and city centre, then take New Elvet Bridge and take left into Old Elvet for Green Lane and ground. *From east:* A690 for Durham and city centre then

↑ North direction (approx.)

Entrances
E1 Green Lane
E2 Towpath

P Pavilion
SB Scoreboard
CP Car Parking
T Toilets
CS Club Shop
CO Durham CCC Club Office
N1 City End
N2 Pavilion End
R DR Durham (direction)
C City Centre (direction)

1 Hilton Cottage
2 Squash Club
3 Durham City Cricket Ground
4 River Wear

Streets
5 Green Lane

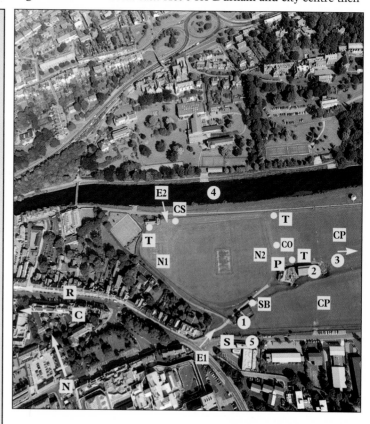

Above Right: Top of Durham's first-class batting averages in 1994, Wayne Larkins hit 960 runs (av 41.73), with a top score of 158 not out versus Gloucestershire at Gateshead Fell.

as north or A1(M) to Durham City Junction (south), then follow A177 for Durham and city centre, then as north.

From west: A167 then follow signs Durham and city centre, take Leazes Bridge and New Elvet Bridge, then as north.

From south: A1(M) to Durham City Junction (south), then follow A177 for Durham and city centre, then as north or A167, then as west and then as north.

WHERE TO STAY AND OTHER INFORMATION

Tourist Information: 0191 384 3720.
Weather: 0898 500418.
Local Hotels: Post House Hotel, Washington (0191 416 2264) or several guesthouses in Durham.
Local Radio Stations: TFM (96.6 MHz FM/1170 KHz MW), BBC Radio Newcastle (96.0 MHz FM/1458 KHz MW), BBC Radio Cleveland (95.0 MHz FM/1548 KHz MW).
Local Newspapers: Northern Echo, Journal, Evening Chronicle, Sunderland Echo, Durham Advertiser.

GATESHEAD FELL

Durham

Address: Gateshead Fell Cricket Club, The Pavilion, Eastwood Gardens, Low Fell, Gateshead, Tyne and Wear NE9 5UB.

Telephone Number for Prospects of Play: 0191 487 5746.

Entrances: Eastwood Gardens (Players, Officials, Members), Salkeld Road (Members, Public), Elvistones Path (Members), Rugby Ground – via car park in Hedley Lawson Park entered off Eastwood Gardens (Members, Public).

Members' Enclosure: Defined area between Players' Pavilion and Store at Pavilion End of the ground including temporary and permanent raised seating areas.

Public Enclosure: Rest of the ground.

Covered Stands: Players' Pavilion, Members' Clubhouse, Store.

Open Stands: Temporary raised seating areas and ground level seating surrounding the playing area.

Disabled Areas: Special position at Rugby Ground End near sightscreen, car parking in ground by prior arrangement.

Car Parking Facilities: Car parking available to the rear of the pavilion for 30 Players' and Officials' cars, at the Rugby Ground End of the ground for 500+ cars in Hedley Lawson Park, and in the nearby St Peter's and Dryden Senior High School grounds for 1,000+ cars. Otherwise street parking to south and north of the ground.

Ground Dimensions: 120m x 126m.

Ground Capacity: 5,500.

Best Crowd: First-Class Match: 4,400 v Middlesex 1993. Limited-Overs Match: 4,000 Leicestershire (SL) 1992.

HOW TO GET THERE

Rail: Newcastle-Upon-Tyne Central (BR) 5 miles. Gateshead Interchange (Tyne and Wear Metro Green/Red/Yellow Lines) 2 miles.

Bus: G2, G3, 27, 35, 93 from Stand H Go-Ahead Northern/Tyne & Wear County bus service from Gateshead Interchange Metro to Low Fell via

↑ North direction (approx.)

Entrances
E1 Eastwood Gardens
E2 Elvistones Path
E3 Car Park
E4 Salkeld Road

P Pavilion
SB Scoreboard
CP Car Parking
CO Club Office
T Toilets
CS Club Shop
N1 Pavilion End
N2 Rugby End
R Gateshead Interchange Tyne & Wear Metro (direction)
C City Centre (direction)

Stands
S1 Clubhouse

1 Hedley Lawson Park
2 Gateshead Rugby Ground
3 Dryden Senior School

Streets
4 Eastwood Gardens
5 Salkeld Road
6 Elvistones Path

Above Right: Born at New Brunswick, USA, Jonathan Longley, seen here on the front foot, scored 100 not out for Durham against Derbyshire at Chesterfield in his first championship innings for his new county in 1994.

Dryden Road for ground. (0191 222 0404).
Car: *From north:* A167 from Newcastle-Upon-Tyne to Gateshead using Durham Road, then take Dryden Road for ground in Eastwood Gardens, follow signs County Cricket.
From east: A184 follow signs Gateshead and Felling, then follow signs County Cricket.
From west: A692, A69, A6528 or A694 signposted Gateshead, then follow signs County Cricket.
From south: A1(M) take A167 signposted Gateshead (South) prior to Gateshead College, then turn right into Valley Drive and at first junction turn right into Dryden Road and then first left for Eastwood Gardens and car parking.

WHERE TO STAY
AND OTHER INFORMATION
Tourist Information: 0191 261 0691.
Weather: 0898 500418.
Local Hotels: Springfield Hotel (0191 477 4121), Swallow Hotel (0191 477 1105), Post House Hotel (0191 416 2264), Metropark Hotel (0191 493 2233).
Local Radio Stations: BBC Radio Newcastle (96.0 MHz FM/1458 KHz MW), TFM Radio (96.6 MHz FM/1170 KHz FM).
Local Newspapers: Newcastle Journal, Newcastle Evening Chronicle, Sunderland Echo, Northern Echo, Sunday Sun, South Shields Gazette.

HARTLEPOOL

Address: Hartlepool Cricket Club, The Pavilion, Park Drive, West Park, Hartlepool, Cleveland TS26 ODA.
Telephone Number for Prospects of Play: 01429 260875.
Entrances: Park Drive (Players, Officials, Members, Public, Vehicles).
Members' Enclosure: Pavilion, Pavilion terrace, Clubhouse and defined Members' Enclosure to the east of the playing area.
Public Enclosure: Rest of the ground.
Covered Stands: Pavilion, Clubhouse.
Open Stands: Pavilion terrace, temporary raised seating and ground level seating surrounding the playing area.
Disabled Areas: Special area at Egerton Road End of the ground, car parking available in the ground by prior arrangement.
Car Parking Facilities: Car parking is available within the ground for 80 Players' and Officials'

cars only. Car parking for Members, Public for 500+ cars at the High Tunstall Comprehensive School off Elwick Road and for 500+ cars at English Martyrs RC Comprehensive School in Catecote Road, although the former is some distance walk from the ground. Alternatively parking is available on the neighbouring streets.
Ground Dimensions: 99m x 93m.
Ground Capacity: 5,000.
Best Crowd: First-Class Match: 5,000 v Essex 1993. Limited-Overs Match: 5,500 v Essex (AELL) 1993.

HOW TO GET THERE
Rail: Hartlepool (BR) 1.5 miles.
Bus: Hartlepool Bus Station 1.5 miles. Bus 15 stops close to ground. Nos 22, 241, 242, 244 United/Favourite link Hartlepool with surrounding areas. (0191 386 4411 ext 2337).
Car: Ground situated near Ward Jackson Park to

↑ North direction (approx.)

Entrances
E1 Park Drive

P Pavilion
SB Scoreboard
CP Car Parking
T Toilets
CO Club Office
CS Club Shop
N1 Park Drive End
N2 Egerton Road End
R BR Hartlepool (direction)
C Town Centre (direction)

Stands
S1 Clubhouse

Streets
1 Ward Jackson Park
2 Elwick Road
3 Park Drive
4 Egerton Road
5 A19 (direction)

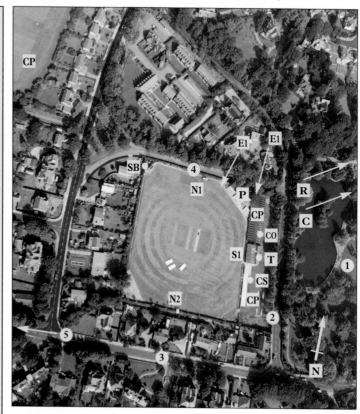

Above Right: Top run scorer for the county in first-class matches in 1994 with 1,376 runs (av 41.69), John Morris, seen sweeping, hit 204 for Durham versus Warwickshire at Edgbaston out of a total of 556 for 8 declared.

the west of the town.

From north: A19 then take Elwick Road signposted County Cricket for Park Drive and ground.

From west: As north.

From south: A19 then as north and west.

WHERE TO STAY
AND OTHER INFORMATION

Tourist Information: 0191 384 3720.

Weather: 0898 500418.

Local Hotels: The Grand Hotel (01429 266345), Staincliffe Hotel (01429 264301), also smaller hotels and guesthouses.

Local Radio Stations: BBC Radio Cleveland (95.0 MHz FM/1548 KHz MW), TFM Radio (96.6 MHz FM/1170 KHz MW).

Local Newspapers: The Northern Echo, Hartlepool Mail, The Journal.

STOCKTON-ON-TEES

Address: Stockton Cricket Club, The Pavilion/Clubhouse, The Grangefield Road Ground, Oxbridge Avenue, Stockton-On-Tees, Cleveland TS18 4JF.

Telephone Number for Prospects of Play: 01642 672835.

Entrances: Grangefield Road – via Herbert Trenholm MBE Gates (Players, Officials, Members, Vehicles), Oxbridge Road/Grangefield Road (Members, Public), Oxbridge Road (Members, Public).

Members' Enclosure: Clubhouse, Chris Old Room and defined Members' Enclosure.

Public Enclosure: Rest of the ground.

Covered Stands: Players' Pavilion, Clubhouse, Chris Old Room, Tea Room.

Opens Stands: Temporary raised seating and ground level seating surrounding the playing area.

Disabled Areas: No special area, request position. Car parking available within ground by prior arrangement.

Car Parking Facilities: Car parking is available in three nearby fields for some 3,000+ cars: at Stockton Comprehensive School (school holidays only), opposite ground in Oxbridge Road; Stockton and Billingham Technical College in Oxbridge Avenue, 5min walk away from the ground; Rudds Recreation Ground in Grangefield Road. Car parking within the ground for 62 cars for Players, Officials only.

Ground Dimensions: 137m x 122m.

Ground Capacity: 5,000.

Best Crowd: First-Class Match: 3,750 v Northamptonshire 1993. Limited-Overs Match: 3,750 v Gloucestershire (AELL) 1993.

HOW TO GET THERE

Rail: Stockton (BR) 1 mile, connections from Darlington (BR) Inter City.

Bus: 55A, 61, 163, 235 OK Travel/United alight at Grangefield Road and Grays Road close to ground. (0191 386 4411 ext 2337).

↑ North direction (approx.)

Entrances
E1 Grangefield Road
E2 Grangefield Road/Oxbridge Road
E3 Oxbridge Road

P Pavilion
SB Scoreboard
CP Car Parking
T Toilets
CS Club Shop
N1 Askrigg Road End
N2 Grangefield Road End
R BR Stockton (direction)
C Town Centre (direction)

1 Tea Room
2 Chris Old Room
3 Groundsman's House
4 Herbert Trenholm Gates

Streets
5 Oxbridge Road
6 Grangefield Road
7 A19 (direction)

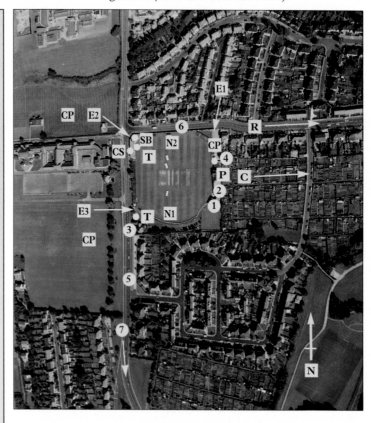

Above Right: Former Nottinghamshire batsman, Mark Saxelby hit 1,102 first-class runs (av 34.43) for the county in his first season with knocks of 181 versus Derbyshire at Chesterfield and 131 versus Essex at Stockton-on-Tees.

Car: *From north:* A19 or A689 to A19 turn off at Billingham/Norton junction, then follow A1027 Stockton Ring Road to Oxbridge Road for Grangefield Road ground and car parking.
From east: A178 to Stockton, then follow signs Ring Road for Grangefield Road ground and car parking or as north.
From west: A177, A66 or A67 to Stockton, then follow signs Ring Road for Grangefield Road ground and car parking or as south.
From south: A66 from Darlington to Middlesbrough, then take Eaglescliffe junction and approach ground via Darlington Road, Hartburn Avenue on to the Ring Road and Oxbridge Avenue for ground and car parking or A19 signposted Stockton and Ring Road for Grangefield Road ground.

WHERE TO STAY
AND OTHER INFORMATION

Tourist Information: 01642 243425.
Weather: 0898 500418.
Local Hotels: Swallow Hotel (01642 679721), The Post House (01642 591213), Parkmore Hotel & Leisure Club (01642 786815), Stonyroyd Hotel (01642 607734).
Local Radio Stations: BBC Radio Cleveland (95.0 MHz FM/1548 KHz MW), TFM Radio (96.6 MHz FM/1170 KHz MW).
Local Newspapers: Northern Echo, Evening Gazette, Darlington and Stockton Times, Hartlepool Mail, Yorkshire Post, Journal, Sunday Sun.

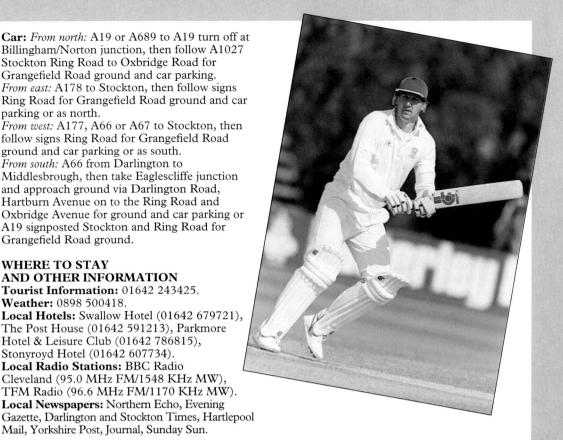

Essex

CHELMSFORD

Address: County Cricket Ground, New Writtle Street, Chelmsford, Essex CM2 0PG.

Telephone Number for Prospects of Play: 01245 287921.

Entrances: New Writtle Street (Players, Officials, Members, Public, Vehicles), Parkway (Members, Public).

Members' Enclosure: Pavilion, Pavilion Terrace, Tom Pearce Stand Upper/Lower, River End Stand (part), Hayes Close End (part).

Public Enclosure: Rest of the ground.

Covered Stands: Pavilion (part), Tom Pearce Stand Lower, River Restaurant Stand (part), Popular Side (part).

Open Stands: Pavilion (part), Pavilion Terrace, Tom Pearce Stand Upper, River Restaurant Stand (part), River End Stand (part), Popular Side (part), Hayes Close End (part).

Disabled Areas: No restrictions – several suitable positions on hardstanding. Wheelchairs may be difficult on the Popular Side. Request position in advance.

Car Parking Facilities: Car parking is available to the rear of the Pavilion for Players, Officials only, with car parking for some Members to the rear of the Essex CCC Indoor Cricket School. Alternative car parking for Members is available adjoining the Members' entrance gate in New Writtle Street and in a school field off New Writtle Street. Car parking for the Public is available in the multi-storey car parking on the north side of the River Can close to the town centre. Some street parking is available off London Road a short walk from the ground.

Ground Dimensions: 132m x 128m.

Ground Capacity: 9,500.

Best Crowd: First-Class Match: 9,500 v West Indians 1991. Limited-Overs Match: 9,500 v Worcestershire (BHC) 1991.

HOW TO GET THERE

Rail: Chelmsford (BR) 0.5 mile.

↑ North direction (approx.)

Entrances
E1 New Writtle Street
E2 Parkway

P Pavilion
SB Scoreboard
CP Car Parking
T Toilets
CO Essex CCC Club Offices
CS Club Shop
N1 Hayes Close End
N2 River End
R BR Chelmsford (direction)
C Town Centre (direction)

Stands
S1 Tom Pearce Stand
S2 River Restaurant Stand
S3 Executive Suites

1 Essex CCC Indoor Cricket
  School
2 River Can
3 Chelmsford FC Ground

Streets
4 New Writtle Street
5 A130 Parkway
6 London Road

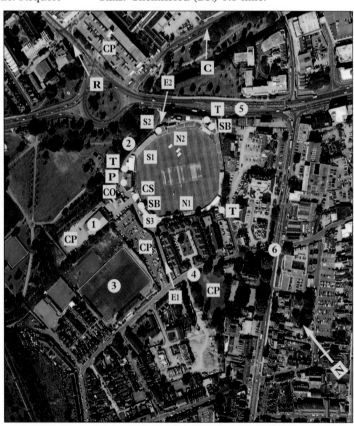

Above Right Watford born Mark Illott who achieved a career best 7 for 85 versus Surrey at The Foster's Oval in 1993.

Bus: From surrounding areas to Bus Station, thence 0.5 mile walk.

Car: Ground situated close to town centre, on the southern bank of the River Can, in New Writtle Street off Parkway A130.

From north: M1 Junction 8 then A120 and A130 to Chelmsford or M1 Junction 6A/M25 interchange to M25 Junction 28 then A12 to Chelmsford.

From east: A414 or A12 or A130, then as north.

From south: M25 Junction 28, then as north.

From west: A414 or as from south, then as north.

WHERE TO STAY
AND OTHER INFORMATION

Tourist Information: 01621 856503.

Weather: 0898 500407.

Local Hotels: County Hotel (01245 266911), Beechcroft Hotel (01245 352462), South Lodge Hotel (01245 264564) – all within walking distance.

Local Radio Stations: Greater London Radio (94.9 MHz FM/1458 KHz MW), BBC Essex (103.5 MHz FM/765 KHz MW), Essex Radio (96.3 MHz FM/1431 KHz MW).

Local Newspapers: Essex Chronicle, Chelmsford Weekly News, Yellow Advertiser.

COLCHESTER

Address: Colchester and East Essex Cricket Club, Castle Park (Lower), Sportsway, off Catchpool Road, Colchester, Essex.

Telephone Number for Prospects of Play: 01206 574028.

Entrances: Sportsway – off Catchpool Road (Players, Officials, Members, Public, Vehicles), King's Meadow (Members), Castle Park Grounds – via Footbridge (Members, Public).

Members' Enclosure: Pavilion and defined Members' Enclosure at Castle Park End of the ground including tiered seating areas.

Public Enclosure: Rest of the ground.

Covered Stands: Pavilion (part).

Open Stands: Temporary raised and ground level seating surrounding the playing area.

Disabled Areas: No restrictions, but there is no hardstanding close to the playing area so wheelchairs may be difficult when weather is poor.

Car Parking Facilities: Parking is available in King's Meadow to the west of the ground off Sportsway for 1,000+ cars.

Ground Dimensions: 132m x 128m.

Ground Capacity: 6,500.

Best Crowd: First-Class Match: 8,000 v Middlesex 1947. Limited-Overs Match: 9,000 v Worcestershire (RAL) 1989.

HOW TO GET THERE

Rail: Colchester (BR) 0.75 mile.

Bus: Eastern National and Colchester Corporation from surrounding areas to Bus Station, thence 0.75 mile walk to ground. Some buses from the north do pass closer to the ground.

Car: *From north:* A12 or A134 follow signs Colchester, then Castle Park off A12 for County Cricket.

From east: A120, A137 or A133 follow signs Colchester, then as north.

↑ North direction (approx.)

Entrances
E1 Sportsway
E2 Castle Park

P Pavilion
SB Scoreboard
CP Car Parking
T Toilets
CS Club Shop
N1 Sportsway End
N2 Castle Park End
R BR Colchester (direction)
C City Centre (direction)

Streets
1 Sportsway
2 A12

3 River Colne

Above Right: Forgotten by England during the home Cornhill Test series despite touring West Indies in 1994, Nasser Hussain responded with 922 first-class runs (av 31.79) with 115 not out versus Hampshire at Southampton and 101 versus Durham at Stockton-on-Tees.

From south: A12 to Colchester, then as north, or B1025 or B1026, then as north.
From west: A120 or A604 to Colchester, then as north, or follow A12, then as north.

WHERE TO STAY
AND OTHER INFORMATION
Tourist Information: 01206 46379.
Weather: 0898 500407.
Local Hotels: George Hotel (01206 578494), Marks Tey Hotel (01206 210001).
Local Radio Stations: Essex Radio (96.3 MHz FM/1431 Khz MW), Radio Orwell (97.1 MHz FM/1170 KHz MW).
Local Newspapers: Colchester Leader, Essex County Standard, Evening Gazette, Yellow Advertiser.

Address: Ilford Cricket Club, The Pavilion, Valentine's Park, Cranbrook Road, Ilford, Essex.
Telephone Number for Prospects of Play: 0181 554 8383.
Entrances: Cranbrook Road (Players, Officials, Members, Public, Vehicles), Valentine's Park (Members, Public).
Members' Enclosure: Pavilion and defined Members' Enclosure between Cranbrook Road Terrace (part) and the main Scoreboard at the Lake End of the ground.
Public Enclosure: Cranbrook Road Terrace (part) and the Lake End of the ground.
Covered Stands: Pavilion (part) and small Members' temporary covered stand adjoining the Pavilion.
Open Stands: Cranbrook Road Terrace together with all temporary raised and ground level seating surrounding the playing area.
Disabled Areas: No restrictions but suggested

positions by the sightscreen or in front of the Pavilion to the left on the hardstanding.
Car Parking Facilities: Car parking is available at the Lake End and in adjoining streets.
Ground Dimensions: 124m x 122m.
Ground Capacity: 10,000.
Best Crowd: First-Class Match: 13,000 v Glamorgan 1948. Limited-Overs Match: 8,000 v Middlesex (JPL) 1970.

HOW TO GET THERE
Rail: Ilford (BR) or Gants Hill (London Underground Central Line) both 0.75 mile.
Bus: LRT 123, 124, 125, 126, 127, 128, 129, 144, 150, 167, 179, 247, 296 all pass BR Ilford and Gants Hill Underground. (0171 222 1234).
Car: Ground is 10 miles north-east of Central London in the district of Redbridge.
From north: M25 Junction 27, then M11 and A12 to Gants Hill, then at roundabout follow

↑ North direction (approx.)

Entrances
E1 Cranbrook Road
E2 Valentine's Park
E3 Valentine's Park (Lake End)

P Pavilion
SB Scoreboard
CP Car Parking
T Toilets
CS Club Shop
N1 Pavilion End
N2 Lake End
T Gants Hill Underground
   (direction)
R BR Ilford (direction)

Stands
S1 Cranbrook Terrace

2 Lake
3 Bowling Green/Tennis Courts
4 Valentine's Park

Streets
1 A12 (direction)
5 Cranbrook Road

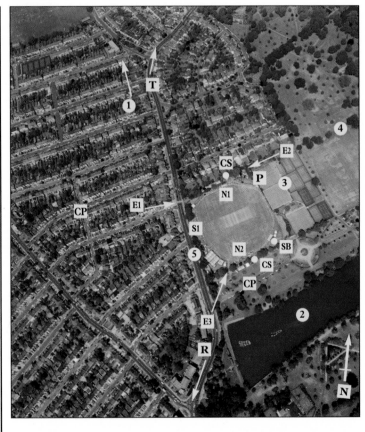

Above Right: Essex's new skipper this season will be Brentwood born, right-handed top order batsman, Paul Pritchard, seen playing the cover drive.

Cranbrook Road, ground situated on your left off this road.

From east: M25 Junctions 28 or 29 then A12 or A126 to Ilford, ground situated close to A118, A1083 and A124, then as north.

From west or south: A13 then A117 and A124 to Ilford, then as north.

WHERE TO STAY
AND OTHER INFORMATION

Tourist Information: 0181 760 5630.

Weather: 0898 500401.

Local Hotels: Cranbrook Hotel (0181 554 6544), Park Hotel (0181 554 9616).

Local Radio Stations: Greater London Radio (94.9 MHz FM/1458 KHz MW), Essex Radio (96.3 MHz FM/1431 KHz MW), Capital Radio/Capital Gold (95.8 MHz/1548 KHz MW), LBC (97.3 MHz FM/1152 KHz MW).

Local Newspapers: Ilford Independent, Ilford Recorder, Walthamstow Guardian Group, Yellow Advertiser.

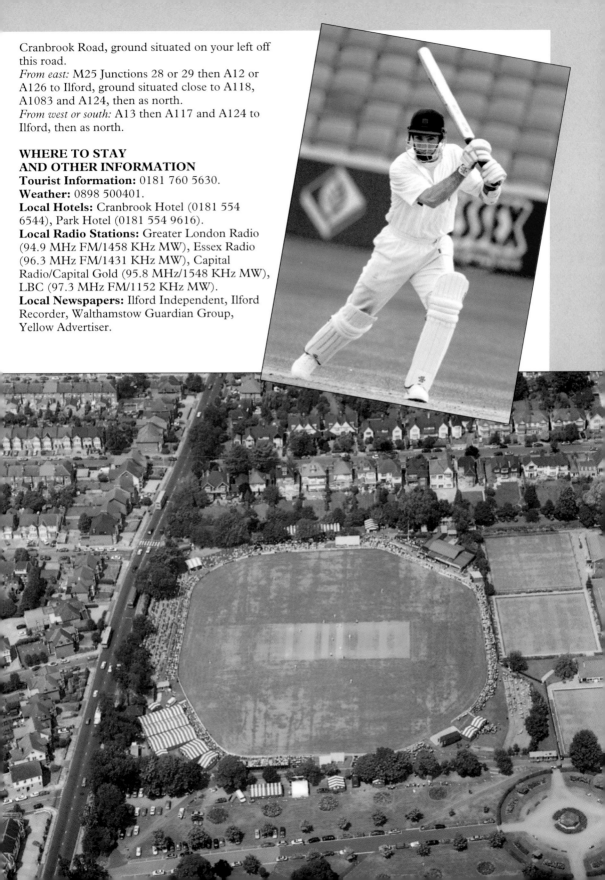

SOUTHEND-ON-SEA

Essex

Address: Southend-On-Sea Cricket Club, The Pavilion, Southchurch Park, Northumberland Crescent, Southend-On-Sea, Essex.

Telephone Number for Prospects of Play: 01702 615195.

Entrances: Kensington Road – via Boat Lake (Members), Kensington Road (Members, Public, Vehicles), Northumberland Crescent (Players, Officials, Members, Public, Vehicles).

Members' Enclosure: Pavilion and defined Members' Enclosure between Players' Pavilion and Members' Pavilion at Boating Lake End, together with temporary raised seating and ground level seating surrounding the playing area.

Public Enclosure: Northumberland Crescent Terrace and the rest of the ground.

Covered Stands: Players' and Members' Pavilions together with small covered temporary Members' stand.

Open Stands: Temporary raised seating and ground level seating surrounding the playing area.

Disabled Areas: No restrictions, but request position on hardstanding at Boating Lake End.

Car Parking Facilities: Car parking is available to the east of the playing area for Players, Officials, Members only. Alternative car parking can be found in neighbouring streets, seafront, or town centre multi-storey car parking a short walk away.

Ground Dimensions: 170m x 123m.

Ground Capacity: 8,000.

Best Crowd: First-Class Match: 16,000 v Australians 1948. Limited-Overs Match: 5,000 v Glamorgan (JPL) 1983.

HOW TO GET THERE

Rail: Southend East (BR) 0.5 mile.

Bus: Eastern National 20 Shoeburyness-Hullbridge passing BR Southend Central and Victoria, (01702 430534); Nos 7, 8, 67, 68 also

↑ North direction (approx.)

Entrances
E1 Kensington Road via Boating Lake
E2 Kensington Road
E3 Northumberland Crescent

P Pavilion (Players')
SB Scoreboard
CP Car Parking
T Toilets
CS Club Shop
N1 Northumberland Crescent End
N2 Boating Lake End
R BR Southend East (direction)
C Town Centre (direction)

Stands
S1 Members' Pavilion
S2 Northumberland Crescent Terrace

Streets
1 Northumberland Crescent
2 Kensington Road

3 Southchurch Park
4 Boating Lake
5 Seafront/Beach

Above Right: Graham Gooch on his way to 210, seen sweeping against Kiwi Matthew Hart, as Adam Parore looks on, during the First Cornhill Test Match between England and New Zealand at Trent Bridge in 1994. Graham Gooch will be taking a well-earned testimonial in 1995.

pass close to the ground.
Car: Ground situated 1.5 miles east of town
centre.
From north and west: M25 Junction 29, then A127
or A130 follow signs Southend, then to
Southchurch and County Cricket.

WHERE TO STAY
AND OTHER INFORMATION
Tourist Information: 01702 355120.
Weather: 0898 500455.
Local Hotels: Airport Moat House (01702
546344), Argyle Hotel (01702 339483), Balmoral
Hotel (01702 342947), plus many other seaside
hotels and guesthouses.
Local Radio Station: Essex Radio (96.3 MHz
FM/1431 KHz MW).
Local Newspapers: Evening Echo, Yellow
Advertiser, Southend Standard, Southend
District News, London Advertiser.

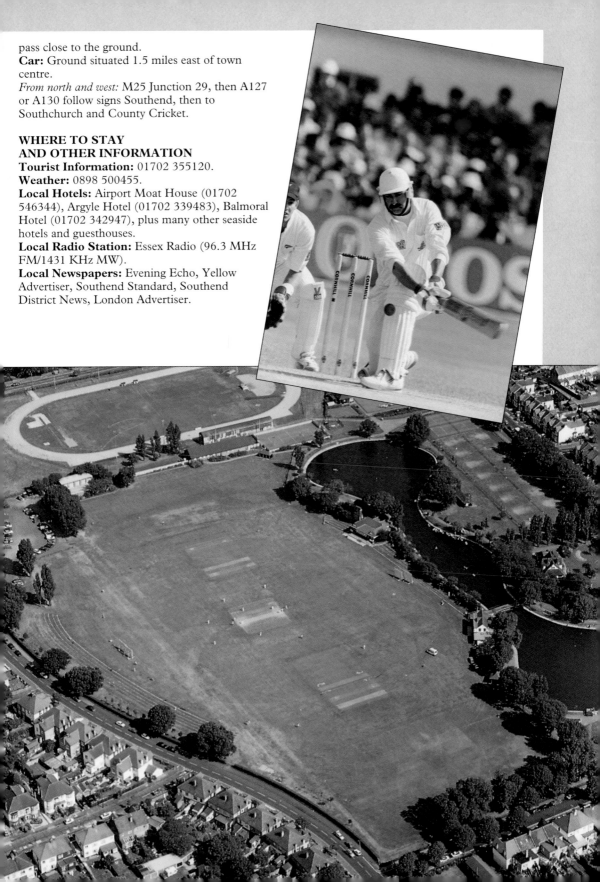

CARDIFF

Address: Cardiff Athletic Club, The Pavilion, Sophia Gardens, Cathedral Road, Cardiff, Wales CF1 9XR.

Telephone Number for Prospects of Play: 01222 43478/29956.

Entrances: Cathedral Road – via car park from National Sports Centre for Wales (Players, Officials, Members, Public, Vehicles).

Members' Enclosure: Pavilion, Pavilion terraces and defined Members' Enclosure.

Public Enclosure: River Stand, Press Box Stand, together with raised and ground level seating surrounding the playing area.

Covered Stands: Pavilion, River Stand, Executive Suites, Press Box Stand.

Open Stands: Pavilion terraces together with permanent and temporary raised seating at the Cathedral Road End of the ground and the ground level seating on the rugby ground to the north of the playing area.

Disabled Areas: No special area, request suitable position. Car parking available within ground by prior arrangement.

Car Parking Facilities: Car parking within the ground for Players, Officials, Committee Members. Outside the ground car parking for Members, Public adjoining the Sports Centre for Wales and car parks south of the Sports Centre complex. During popular matches car parking is sometimes available on the rugby field to the north of the playing area.

Ground Dimensions: 142m x 146m.

Ground Capacity: 10,000.

Best Crowd: First-Class Match: 16,000 v Worcestershire 1969. Limited-Overs Match: 11,000 v Somerset (JPL) 1976.

Anticipated Developments: Club presently looking at possibility of relocating ground to Cardiff Docklands Development Corporation land.

HOW TO GET THERE

Rail: Cardiff Central (BR) 1 mile.

Bus: Cardiff Bus 32, 62 from BR Cardiff Central

↑ North direction (approx.)

Entrances
E1 Cathedral Road via Sports
    Centre car park

P Pavilion
SB Scoreboard
CP Car Parking
T Toilets
CO Glamorgan CCC Club Offices
CS Club Shop
N1 River Taff End
N2 Cathedral Road End
R BR Cardiff Central (direction)
C City Centre (direction)

Stands
S1 River Stand

1 River Taff
2 Rugby Ground
3 National Sports Centre for Wales
4 Tennis Courts and Hockey
    Pitches

Streets
5 A48 Cathedral Road

Above Right: West Indian all-rounder Ottis Gibson who played for the Welsh county in the 1994 season.

and also 21, 25, 33 from city centre pass close to ground. (01222 396521).

Car: *From north:* A470 follow signs to Cardiff until Junction with Cardiff bypass, then A48 Port Talbot and city centre, ground is situated off A48 Cathedral Road for Sophia Gardens.
From east: M4 Junction 29, then A48, then as north.
From west: A4160 follow signs Cardiff, then A48, then as north.

WHERE TO STAY
AND OTHER INFORMATION
Tourist Information: 01222 227281.
Weather: 0898 500409.
Local Hotels: Crest Hotel (01222 388681), Forte Post House (01222 731212), Park Hotel (01222 383471), Inn on the Avenue (01222 732520).
Local Radio Stations: BBC Radio Wales (882 KHz MW), Red Dragon Radio (97.4 MHz FM/1359 KHz MW).
Local Newspapers: South Wales Evening Post, South Wales Echo, Western Mail, Cardiff Independent, Cardiff Post Series.

ABERGAVENNY

Address: Abergavenny Cricket Club, The Pavilion, Pen-y-Pound Cricket Ground, Avenue Road, Abergavenny, Gwent, Wales.

Telephone Number for Prospects of Play: 01873 852350.

Entrances: Avenue Road (Players, Officials, Members, Public, Vehicles). Hill Road – via Pen-y-Pound (Members, Public).

Members' Enclosure: Pavilion, Pavilion terrace and defined Members' Enclosure between pavilion and electronic scoreboard.

Public Enclosure: Rest of the ground.

Covered Stands: Pavilion.

Open Stands: Temporary tiered seating and ground level seating surrounding the playing area.

Disabled Areas: No special area, request suitable position. Car parking available within ground at Avenue Road End by prior arrangement.

Car Parking Facilities: Car parking within the ground for Players, Officials, Members only at the Avenue Road End. Car parking is also available at Abergavenny Football Ground off Hill Road and in surrounding residential streets.

Ground Dimensions: 117m x 118m.

Ground Capacity: 5,000.

Best Crowd: First-Class Match: 5,000 v Worcestershire 1988. Limited-Overs Match: 3,000 v Northamptonshire (JPL) 1982.

HOW TO GET THERE

Rail: Abergavenny (BR) 2 miles.

Bus: National Welsh 20 Newport to Hereford; 21 Newport to Brecon alight at Bus Station, thence 1.5 mile walk to ground. (01222 371331).

Car: *From north:* A465 or A40 follow signs Abergavenny, ground situated in Avenue Road off A40 Brecon Road.

From east: A40 or A465, then as north.

From west: A465 or A40, then as north.

↑ North direction (approx.)

Entrances
E1/2 Avenue Road
E3/4 Hill Road

P Pavilion
SB Scoreboard
CP Car Parking
T Toilets
CS Club Shop
N1 Hill Road End
N2 Avenue Road End
R BR Abergavenny (direction)
C Town Centre (direction)

1 River Cibi
2 Bowling Green
3 Tennis Courts

Streets
4 Avenue Road
5 Hill Road
6 A40 (direction)

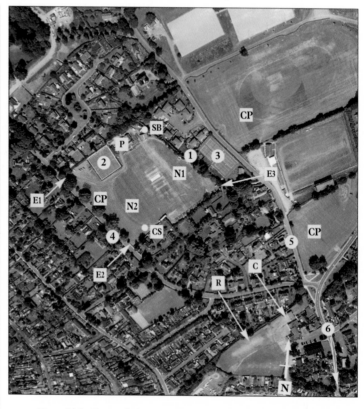

Above Right: Rewarded with a place on the England 'A' Tour to India in 1995, Bermuda born left-hand batsman, David Hemp was Glamorgan's leading run scorer in 1994 with 1,452 first-class runs (av 42.70), with a top score of 136 versus Gloucestershire at Bristol.

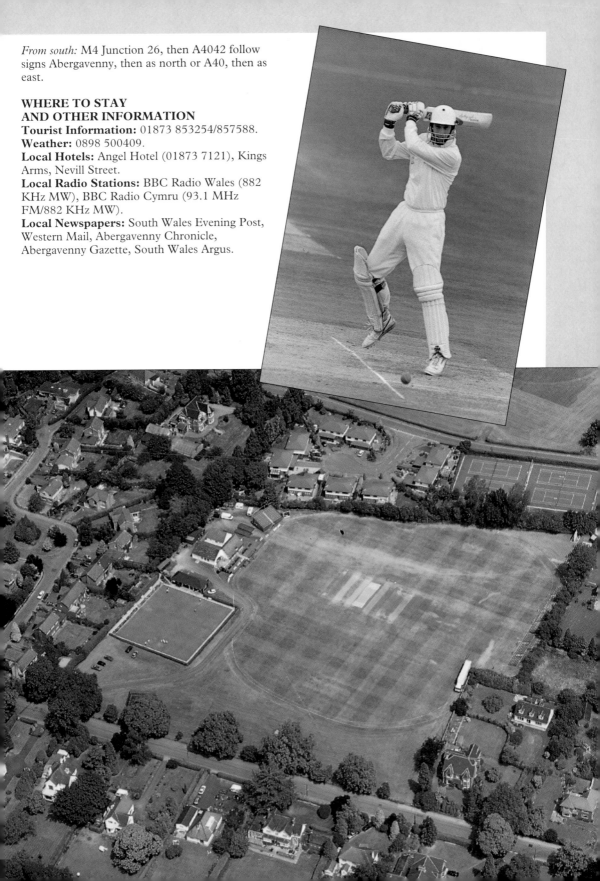

From south: M4 Junction 26, then A4042 follow signs Abergavenny, then as north or A40, then as east.

**WHERE TO STAY
AND OTHER INFORMATION**
Tourist Information: 01873 853254/857588.
Weather: 0898 500409.
Local Hotels: Angel Hotel (01873 7121), Kings Arms, Nevill Street.
Local Radio Stations: BBC Radio Wales (882 KHz MW), BBC Radio Cymru (93.1 MHz FM/882 KHz MW).
Local Newspapers: South Wales Evening Post, Western Mail, Abergavenny Chronicle, Abergavenny Gazette, South Wales Argus.

COLWYN BAY

Address: Colwyn Bay Cricket Club, The Pavilion, 77 Penrhyn Avenue, Rhos-on-Sea, Colwyn Bay, Clwyd, North Wales LL28 4LR.
Telephone Number for Prospects of Play: 01492 44103.
Entrances: Penrhyn Avenue (Players, Officials, Members, Vehicles). Church Road – car park (Members, Public, Vehicles).
Members' Enclosure: Pavilion, Clubhouse and defined Members' Enclosure between Tea Pavilion and Scoreboard and the Sea End of the ground.
Public Enclosure: Rest of the ground.
Covered Stands: Pavilion, Tea Pavilion and two temporary stands.
Open Stands: Rest of the ground including temporary raised seats, ground level seats/benches surrounding the playing area and deck chairs on the embankment at the Town End of the ground.
Disabled Areas: Special area provided on hardstanding path between Scoreboard and Pavilion at Penrhyn Avenue end of the ground, close to pedestrian entrance.
Car Parking Facilities: Car parking is available at the rear of the pavilion for Players, Officials and in an adjoining field off Church Road to the south-west of the playing area for Members, Public. Alternatively street parking is available locally.
Ground Dimensions: 115m x 107m.
Ground Capacity: 6,000.
Best Crowd: First-Class Match: 6,000 v Derbyshire 1966. Limited-Overs Match: 5,500 v Lancashire (RAL) 1990.

HOW TO GET THERE
Rail: Colwyn Bay (BR) 1.5 miles.
Bus: Crosville Bus service M16 passes ground and links BR Colwyn Bay with Rhos-on-Sea.
Car: *From north:* A470 or A546 signposted Rhos-on-Sea or as east.
From east: A55 or A547 signposted Colwyn Bay,

↑ North direction (approx.)

Entrances
E1 Penrhyn Avenue
E2 Church Road

P Pavilion
SB Scoreboard
CP Car Parking
T Toilets
CS Club Shop
N1 Sea End
N2 Embankment End
R BR Colwyn Bay (direction)
C Town Centre (direction)

Stands
S1 Tea Pavilion

1 Seafront

Streets
2 Penrhyn Avenue
3 Church Road
4 A55 (direction)

Above Right: Glamorgan spinner Robert Croft, seen bowling versus Lancashire at Colwyn Bay in 1994, is watched by former county player and umpire Kevin Lyons.

then follow A55 to junction signposted Rhos-on-Sea, then take exit and follow Llandudno Road for Church Road for car parking and Colwyn Bay CC.
From west: A5 and A55 signposted Colwyn Bay, take junction signposted Rhos-on-Sea, then as east for ground.
From south: A470 or B5106 or B5113 signposted Colwyn Bay, then follow A55 and signs Rhos-on-Sea for ground in Penrhyn Avenue.

WHERE TO STAY
AND OTHER INFORMATION
Tourist Information: 01492 530478.
Weather: 0898 500460
Local Hotels: Hotel Seventy Degrees (01492 534626), The Cedar Tree (01492 45867), Norfolk House Hotel (01492 531757).
Local Radio Stations: Radio Clwyd (657 KHz MW), Radio City (96.7 MHz FM/1548 KHz MW), BBC Radio Wales (882 KHz MW).
Local Newspapers: North Wales Weekly News, North Wales Pioneer.

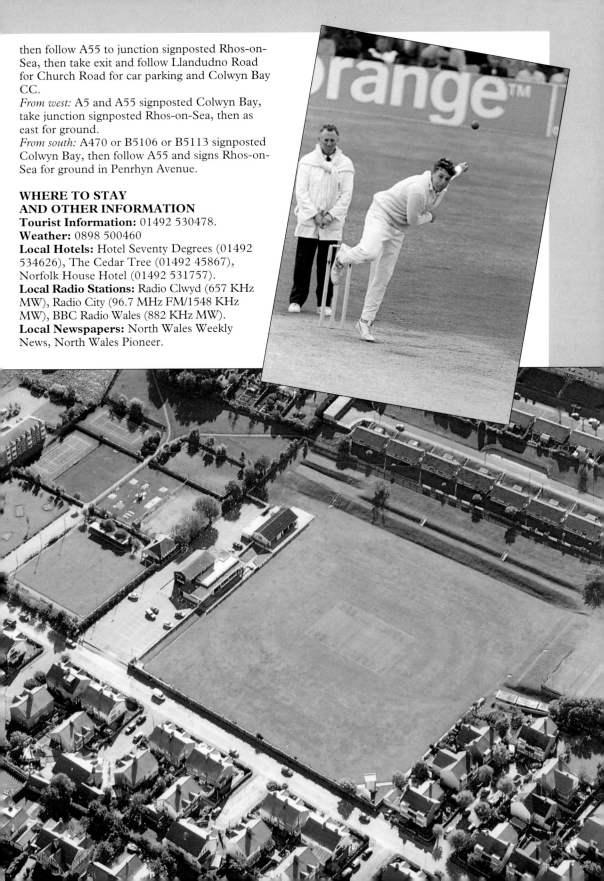

EBBW VALE

Address: Ebbw Vale Cricket Club, The Pavilion, Eugene Cross Park, Newchurch Road, Ebbw Vale, Gwent, Wales.

Telephone Number for Prospects of Play: 01495 305368.

Entrances: Newchurch Road (Players, Officials, Members, Public, Vehicles), Beaufort Road (Members, Public), Ebbw Vale Rugby Football Ground – via footbridge (Members, Public, Vehicles).

Members' Enclosure: Pavilion, terrace in front of the Pavilion, adjacent terraced area.

Public Enclosure: Rest of the ground including East Terrace and temporary seating at Rugby Ground End of the ground.

Covered Stands: Pavilion, Glamorgan CCC Indoor Cricket School, Ebbw Vale Rugby Club Clubhouse.

Open Stands: Pavilion terraces, East terrace and temporary raised seating and ground level seating surrounding the playing area.

Disabled Areas: No special area, request suitable position. Car parking available at Rugby Ground End.

Car Parking Facilities: Car parking is available for Players, Officials at the rear of the pavilion and there is limited space for Members on the Ebbw Vale rugby field. Alternatively car parking can be found at the Ebbw Vale Leisure Centre and town centre car parks a short walk away.

Ground Dimensions: 126m x 102m.

Ground Capacity: 5,000.

Best Crowd: First-Class Match: 12,000 v Worcestershire 1947. Limited-Overs Match: 5,500 v Derbyshire (JPL) 1984.

HOW TO GET THERE

Rail: Rhymney (BR) 6 miles.

Bus: Inter Valley Link 49 from close to BR Rhymney, (01222 851506); National Welsh X4, 444 from Abergavenny (0.5 mile from BR

↑ North direction (approx.)

Entrances
E1 Newchurch Road
E2 Beaufort Road

P Pavilion
SB Scoreboard
CP Car Parking
T Toilets
CS Club Shop
N1 Pavilion End
N2 Rugby Ground End

Stands
S1 Pavilion Terrace
S2 Rugby Terrace

1 Glamorgan CCC Indoor Cricket School
2 Bowling Green
3 Ebbw Vale RFC Ground
4 Ebbw Vale RFC Clubhouse

Streets
5 A4046 Newchurch Road

Above Right: Wicket-keeper Colin Metson achieved 61 dismissals during the 1994 season with 54 catches and 7 stumpings, together with making 398 runs (av 22.11), but was still overlooked by the tour selectors.

Abergavenny) and surrounding areas; National Welsh 151 from BR Newport; all pass close to ground. (01222 371331).

Car: Ground situated close to town centre adjoining Ebbw Vale RFC ground off A4046.
From north and east: A465 and A4046 follow signs Ebbw Vale, then as above.
From west: A465 and A4046 follow signs Ebbw Vale, then as north.
From south: M4 Junction 28, then follow A467 and A4046 signposted Ebbw Vale, then as north.

WHERE TO STAY
AND OTHER INFORMATION
Tourist Information: 01873 853254/857588.
Weather: 0898 500409
Local Hotels: County Hotel (01495 302418).
Local Radio Stations: BBC Radio Wales (882 KHz FM), Radio Gwent (95.9 MHz FM), Red Dragon Radio (97.4 MHz FM/1359 KHz MW).
Local Newspapers: South Wales Echo, Western Mail, South Wales Evening Post, Newport Argus, Gwent Gazette.

NEATH

Address: Neath Cricket Club, The Pavilion, The Gnoll Cricket Ground, Dyfed Road, Gnoll, Neath, West Glamorgan, Wales.

Telephone Number for Prospects of Play: 01639 643719.

Entrances: Dyfed Road (Players, Officials, Members, Public, Vehicles), Gnoll Park Road – Neath Rugby Football Ground (Members, Public, Vehicles), Llantwit Road (Members, Public).

Members' Enclosure: Pavilion, Pavilion terraces and defined Members' Enclosure.

Public Enclosure: Rest of the ground.

Covered Stands: Pavilion, Glamorgan CCC Indoor Cricket School.

Open Stands: Pavilion terraces together with temporary raised seating and ground level seating surrounding the playing area.

Disabled Areas: No special area, request suitable position.

Car Parking Facilities: Car parking within the ground is limited to Players, Officials, Committee Members. Limited Members' parking on the Neath Rugby field. Alternative car parks in the town centre a short walk away or in neighbouring streets.

Ground Dimensions: 133m x 115m.

Ground Capacity: 6,000.

Best Crowd: First-Class Match: 12,000 v Warwickshire 1948. Limited-Overs Match: 4,000 v Somerset (RAL) 1990.

HOW TO GET THERE

Rail: Neath (BR) 0.5 mile.

Bus: South Wales Transport from surrounding areas to Neath Bus Station thence 0.25 mile.

Car: Ground is situated north-west of town centre between River Neath and B4434 adjoining Neath Sports Centre and Neath RFC.

From north: A465 or A474 follow signs Neath.

↑ North direction (approx.)

Entrances
E1 Dyfed Road
E2 Llantwit Road
E3 via Neath Rugby Ground

P Pavilion
SB Scoreboard
CP Car Parking
T Toilets
CS Club Shop
N1 Llantwit Road End
N2 Dyfed Road End
R BR Neath (direction)
C Town Centre (direction)

Stands
S1 Pavilion Terrace

1 Glamorgan CCC Indoor Cricket School
2 Neath RFC Ground
3 Neath RFC Clubhouse
4 Neath Sports Centre
5 Tennis Courts/Bowling Greens

Streets
6 Dyfed Road
7 B4434 (direction)

Above Right: Despite touring the West Indies in 1994, Matthew Maynard missed much of the 1994 season due to injury but still hit 974 first-class runs (av 36.07) with a best performance of 118 versus Derbyshire at Cardiff.

From east and south: M4 Junction 41, then follow A48 and A474 signposted Neath.
From west: M4 Junction 44, then follow A48 and A465 signposted Neath.

WHERE TO STAY AND OTHER INFORMATION

Tourist Information: 01639 63353.
Weather: 0898 500409.
Local Hotels: Cimla Court Hotel (01639 3771), Castle Hotel (where Welsh Rugby Union was founded).
Local Radio Stations: BBC Radio Wales (882 KHz MW), BBC Radio Cymru (93.1 MHz FM/882 KHz MW), Swansea Sound (96.4 MHz FM/1170 KHz MW).
Local Newspapers: South Wales Evening Post, South Wales Echo, Western Mail, Neath Guardian Series.

PONYTPRIDD

Address: Pontypridd Cricket Club, The Pavilion, Ynysangharad Park, Pontypridd, Mid Glamorgan, Wales.

Telephone Number for Prospects of Play: 01443 400785.

Entrances: From Ynysangharad Park (Players, Officials, Members, Vehicles).

Members' Enclosure: Pavilion, Pavilion terrace and defined Members' Enclosure.

Public Enclosure: Rest of the ground.

Covered Stands: Pavilion.

Open Stands: Temporary raised seating together with ground level seating and benches on the bank at the Pavilion End.

Disabled Areas: No special area, request suitable position. Car parking available within park by prior arrangement.

Car Parking Facilities: Car parking is limited to Players, Officials within the park and ground. Car parking for Members, Public is available a short walk away in town centre car parks. Alternatively there is limited street parking locally.

Ground Dimensions: 120m x 114m.

Ground Capacity: 6,000.

Best Crowd: First-Class Match: 6,000 v Gloucestershire 1933. Limited-Overs Match: 3,000 v Essex (JPL) 1970.

HOW TO GET THERE

Rail: Pontypridd (BR) 0.25 mile.

Bus: Local bus to Ynysangharad Park via Ynysybwl Road from surrounding areas to Pontypridd Bus Station, thence 0.5 mile.

Car: Ground is situated off B4273 Ynysybwl Road adjoining Ynysangharad Park.

From north: A470 follow signs Pontypridd.

From east and south: M4 Junction 32, then follow A470 signs Pontypridd and town centre.

From west: A4058 or A473 follow signs Pontypridd and town centre.

↑ North direction (approx.)

Entrances
E1 Ynysangharad Park

P Pavilion
SB Scoreboard
CP Car Parking
T Toilets
CS Club Shop
N1 Pavilion End
N2 River Taff End
R BR Pontypridd (direction)
C Town Centre (direction)

Stands
S1 Pavilion Terrace

1 River Taff
2 Ynysangharad Park
3 Rugby Ground

Streets
4 B4273 Ynysybwl Road
5 A470

Above Right: Glamorgan captain and left-handed opening batsman, Hugh Morris scored 885 first-class runs (av 30.51) last season with a top score of 106 versus Sussex at Hove.

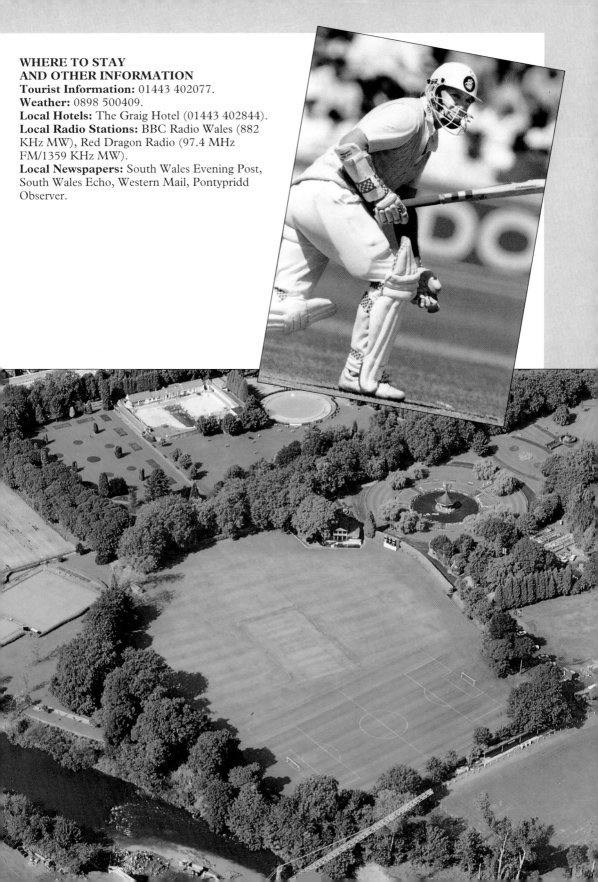

**WHERE TO STAY
AND OTHER INFORMATION**
Tourist Information: 01443 402077.
Weather: 0898 500409.
Local Hotels: The Graig Hotel (01443 402844).
Local Radio Stations: BBC Radio Wales (882 KHz MW), Red Dragon Radio (97.4 MHz FM/1359 KHz MW).
Local Newspapers: South Wales Evening Post, South Wales Echo, Western Mail, Pontypridd Observer.

Glamorgan

Address: Swansea Cricket and Football Club, The Pavilion, St Helen's Cricket Ground, Bryn Road, Swansea, West Glamorgan, Wales.
Telephone Number for Prospects of Play: 01792 466321.
Entrances: Bryn Road (Players, Officials, Members), Gorse Lane (Members, Public), Mumbles Road (Members, Public), Swansea Rugby Ground – via Mumbles Road (Members, Public).
Members' Enclosure: Pavilion, Clubhouse, St Helen's Lounge and defined Members' terrace enclosure at Pavilion End of the ground.
Public Enclosure: Rest of the ground.
Covered Stands: Pavilion, Clubhouse, St Helen's Lounge, Main Rugby Stand.
Open Stands: Pavilion terrace enclosure together with all permanent tiered terraces and seating surrounding the playing area.
Disabled Areas: No special area, request suitable position. Pavilion enclosure not recommended due to steep steps. Ideal position at Sea End near sightscreen.
Car Parking Facilities: Car parking within the ground for Players, Officials, Committee Members only. Car parking for Members, Public in Bryn Road, King Edward Road, St Helen's Avenue or the Mumbles car park on the seafront.
Ground Dimensions: 130m x 118m.
Ground Capacity: 16,000.
Best Crowd: First-Class Match: 50,000 v Australians 1964. Limited-Overs Match: 6,000 v Leicestershire (GC) 1977.

HOW TO GET THERE
Rail: Swansea (BR) 1.5 miles.
Bus: South Wales Transport 1, 2, 3, 14 from Swansea Bus Station 0.75 mile from BR Swansea – numerous services link BR Station with Bus Station, also South Wales Transport to Mumbles, Sketty, Oystermouth and Brynmill pass close to ground. (01792 485511).
Car: Ground shared with Swansea RFC near

↑ North direction (approx.)

Entrances
E1 Bryn Road
E2/3 Gorse Lane
E4 Mumbles Road

P Pavilion
SB Scoreboard
CP Car Parking
T Toilets
CS Club Shop
N1 Pavilion End
N2 Sea End
R BR Swansea (direction)
C City Centre (direction)

Stands
S1 Pavilion Terrace
S2 Rugby Stand
S3 St Helen's Lounge

1 Swansea RFC Ground
2 Swansea Seafront
7 The Cricketers Public House

Streets
3 Bryn Road
4 King Edward Road
5 Gorse Lane
6 A4067 Mumbles Road

Above Right: Right-arm medium pacer Stephen Barwick seen bowling at Colwyn Bay in 1994, watched by Neil Fairbrother.

seafront, 1.5 miles west of city centre off A4067 Mumbles Road close to Gorse Lane and Bryn Road.
From north: A465, A4067 or A48, follow signs city centre.
From west: M4 Junction 47, then follow A483 and A4216 to Mumbles Road.
From east: M4 Junction 44, then follow signs Swansea on A4217 and A4067 to Mumbles Road.

WHERE TO STAY
AND OTHER INFORMATION
Tourist Information: 01792 468321.
Weather: 0898 500459.
Local Hotels: Dragon Hotel (01792 51074), Beaumont Hotel (01792 43044), Dolphin Hotel (01792 50011).
Local Radio Stations: BBC Radio Wales (882 KHz MW), BBC Radio Cymru (93.1 MHz FM/882 KHz MW), Swansea Sound (96.4 MHz FM/1170 KHz MW).
Local Newspapers: South Wales Evening Post, Western Mail, South Wales Echo.

Address: Sun Alliance County Cricket Ground, Nevil Road, Bishopston, Bristol, BS7 9EJ.

Telephone Number for Prospects of Play: 0117 924 8461.

Entrances: Nevil Road – via Grace Gates (Players, Officials, Members, Public, Vehicles), Ashley Down Road (Members, Public, Vehicles).

Members' Enclosure: Pavilion and defined area at Pavilion End of the ground.

Public Enclosure: Rest of the ground.

Covered Stands: Pavilion (part), Mound Stand, Jessop Tavern, New Sports Complex (part).

Open Stands: Pavilion (part), Jessop Terrace, temporary seating surrounding the playing area.

Disabled Areas: No special area, request suitable position. Car parking available within the ground in a position to view the cricket.

Car Parking Facilities: Car parking is available within the ground to the rear of the New Sports Complex and Mound Stand, together with an area to the north of the playing area from where cricket can be viewed from cars and at the Ashley Down End. Street parking is also available locally.

Ground Dimensions: 154m x 156m.

Ground Capacity: 8,000.

Best Crowd: First-Class Match: 15,000 v Australians 1930 and 1948. Limited-Overs Match: 7,500 v Nottinghamshire (NWBT) 1987.

HOW TO GET THERE

Rail: Montpelier (BR) 0.75 mile, Bristol Temple Meads (BR) 2.5 miles, Bristol Parkway (BR) 5 miles.

Bus: City Line 78 from BR Bristol Temple Meads Station Approach Road, 72, 73 from BR Bristol Parkway, 71, 72, 73, 74, 75, 76, 77, 78 from City Centre pass close to the ground. (0117 955 3231).

Car: *From north:* M5 Junction 17, then follow signs A38 Bristol and city centre, then follow signs for County Cricket in Nevil Road off A38

↑ North direction (approx.)

Entrances
E1 Nevil Road
E2 Ashley Down Road

P Pavilion/Gloucestershire CCC
   Club Office
SB Scoreboard
CP Car Parking
T Toilets
CS Club Shop
N1 Pavilion End
N2 Ashley Down End
R BR Bristol Temple Meads
   (direction)
C City Centre (direction)

Stands
S1 Pavilion Terrace
S2 Mound Stand
S3 Jessop Tavern
S4 Jessop Terrace
S5 New Stand

1 Tennis Courts
2 Squash Club

Streets
3 Nevil Road
4 A38 Gloucester Road

Above Right: Stevenage born Tony Wright was Gloucestershire's leading run scorer in 1994 with 1,203 first-class runs (av 36.45), which included a career best 184 not out versus Leicestershire at Bristol.

Gloucester Road.

From east: M4 Junction 19, then follow M32 to Junction 2, then follow signs to Bristol and city centre on A38, then as north.

From south: A37 or A4 to Bristol city centre, then as west.

From west: As north or A370, A369 or A38 to Bristol and city centre, then follow A38 Gloucester Road for Nevil Road and county cricket.

WHERE TO STAY AND OTHER INFORMATION

Tourist Information: 0117 926 0767.
Weather: 0898 500405/500409.
Local Hotels: Grand Hotel (0117 929 1645), Holiday Inn (0117 929 4281), Clifton Hotel (0117 973 6882), Unicorn Hotel (0117 923 0333).
Local Radio Stations: BBC Radio Bristol (95.5 MHz FM/1548 KHz MW), Great Western Radio (96.3 MHz FM/1260 KHz MW).
Local Newspapers: Bristol Evening Post, Western Daily Press, Bristol Journal, Bristol Observer, Sunday Independent.

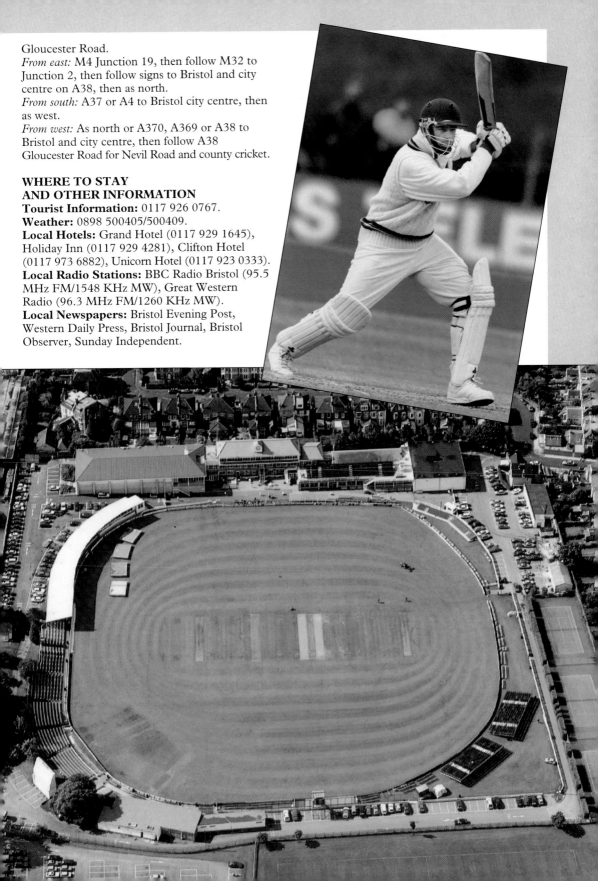

Address: Cheltenham College, College Sports Ground, Thirlestaine Road, Cheltenham, Gloucestershire.

Telephone Number for Prospects of Play: 01242 522000.

Entrances: Thirlestaine Road (Players, Officials, Members, Public, Vehicles), Sandford Road (Members, Public).

Members' Enclosure: Gymnasium (used as a Pavilion by Players, Members) and defined Members' Enclosure to the south of the playing area.

Public Enclosure: Rest of the ground.

Covered Stands: Gymnasium.

Open Stands: Temporary ground level and tiered seating surrounding the playing area.

Disabled Areas: No special area, request suitable position.

Car Parking Facilities: Car parking is available within the ground at the College Lawn End for Players, Officials, Members, through the entrance to the south of the ground. Car parking is also available in the adjacent College fields and in Thirlestaine Road for the Public.

Ground Dimensions: 120m x 150m.

Ground Capacity: 8,000.

Best Crowd: First-Class Match: 15,000 v Middlesex 1947. Limited-Overs Match: 6,750 v Essex (JPL) 1975.

HOW TO GET THERE

Rail: Cheltenham Spa (BR) 1 mile.

Bus: Cheltenham and District L from town centre, F/G link BR Cheltenham Spa with town centre. (01242 522021).

Car: Ground is situated in Thirlestaine Road, adjoining Cheltenham College, reached by A435 from town centre.

From north: M5 Junction 10, then follow A4019 signposted Cheltenham and town centre,

↑ North direction (approx.)

Entrances
E1/2 Thirlestaine Road
E3/4 Sandford Road

P Gymnasium (Players' Pavilion)
SB Scoreboard
CP Car Parking
T Toilets
CS Club Shop
N1 College End
N2 College Lawn End
R BR Cheltenham Spa (direction)
C City Centre (direction)

1 Cheltenham College Buildings

Streets
2 Thirlestaine Road
3 Sandford Road

Above Right: Mark Alleyne became the youngest player to score a double century for the county in 1990 when he hit a career best 256 against Northamptonshire at Northampton.

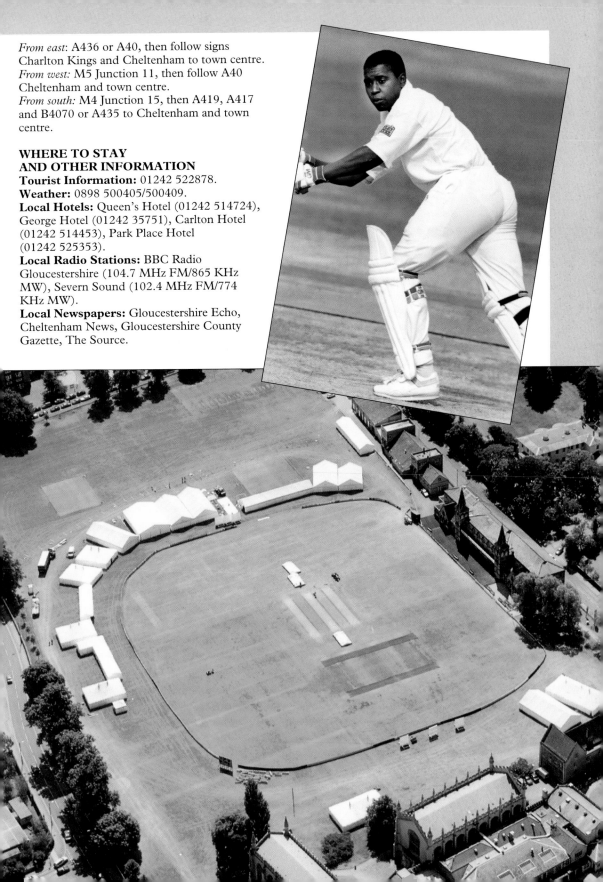

From east: A436 or A40, then follow signs
Charlton Kings and Cheltenham to town centre.
From west: M5 Junction 11, then follow A40
Cheltenham and town centre.
From south: M4 Junction 15, then A419, A417
and B4070 or A435 to Cheltenham and town
centre.

WHERE TO STAY
AND OTHER INFORMATION
Tourist Information: 01242 522878.
Weather: 0898 500405/500409.
Local Hotels: Queen's Hotel (01242 514724),
George Hotel (01242 35751), Carlton Hotel
(01242 514453), Park Place Hotel
(01242 525353).
Local Radio Stations: BBC Radio
Gloucestershire (104.7 MHz FM/865 KHz
MW), Severn Sound (102.4 MHz FM/774
KHz MW).
Local Newspapers: Gloucestershire Echo,
Cheltenham News, Gloucestershire County
Gazette, The Source.

Address: King's School, The Pavilion, Archdeacon Meadow, St Oswald's Road, Gloucester, Gloucestershire.

Telephone Number for Prospects of Play: 01452 423011.

Entrances: St Oswald's Road (Players, Officials, Members, Public, Vehicles).

Members' Enclosure: Pavilion, defined Members' Enclosure.

Public Enclosure: Rest of the ground.

Covered Stands: Pavilion.

Open Stands: Temporary ground level seating surrounding the playing area.

Disabled Areas: No special area, request suitable position. Cars can be taken into the ground and parked at the Scoreboard End.

Car Parking Facilities: Car parking is available within the ground at the Pavilion End for Players, Officials, Members, through the main entrance to the rear of the Pavilion off St Oswald's Road. Car parking is also available a short walk away from the ground in Lower Westgate Street.

Ground Dimensions: 145m x 135m.

Ground Capacity: 7,500.

Best Crowd: First-Class Match: 3,500 v Worcestershire 1993. Limited-Overs Match: 4,500 v Worcestershire (AELL) 1993.

HOW TO GET THERE

Rail: Gloucester Central (BR) 0.5 mile.

Bus: City of Gloucester Bus Company services from city centre pass outside the ground 300m from BR Gloucester Central. (01452 27516).

Car: *From north:* M5 Junction 11, then follow signs Gloucester city centre.

From east: A436, A417 to Gloucester city centre.

From west: A417, A48 and B4215 follow signs Gloucester city centre.

From south: M5 Junction 12, then follow signs Gloucester city centre.

↑ North direction (approx.)

Entrances
E1/2 St Oswald's Road

P Pavilion
SB Scoreboard
CP Car Parking
T Toilets
CS Club Shop
N1 Pavilion End
N2 Sports Centre End
R BR Gloucester Central
   (direction)
C City Centre (direction)

Streets
1 A417 St Oswald's Road

2 Sports Centre/Tennis Courts

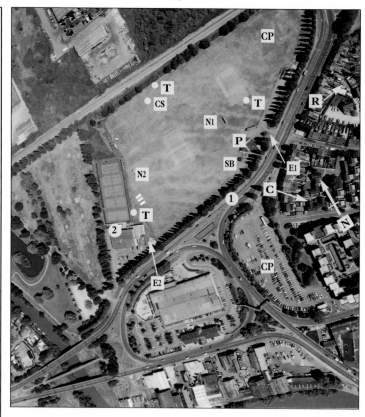

Above Right: Gloucestershire wicket-keeper Jack Russell who scored 901 first-class runs (av 34.65) and achieved 60 dismissals (59 catches and 1 stumping) during his Benefit last season.

WHERE TO STAY
AND OTHER INFORMATION

Tourist Information: 01452 421188.
Weather: 0898 500405/500409.
Local Hotels: New County Hotel
(01452 24977), Fleece Hotel (01452 22762),
Bowden Hall (01452 64121), Crest Hotel
(01452 63311).
Local Radio Stations: BBC Radio
Gloucestershire (104.7 MHz FM/865 KHz MW),
Severn Sound (102.4 MHz FM/774 KHz MW),
BBC Radio Hereford and Worcester
(94.7 MHz FM).
Local Newspapers: Gloucester Citizen,
Gloucestershire Echo, Gloucester Express,
Gloucester News, The Source.

SOUTHAMPTON

Address: County Cricket Ground, Northlands Road, Southampton, Hampshire SO9 2TY.
Telephone Number for Prospects of Play: 01703 333788/333789.
Entrances: Northlands Road (Players, Officials, Members, Public, Vehicles), Hulse Road (Members, Public).
Members' Enclosure: Pavilion, Pavilion terrace seating and areas defined as Members' Enclosure.
Public Enclosure: Rest of the ground.
Covered Stands: Pavilion, Phil Mead Stand, City End Stand.
Open Stands: Permanent and temporary raised and ground level seating surrounding the playing area.
Disabled Areas: No special area, request suitable position.
Car Parking Facilities: Car parking is available within the ground for Players, Officials, Members only. Alternative car parking is available in neighbouring streets or on the nearby Southampton Common.

Ground Dimensions: 130m x 128m.
Ground Capacity: 7,000.
Best Crowd: First-Class Match: 15,000 v Australians 1935. Limited-Overs Match: 7,500 v Northamptonshire (GC) 1976.
Anticipated Developments: Designs being prepared for new County Ground outside urban area of Southampton.

HOW TO GET THERE

Rail: Southampton Central (BR) 1 mile.
Bus: Hampshire Bus 47, 147 Southampton-Winchester and Solent Blue Line 48 Southampton-Eastleigh all pass within 0.25 mile of the ground. (01962 52352).
Car: Ground situated in Northlands Road off The Avenue (A33), west of Southampton Common and 0.75 mile north of the city centre. *From north:* M3 to Junction 10, then follow A33 Southampton and city centre, or A3037 and A35 to city centre.

⬆ North direction (approx.)

Entrances
E1/2 Northlands Road
E3 Hulse Road

P Pavilion
SB Scoreboard
CP Car Parking
T Toilets
CO Hampshire CCC Club Office
CS Club Shop
N1 Northlands Road End
N2 City End
R BR Southampton (direction)
C City Centre (direction)

Stands
S1 Pavilion Terrace
S2 Phil Mead Stand
S3 City End Stand

1 Hampshire CCC Indoor Cricket School and Squash Club
4 Southampton Common

Streets
2 Northlands Road
3 A33 The Avenue

Above Right Hampshire opener Paul Terry topped the county's first-class batting averages in 1994 with 1,286 runs (av 38.96) including 164 against Durham at Portsmouth.

From east: M27 Junction 5, then follow signs Southampton and city centre, A35 and A33, then as north.
From west: M27 Junction 3, then M271, A35 or A3024 follow Southampton and city centre, then as north.

WHERE TO STAY
AND OTHER INFORMATION
Tourist Information: 01703 832615.
Weather: 0898 500403/500457.
Local Hotels: Northlands Hotel (01703 333871), Dolphin Hotel (01703 226178), The Polygon (01703 330055), Forte Post House Hotel (01703 330777).
Local Radio Stations: BBC Radio Solent (96.1 MHz FM/1359 KHz MW), Radio Victory (95.0 MHz FM/1170 KHz MW).
Local Newspapers: Evening Echo & Hampshire Chronicle, Southern Evening Echo, The News, Southampton Advertiser, Southampton Guardian, Portsmouth News.

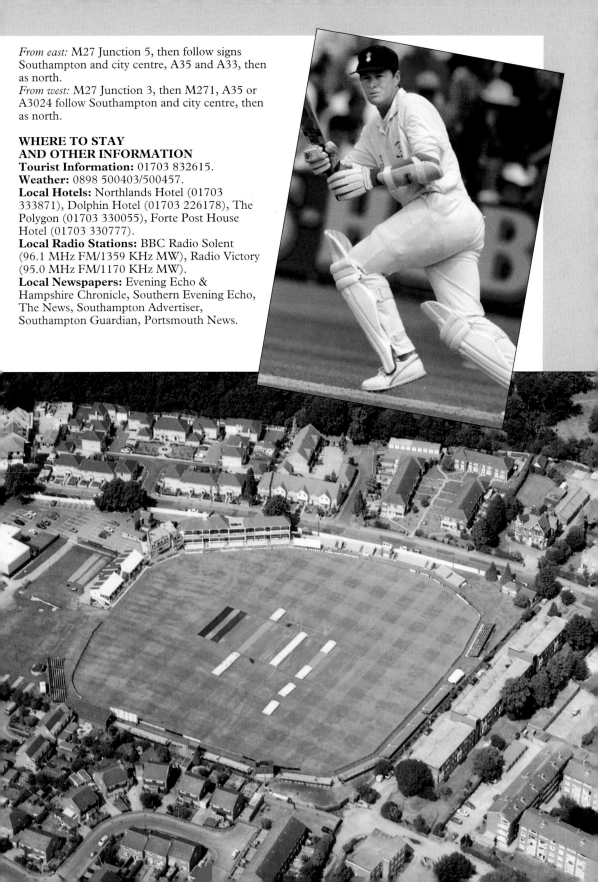

BASINGSTOKE

Address: Basingstoke and North Hants Cricket Club, May's Bounty, Bounty Road, Basingstoke, Hampshire.

Telephone Number for Prospects of Play: 01256 473646.

Entrances: Fairfields Road (Players, Officials, Members, Public), Bounty Road (Members, Public, all Vehicles).

Members' Enclosure: Pavilion, Pavilion terrace and defined Members' Enclosure between Pavilion and Press/Scorers' Tent at the Castle Field End of the ground.

Public Enclosure: Rest of the ground.

Covered Stands: Pavilion.

Open Stands: Temporary ground level seating surrounding the playing area.

Disabled Areas: No special area, request suitable position.

Car Parking Facilities: Car parking is available in adjoining Castle Field to the west and south of the ground for 2,500+ vehicles and is entered from Bounty Road.

Ground Dimensions: 120m x 115m.

Ground Capacity: 5,000.

Best Crowd: First-Class Match: 5,000 v Surrey 1986. Limited-Overs Match: 4,300 v Warwickshire (JPL) 1977.

HOW TO GET THERE

Rail: Basingstoke (BR) 0.75 mile.

Bus: Hampshire Bus 322, 323, 324 from BR Basingstoke to within 0.25 mile of ground. (01256 464501).

Car: Ground is situated 0.5 mile from the town centre south-west of the town off the A30 Winchester Road in Bounty Road.

From north: M4 Junction 11, then A33 follow signs Basingstoke, or M4 Junction 12, then A4 and A340 follow signs Basingstoke, then as above.

From east: M3 Junction 6, then follow signs

↑ North direction (approx.)

Entrances
E1 Bounty Road
E2 Car Park via Bounty Road
E3 Fairfields Road

P Pavilion
SB Scoreboard
CP Car Parking
T Toilets
CS Club Shop
N1 Town End
N2 Castle Field End
R BR Basingstoke (direction)
C Town Centre (direction)

Stands
S1 Pavilion Terrace

Streets
1 Bounty Road
2 Fairfields Road
3 A340 (direction)

Above Right: Shaun Udal, who toured Australia last winter, is seen eagerly twitching his spinning finger during net practice.

Basingstoke and A30 Winchester Road, then into
Bounty Road, or A30.
From west: M3 Junction 7, then follow signs
Basingstoke, then as above.
From south: A339 or A32 and A30 to Basingstoke,
then as above.

WHERE TO STAY
AND OTHER INFORMATION
Tourist Information: 01734 566226.
Weather: 0898 500406.
Local Hotels: Crest Hotel (01256 468181), Red
Lion Hotel (01256 28525).
Local Radio Stations: Radio 210 (97.0 MHz
FM/1431 KHz MW), County Sound (96.4 MHz
FM/1476 KHz MW).
Local Newspapers: Southern Evening Echo,
The News, Basingstoke and North Hants
Gazette.

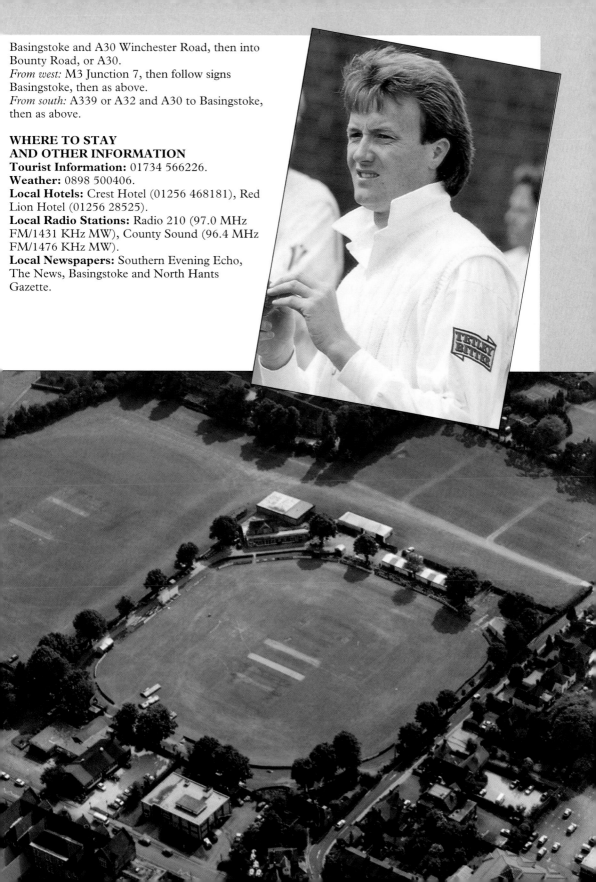

Hampshire

Address: United Services Portsmouth Cricket Club, United Services Officers' Sports Ground, Burnaby Road, Portsmouth, Hampshire.

Telephone Number for Prospects of Play: 01705 22351.

Entrances: Burnaby Road (Players, Officials, Members), King James Gate – via Burnaby Road (Public), Rugby Ground – via Park Road (Members, Public, Vehicles).

Members' Enclosure: Pavilion and defined area in front of the Pavilion and Clubhouse/bar area.

Public Enclosure: Rest of the ground.

Covered Stands: Pavilion, Clubhouse, Rugby Stand.

Open Stands: Permanent and temporary raised and ground level seating surrounding the playing area.

Disabled Areas: No special area, request suitable position.

Car Parking Facilities: Car parking is available on the rugby field for Players, Officials, Members. Alternative car parking can be found in local streets, city centre car parks a short walk away and the Portsmouth University car park (out of term time or at weekends).

Ground Dimensions: 145m x 140m.

Ground Capacity: 8,000.

Best Crowd: First-Class Match: 10,000 v Sussex 1948. Limited-Overs Match: 5,000 v Surrey (JPL) 1983.

HOW TO GET THERE

Rail: Portsmouth & Southsea (BR) 500m, Portsmouth Harbour (BR) 0.5 mile.

Bus: From surrounding areas to The Hard Interchange, thence 0.5 mile.

Car: Ground is situated in Old Portsmouth off the A3 London Road, close to the Guildhall and United Services' Sports Club. The ground is shared with USO Portsmouth Royal Navy.

↑ North direction (approx.)

Entrances
E1-E3 Burnaby Road
E4 Rugby Ground

P Pavilion/Club Office
SB Scoreboard
CP Car Parking
T Toilets
CS Club Shop
N1 Railway End
N2 United Services Club End
R BR Portsmouth & Southsea
   (direction)
C City Centre (direction)

Stands
S1 United Services Portsmouth
   Clubhouse
S2 Rugby Stand

1 Pay Gate
2 United Services Rugby Ground
3 United Services Officers' Club
4 Portsmouth University
5 Railway line
6 Tennis Courts

Streets
7 Burnaby Road
8 A3 London Road

Above Right: Robin Smith seen hitting to leg during England's tour match with Barbados at Bridgetown in 1994

From *north:* A3 or A3(M) follow signs Portsmouth and Isle of Wight Ferry Terminal.
From *east:* A27 then A2030 signposted Portsmouth and Ferry Terminal.
From *west:* M27 Junction 12, then M275 follow signs Portsmouth Harbour and Ferry Terminal.

**WHERE TO STAY
AND OTHER INFORMATION**
Tourist Information: 01705 826722.
Weather: 0898 500403/500457.
Local Hotels: Crest Hotel (01705 827651), Holiday Inn (01705 383151), Keppel's Head Hotel (01705 833231).
Local Radio Stations: BBC Radio Solent (96.1 MHz FM/1359 KHz MW), Ocean Sound (103.2 MHz FM/1557 KHz MW).
Local Newspapers: Southern Evening Echo & Hampshire Chronicle, Portsmouth Evening News.

CANTERBURY

Address: St Lawrence Cricket Ground, Old Dover Road, Canterbury, Kent CT1 3NZ.
Telephone Number for Prospects of Play: 01227 457323.
Entrances: Old Dover Road (Players, Officials, Members, Public, Vehicles), Nackington Road (Members, Public, Vehicles).
Members' Enclosure: Pavilion, Pavilion Annexe, Frank Woolley Stand, Colin Cowdrey Stand (Ground and First Floor Only).
Public Enclosure: Rest of the ground.
Covered Stands: Pavilion (part), Pavilion Annexe, Frank Woolley Stand (part), Colin Cowdrey Stand (part), Leslie Ames Stand (Executive Suites).
Open Stands: Pavilion (part), Frank Woolley Stand (part), Colin Cowdrey Stand (part) together with permanent ground level and tiered seating surrounding the playing area.
Disabled Areas: In Frank Woolley Stand and elsewhere in the ground by arrangement.

Car Parking Facilities: Ample car parking is available at most matches for Members and Public although this depends on weather conditions. During Canterbury Festival week and Benson and Hedges or National Westminster Bank Trophy Quarter and Semi-Finals space may be limited to Members' only – there is an overflow car park off Nackington Road in the nearby school field. There is also limited street parking surrounding the ground and in city centre car parks approximately 15min walk away. Cricket can be viewed from cars on the ring to the south but space is limited – arrive early!
Ground Capacity: 14,000.
Best Crowd: First-Class Match: 26,500 v Australians 1948. Limited-Overs Match: 14,000 v Somerset (GC) 1974.

HOW TO GET THERE
Rail: Canterbury East (BR) 1 mile, Canterbury West (BR) 1.5 miles.

↑ North direction (approx.)

Entrances
E1/2 Old Dover Road
E3 Nackington Road

P Pavilion
SB Scoreboard
CP Car Parking
T Toilets
CO Kent CCC Club Office
M Kent CCC Museum/Library
CS Club Shop
N1 Pavilion End
N2 Nackington Road End
R BR Canterbury East (direction)
C City Centre (direction)

Stands
S1 Frank Woolley Stand
S2 Colin Cowdrey Stand
S3 Leslie Ames Stand
S4 Pavilion Annexe

1 Kent CCC Indoor Cricket School
2 War Memorial
3 Lime Tree

Streets
4 A290 Old Dover Road
5 Nackington Road
6 New Dover Road

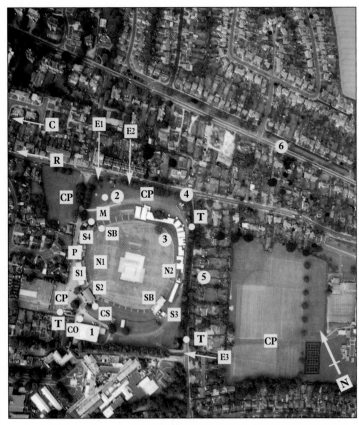

Above Right: Kent skipper Mark Benson will be hoping for an improved season in 1995 with some greater success for his county.

Bus: East Kent Buses 15, 16, 17 from Canterbury Bus Station or Folkestone pass ground, also 339 from City Centre; C1, C2, C5 link BR Canterbury Stations with the Bus Station. (01843 581333).

Car: Ground is situated 0.5 mile south of city centre off Old Dover Road.

From north: A290, A291 and A28 follow signs Canterbury and city centre.

From east: A257 to Canterbury, then as north.

From west: M2 to Junction 7, then A2 to Bridge turn off on Canterbury bypass, then A290 to Canterbury and Old Dover Road signposted County Cricket for St Lawrence Cricket Ground.

From south: A2, A28 and B2068 follow Canterbury signs, then Old Dover Road signposted County Cricket.

WHERE TO STAY
AND OTHER INFORMATION

Tourist Information: 01227 766567.

Weather: 0898 500402.

Local Hotels: County Hotel (01227 466266), The Chaucer Hotel (01227 464427).

Local Radio Stations: BBC Radio Kent (104.2 MHz FM/1035 KHz MW), Invicta Radio (103.1 MHz FM/1242 KHz MW).

Local Newspapers: Evening Post, Kentish Gazette, Kent Messenger, Kent and Sussex Courier.

FOLKESTONE

Address: Folkestone Cricket Club, The Pavilion, Cheriton Road, Cheriton, Folkestone, Kent CT19 5JU.

Telephone Number for Prospects of Play: 01303 253366.

Entrances: Cheriton Road (Players, Officials, Members, Public, Vehicles), Cornwallis Road (Members, Public, Vehicles).

Members' Enclosure: Pavilion, Pavilion Terrace, West Stand (part), South Stand.

Public Enclosure: West Stand (part), rest of the ground.

Covered Stands: Pavilion (part), West Stand, South Stand.

Open Stands: Pavilion (part) together with temporary ground level seating surrounding the playing area.

Disabled Areas: Disabled area at northern end near sightscreen, request suitable position. An area for vehicles is near the main scoreboard at the northern end.

Car Parking Facilities: Car parking for Members is available on the polo ground but spectators can also view cricket from their cars at the northern end of the ground. Car parking at the southern end is entered from Cheriton Road or from Cherry Garden Avenue.

Ground Dimensions: 134m x 170m.

Ground Capacity: 8,000.

Best Crowd: First-Class Match: 5,000 v Gloucestershire 1933. Limited-Overs Match: 7,500 v Essex (JPL) 1976.

HOW TO GET THERE

Rail: Folkestone Central (BR) 0.5 mile, Folkestone West (BR) 0.5 mile, Folkestone TML (Channel Tunnel Station) 0.75 mile.

Bus: From surrounding areas to Bus Station, thence 1 mile. East Kent F1, F3, F6, F9 link Bus Station and BR Folkestone Central with ground.

↑ North direction (approx.)

Entrances
E1 Cheriton Road
E2 Cornwallis Road

P Pavilion
SB Scoreboard
CP Car Parking
T Toilets
CS Club Shop
N1 North Downs End
N2 Cheriton Road End
R BR Folkestone West (direction)
C Town Centre (direction)

Stands
S1 Pavilion Terrace
S2 South Stand
S3 West Stand

1 Channel Tunnel Complex
2 Folkestone FC Ground

Streets
3 A20 Cheriton Road

Above Right: Min Patel, Kent's left-arm spinner, was rewarded with a place on England's 'A' tour of India in 1995 after achieving 90 wickets (av 22.85) in 1994.

(01843 581333).
Car: Ground is situated 0.5 mile west of town centre off A20 Cheriton Road.
From north: A260 to Folkestone, then follow signs Cheriton.
From east: A20 to Folkestone, then as above.
From west: M20 Junction 12, then A20 to Cheriton district.

WHERE TO STAY
AND OTHER INFORMATION
Tourist Information: 01303 58594.
Weather: 0898 500456/500457.
Local Hotels: Clifton Hotel (01303 241231), Burlington Hotel (01303 255301).
Local Radio Stations: BBC Radio Kent (104.2 MHz FM/1035 KHz MW), Invicta Radio (103.1 MHz FM/1242 KHz MW).
Local Newspapers: Evening Post, Folkestone & Dover People, Folkestone Hythe & Romney Marsh Herald.

MAIDSTONE

Address: The Mote Cricket Club, The Pavilion, Mote Park, Willow Way, Maidstone, Kent ME15 7RN.

Telephone Number for Prospects of Play: 01622 754545.

Entrances: Willow Way (Players, Officials, Members, Public, Vehicles), Mote Avenue (Members, Public, Vehicles).

Members' Enclosure: Pavilion, Mote Squash Club and defined Members' Enclosure between raised temporary stand next to the Squash Club building and the Tabernacle.

Public Enclosure: Rest of the ground.

Covered Stands: Pavilion (part).

Open Stands: Pavilion (part) together with permanent and temporary raised seating at bank level and ground level seating surrounding the playing area.

Disabled Areas: No special area, request suitable position. Vehicles can be parked on the motor bank next to the sightscreen at the West Park Road End.

Car Parking Facilities: Car parking is available at the Mote Avenue End for 1,000 cars and at the West Park Road End of the ground for 250 cars on the motor bank area from where cricket can be viewed from the car.

Ground Dimensions: 136m x 135m.

Ground Capacity: 8,000.

Best Crowd: First-Class Match: 8,000 v Essex 1948. Limited-Overs Match: 14,000 v Lancashire (JPL) 1974.

HOW TO GET THERE

Rail: Maidstone East (BR) 1 mile, Maidstone West (BR) 1.25 miles.

Bus: Boro' Line 85 from High Street 0.25 mile from both BR Stations, also routes 5, 12 pass the ground. (01622 690060).

Car: Ground situated off A20 Ashford Road through Square Hill Road and Mote Road for Mote Park.

↑ North direction (approx.)

Entrances
E1 Willow Way
E2 Willow Way
E3 Mote Avenue

P Pavilion
SB Scoreboard
CP Car Parking
T Toilets
CS Club Shop
N1 Mote Avenue End
N2 West Park Road End
R BR Maidstone East (direction)
C Town Centre (direction)

1 Tabernacle
2 Mote Squash Club

Streets
3 Willow Way
4 Mote Road
5 A20 Ashford Road

Above Right: Former member of the Royal Green Jackets, Matthew Fleming, seen under a green batting helmet, hits to leg during the match with Combined Universities at Christ Church, Oxford in 1994.

From north: M20 Junctions 6 or 7, then either A229 or A249 to Maidstone town centre, then as above.
From east: M20 Junction 8, then A20 to town centre, then as above, or A274 or A229 to town centre and as above.
From west: M20 Junction 5, then follow signs Maidstone and town centre, then as above.
From south: A26, A229 or A274 to Maidstone and town centre, then as above.

WHERE TO STAY
AND OTHER INFORMATION
Tourist Information: 01634 843666.
Weather: 0898 500402.
Local Hotels: Great Danes, Hollingbourne (01622 730022), Royal Star Hotel (01622 755721), Larkfield Hotel (01732 846858).
Local Radio Stations: BBC Radio Kent (104.2 MHz FM/1035 KHz MW), Invicta Radio (103.1 MHz FM/1242 KHz MW).
Local Newspapers: Evening Post, Kentish Gazette, East Kent Mercury, Maidstone Borough News.

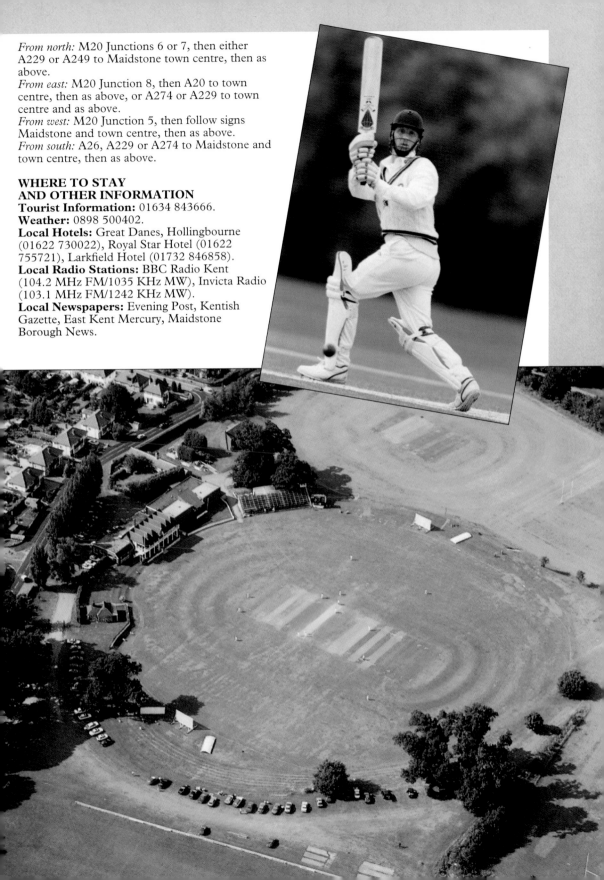

TUNBRIDGE WELLS

Address: Tunbridge Wells Cricket Club, The Pavilion, Nevill Cricket Ground, Nevill Gate, Warwick Park, Tunbridge Wells, Kent TN2 5ES.
Telephone Number for Prospects of Play: 01892 520846.
Entrances: Nevill Gate – via Warwick Park (Players, Officials, Members, Public, Vehicles), Car Park – via path off Warwick Park (Members, Public), Cumberland Walk (Members, Public).
Members' Enclosure: Pavilion together with defined Members' Enclosure at the Pavilion End of the ground.
Public Enclosure: Rest of the ground.
Covered Stands: Pavilion (part).
Open Stands: Pavilion (part) together with temporary raised and ground level seating surrounding the playing area.
Disabled Areas: Defined area available close to main Pavilion, otherwise request suitable position.
Car Parking Facilities: Car parking is available within the ground for Players, Officials and some Members near the hard tennis courts. There is also a 4-acre field available for car parking adjoining the ground and street parking locally.
Ground Dimensions: 138m x 135m.
Ground Capacity: 5,500.
Best Crowd: First-Class Match: 10,000 v Lancashire 1950. Limited-Overs Match: 6,000 v Sussex (GC) 1963.

HOW TO GET THERE
Rail: Tunbridge Wells (BR) 0.75 mile.
Bus: From surrounding areas to Frant Road End routes 252, 254, 256, 280, 283, 791; also via Hawkenbury End route 285. (01622 690060).
Car: Ground is situated 0.5 mile south of the town centre off A267 Hastings Road, then into Roedean Road and Warwick Park.
From north: A21, A26 or A227 to Tunbridge Wells, then as above.

↑ North direction (approx.)

Entrances
E1 Nevill Gate via Warwick Park
E2 Warwick Park via Car Park
E3 Cumberland Walk

P Pavilion
SB Scoreboard
CP Car Parking
T Toilets
CS Club Shop
N1 Railway End
N2 Pavilion End
R BR Tunbridge Wells (direction)
C Town Centre (direction)

Stands
S1 Pavilion Terrace
S2 Martlets Pavilion
S3 Pavilion Enclosure

1 Tennis Courts
2 Railway line

Streets
3 Warwick Park
4 Nevill Gate
5 Cumberland Walk
6 A267 Hastings Road

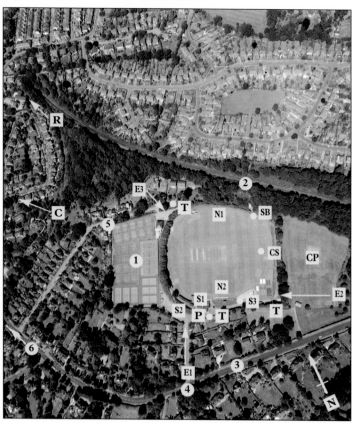

Above Right: Kent quickie, Martin McCague celebrates the wicket of David Boon during the Third Cornhill Test at Trent Bridge in 1993.

From east and west: A264 to Tunbridge Wells, then as above.
From south: A267 to Tunbridge Wells, then as above.

WHERE TO STAY
AND OTHER INFORMATION
Tourist Information: 01892 515675.
Weather: 0898 500402/500403.
Local Hotels: Calverley Hotel (01892 536801), Russell Hotel (01892 544833).
Local Radio Stations: BBC Radio Kent (104.2 MHz FM/1035 KHz MW), Invicta Radio (103.1 MHz FM/1242 KHz MW).
Local Newspapers: Evening Post, Kent and Sussex Courier.

MANCHESTER

Address: Old Trafford Cricket Ground, Talbot Road, Manchester M16 0PX.

Telephone Number for Prospects of Play: 0161 872 0261.

Entrances: Warwick Road (Members, Public), Talbot Road (Players, Officials, Members, Public, Vehicles), Great Stone Road (Members, Public, Vehicles).

Members' Enclosure: Pavilion, Ladies Pavilion and defined permanent enclosure in front of these two buildings.

Public Enclosure: Warwick Road End terraced seating – enclosure A (Archie MacLaren Stand), B (Eddie Paynter Stand), C, D (A.N. Hornby Stand), E (Cyril Washbrook and Brian Statham Stand). Upper/Lower, terraced seating, enclosures F, G, H, J, K.

Covered Stands: Pavilion (part), Red Rose Executive Suites, Washbrook and Statham Stand Lower (part), H Stand (part), Stretford End Executive Suites, Board of Control Stand Suites, Ladies Pavilion.

Open Stands: Pavilion (part), Pavilion enclosure, Stands A (Archie MacLaren Stand), B (Eddie Paynter Stand), C, D (A.N. Hornby Stand), E, F, G, H (part), J, K, together with Washbrook and Statham Stand Upper, Board of Control Stand, Ladies Pavilion enclosure.

Disabled Areas: E Stand enclosure for wheelchairs and for Members' Enclosure in special section adjoining Pavilion.

Car Parking Facilities: Car parking is available for Players, Officials, Members in the main Talbot Road car park for season ticket holders only. Alternative car parking for Members, Public on the practice ground entered off Great Stone Road, in the adjoining government office car parks at weekends only, and in several local school playing fields during Test and International Matches. Street car parking also available nearby.

Ground Dimensions: 143m x 149m.

↑ North direction (approx.)

Entrances
E1 Talbot Road
E2 Warwick Road
E3 Great Stone Road

P Pavilion
SB Scoreboard
CP Car Parking
T Toilets
CO Lancashire CCC Club Office
M Lancashire CCC Museum
CS Club Shop
N1 Stretford End
N2 Warwick Road End
R Old Trafford Metro (direction)
C City Centre (direction)

Stands
S1 Pavilion Terrace
S2 Archie MacLaren Stand
S3 Eddie Paynter Stand
S4 A.N. Hornby Stand
S5 Red Rose Suites/Cardus Press Gallery
S6 Washbrook and Statham Stand
S7 H Stand
S8 Stretford Executive Suites
S9 Board of Control Stand
S10 Ladies Pavilion

1 Tyldesley Suite
2 Trafford Suite
3 Lancashire CCC Indoor Cricket School
4 B&Q Warehouse
5 Metro Tram line
6 Government Offices
7 Manchester United FC Ground (direction)
8 Trafford Town Hall
9 Kellogg's Head Office

Streets
10 Great Stone Road
11 Talbot Road
12 Warwick Road
13 A56 (direction)

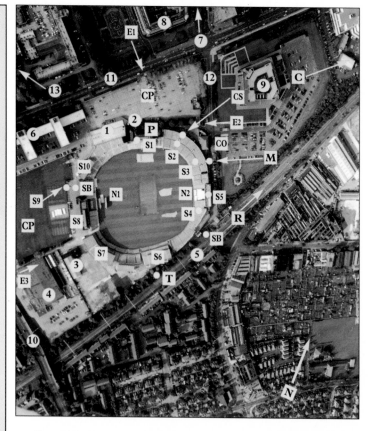

Above Right: Seen batting at The Parks, Lancashire's Neil Fairbrother hit a career best 366 versus Surrey at The Foster's Oval in 1990.

Ground Capacity: 20,000.
Best Crowd: First-Class Match: 78,617 v Yorkshire 1926. Limited-Overs Match: 33,000 v Yorkshire (JPL) 1970.

HOW TO GET THERE
Rail: Old Trafford (Metro) adjacent, connects with Manchester Piccadilly (BR).
Bus: GM Buses 112, 113, 115, 720 from Piccadilly to ground. (0161 228 7811).
Car: The ground is situated 2.5 miles south-west of the city centre on the east side of the main A56 in the Old Trafford district of Manchester.
From north: M61 then M63 Junction 4, follow signs A5081 Manchester, then after 2.5 miles left into Warwick Road and right into Talbot Road for Old Trafford.
From east: M62 Junction 17, then A56 follow signs Manchester, Old Trafford is signposted on your right in Talbot Road.
From west: M62 then M63 Junction 4, then as north.
From south: M6 Junction 19, then follow signs A556 Stockport, then A56 Altrincham, from Altrincham follow signs County Cricket/Test Match for Old Trafford and Manchester. Old Trafford is signposted on your right off Talbot Road.

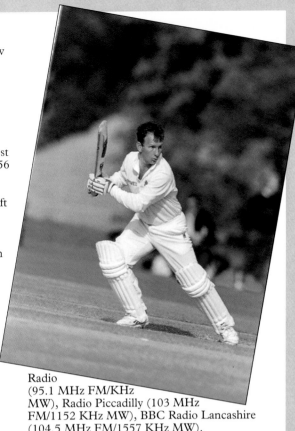

WHERE TO STAY
AND OTHER INFORMATION
Tourist Information: 0161 234 3157.
Weather: 0898 500411.
Local Hotels: Hotel Piccadilly (0161 236 8414), Portland Thistle (0161 228 3567), The Grand Hotel (0161 236 9559), Post House Hotel (0161 998 7090), many others.
Local Radio Stations: Greater Manchester Radio (95.1 MHz FM/KHz MW), Radio Piccadilly (103 MHz FM/1152 KHz MW), BBC Radio Lancashire (104.5 MHz FM/1557 KHz MW).
Local Newspapers: Manchester Evening News, North West Times, Saturday and Sunday Sports Pink.

BLACKPOOL

Address: Blackpool Cricket Club, The Pavilion, Stanley Park, West Park Drive, Blackpool, Lancashire.

Telephone Number for Prospects of Play: 01253 33347/301950.

Entrances: West Park Drive (Players, Officials, Members, Public, Vehicles).

Members' Enclosure: Pavilion and defined Members' Enclosure to the west of the playing area.

Public Enclosure: Rest of the ground.

Covered Stands: Pavilion, Ladies Pavilion.

Open Stands: Permanent tiered seating and temporary ground level surrounding the playing area.

Disabled Areas: Special area at Pavilion End with facility for vehicles by prior arrangement at Northern End.

Car Parking Facilities: Car parking is available within the ground on top of the bank at the Nursery End of the ground where cricket can be viewed from cars. Further car parking is available in Stanley Park and surrounding streets.

Ground Dimensions: 131m x 126m.

Ground Capacity: 9,000.

Best Crowd: First-Class Match: 13,782 v Glamorgan 1950. Limited-Overs Match: 12,000 v Sussex (JPL) 1976.

HOW TO GET THERE

Rail: Blackpool North (BR) 1 mile, Blackpool South (BR) 0.75 mile.

Bus: Blackpool Transport 16, 26 from Talbot Square adjacent to BR Blackpool North to within 0.25 mile of ground. (01253 23931).

Car: Ground is located off the A583 in West Park Drive adjoining Stanley Park which is 0.5 mile south-east of the town centre.

From north: M6 Junction 32, then follow M55 to Junction 4 Blackpool and seafront, or A584,

↑ North direction (approx.)

Entrances
E1 West Park Drive
E2 West Park Drive

P Pavilion
SB Scoreboard
CP Car Parking
T Toilets
CS Club Shop
N1 Pavilion End
N2 Nursery End
R BR Blackpool North (direction)
C Town Centre (direction)

Stands
S1 Pavilion Terrace
S2 Ladies Pavilion

1 Stanley Park
3 Seafront/Beach (direction)

Streets
2 A583 West Park Road

Above Right: Australian-born, Jason Gallian made a super start to his first-class county career with Lancashire last season recording 874 runs (av 43.70) with a career best 171 against Surrey at Old Trafford.

A587, A586 to town centre then A583 as above.
From east: M6 Junction 32, then as north.
From south: A584, A583 or B5261 to Blackpool
town centre, then as above.

WHERE TO STAY
AND OTHER INFORMATION
Tourist Information: 01253 21623.
Weather: 0898 500461.
Local Hotels: Imperial Hotel (01253 23971),
Savoy Hotel (01253 52561), many small hotels
and guesthouses.
Local Radio Stations: Red Rose Radio
(97.3 MHz FM/999 KHz MW), BBC Radio
Lancashire (104.5 MHz FM/1557 KHz MW).
Local Newspapers: Lancashire Evening
Telegraph, Lancashire Evening Post, West
Lancashire Gazette, Blackpool Evening Gazette.

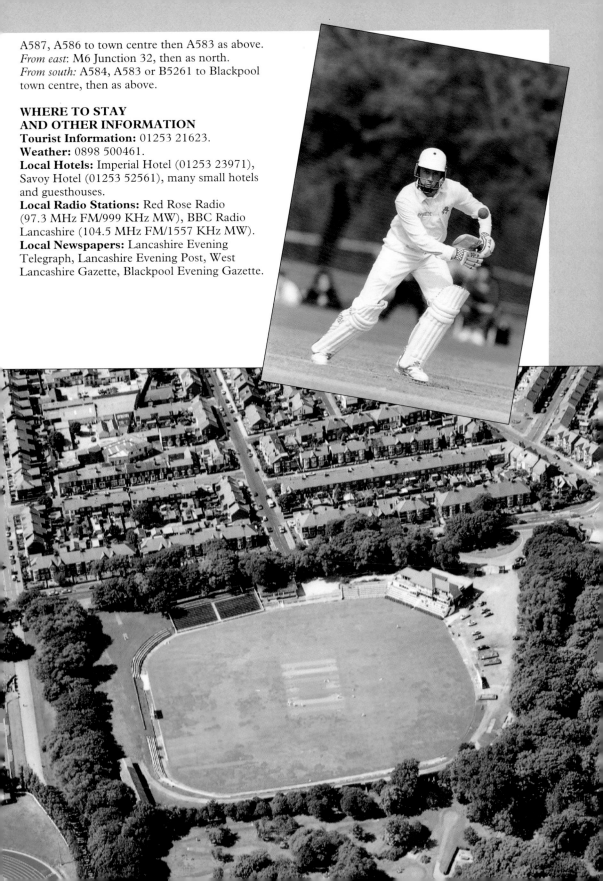

LIVERPOOL

Address: Liverpool Cricket Club, The Pavilion, Aigburth Road, Grassendale, Liverpool, Merseyside L19 3QF.

Telephone Number for Prospects of Play: 0151 427 2930.

Entrances: Aigburth Road (Players, Officials, Members, Vehicles), Riversdale Road (Members, Public, Vehicles).

Members' Enclosure: Pavilion, Ladies Pavilion/Restaurant and defined Members' Enclosure.

Public Enclosure: Rest of the ground including Riversdale Road Stand.

Covered Stands: Pavilion, Pavilion balcony/terrace (part), Ladies Pavilion, Riversdale Road Stand.

Open Stands: Pavilion balcony/terrace (part) together with temporary raised seating areas and ground level seating surrounding the playing area.

Disabled Areas: Special small area sited on Riversdale Road side of the ground or as requested.

Car Parking Facilities: Car parking is available within the ground for Players, Officials only, but Members may park on the lower ground adjoining the Mersey Rail railway line, off Riversdale Road and Beechwood Road. Alternatively street parking is also available a short walk away.

Ground Dimensions: 142m x 138m.

Ground Capacity: 10,000.

Best Crowd: First-Class Match: 15,164 v Northamptonshire 1948. Limited-Overs Match: 4,750 v West Indies (Tour) 1984.

HOW TO GET THERE

Rail: Aigburth Mersey Rail (BR) 0.5 mile, Liverpool Lime Street (BR) 4 miles.

Bus: Merseybus 82, Crosville X5, H25 from BR Liverpool Lime Street pass ground. (0151 236 7676).

Car: Ground is situated south-east of the city

↑ North direction (approx.)

Entrances
E1 Aigburth Road
E2/3 Riversdale Road
E4 Beechwood Road

P Pavilion
SB Scoreboard
CP Car Parking
T Toilets
CS Club Shop
N1 Aigburth Road End
N2 Mersey End
R BR Aigburth (direction)
C City Centre (direction)

Stands
S1 Pavilion Terrace/Balcony
S2 Ladies Pavilion
S3 Riversdale Road Stand

1 Bowling Green
2 Tennis Courts
6 River Mersey (direction)

Streets
3 A561 Aigburth Road
4 Beechurst Road
5 Riversdale Road

Above Right: Bowling against Combined Universities at The Parks, Mike Watkinson had a splendid June last season, scoring 155 against Glamorgan at Colwyn Bay and taking match figures of 11 for 87 versus Hampshire at Old Trafford.

centre in the Aigburth and Grassendale district.
From north: M6 Junction 28, then follow signs
A48 Liverpool and then A562 Aigburth.
From south or east: M6 Junction 21a, then M62 to
Junction 4, then follow signs Aigburth and
County Cricket or B5180 and A561 to ground.
From west: Mersey Tunnel into Liverpool city
centre, then follow A562 to Grassendale and
Aigburth.

WHERE TO STAY
AND OTHER INFORMATION
Tourist Information: 0151 709 3631.
Weather: 0898 500461.
Local Hotels: Holiday Inn (0151 709 0181),
Royal Garden (0151 928 2332), St George's
Hotel (0151 709 7090).
Local Radio Stations: BBC Radio Merseyside
(95.8 MHz FM/1485 KHz MW), Radio City
(96.7 MHz FM/1548 KHz MW).
Local Newspapers: Liverpool Daily Post,
Liverpool Echo, Liverpool Star.

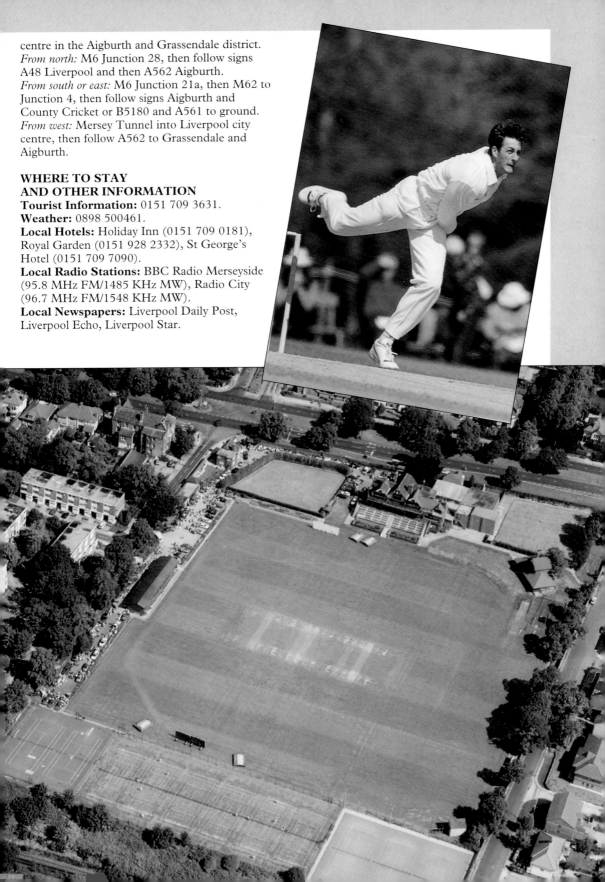

LYTHAM

Address: Lytham Cricket Club, Lytham Cricket and Sports Club, Church Road, Lytham, Lancashire.

Telephone Number for Prospects of Play: 01253 734137.

Entrances: Church Road (Players, Officials, Members, Public, Vehicles), Upper Westby Street (Members, Public, Vehicles).

Members' Enclosure: Pavilion (Players, Officials Only), Clubhouse (Members Only) together with defined Members' Enclosure to the west and south of the playing area.

Public Enclosure: Rest of the ground.

Covered Stands: Pavilion, Clubhouse.

Open Stands: Temporary raised and ground level seating, permanent tiered seating surrounding the playing area.

Disabled Areas: No special area, request suitable position.

Car Parking Facilities: Car parking within the ground for Players, Officials only entered off Church Road, and for Members only to the east of the playing area entered off Upper Westby Street. Alternatively parking is available in nearby car parks or on the seafront.

Ground Dimensions: 136m x 131m.

Best Crowd: First-Class Match: 6,750 v Sussex 1987.

HOW TO GET THERE

Rail: Lytham (BR) 0.5 mile.

Bus: From surrounding areas to town centre, thence 0.5 mile. No 11A to Lytham, 167 St Anne's to Preston and 193 St Anne's to Kirkham also pass the ground.

Car: Ground is situated in Church Road 0.25 mile west of Lytham town centre.

From north or south: M6 Junction 32, then follow M55 to Junction 3, then A585 to Kirkham and B5259 signposted Lytham,

From east: A583 and A584 to Lytham or as north.

⬆ North direction (approx.)

Entrances
E1 Church Road
E2 Upper Westby Street

P Pavilion (Players)
SB Scoreboard
CP Car Parking
T Toilets
CS Club Shop
N1 Railway End
N2 Church Road End
R BR Lytham (direction)
C Town Centre (direction)

Stands
S1 Pavilion (Members)

1 Tennis Courts
2 Railway line
3 St Cuthbert's Church
4 Seafront/Beach

Streets
5 Church Road
6 B5259 (direction)

Above Right: Pakistan's opening bowler, Wasim Akram, in full flight for Lancashire at The Parks in 1994 versus Combined Universities.

WHERE TO STAY
AND OTHER INFORMATION
Tourist Information: 01253 725610.
Weather: 0898 500461.
Local Hotels: Clifton Arms Hotel (01253 739898), Fernlea Hotel (01253 726726), St Ives Hotel (01253 720011), plus many other small hotels and guesthouses. Also consider staying in Blackpool.
Local Radio Stations: BBC Radio Lancashire (104.5 MHz FM/1557 KHz MW), Red Rose Radio (97.3 MHz FM/999 KHz MW).
Local Newspapers: Lancashire Evening Telegraph, Lancashire Evening Post, Lancashire Evening Gazette, Lytham St Anne's Express.

SOUTHPORT

Address: Southport and Birkdale Cricket Club, The Pavilion, Trafalgar Road, Birkdale, Southport, Merseyside PR8 2HF.

Telephone Number for Prospects of Play: 01704 69951.

Entrances: Trafalgar Road (Players, Officials, Members, Public, Vehicles).

Members' Enclosure: Pavilion, Ladies Pavilion and defined Members' Enclosure.

Public Enclosure: Rest of the ground.

Covered Stands: Pavilion, Ladies Pavilion, 'Late-Cut' Bar.

Open Stands: Permanent raised seating in front of the scoreboard together with temporary raised and ground level seating surrounding the playing area.

Disabled Areas: No special area, request suitable position.

Car Parking Facilities: Car parking for Players, Officials and some Members is available via the main entrance at the rear of the Pavilion off Trafalgar Road and space is also available in neighbouring streets and in the large car park at Royal Birkdale Golf Club situated off the main A565 road some 10 minutes' walk from the ground.

Ground Dimensions: 121m x 126m.

Ground Capacity: 6,000.

Best Crowd: First-Class Match: 4,500 v Worcestershire 1959. Limited-Overs Match: 10,500 v Glamorgan (JPL) 1969.

HOW TO GET THERE

Rail: Birkdale Mersey Rail (BR) 0.5 mile, Hillside Mersey Rail (BR) 0.5 mile.

Bus: Merseybus 16, 105, 284 from Southport Monument to within 0.25 mile of the ground also 10, 17 from surrounding area pass ground. (0151 236 7676).

Car: Ground is 1 mile south of Southport town

⬆ North direction (approx.)

Entrances
E1 Trafalgar Road

P Pavilion
SB Scoreboard
CP Car Parking
T Toilets
CS Club Shop
N1 Grosvenor Road End
N2 Harrod Drive End
R1 BR Birkdale (direction)
R2 Hillside Mersey Rail
C Town Centre (direction)

Stands
S1 Pavilion Terrace
S2 Ladies Pavilion

1 Late-Cut Bar
2 Railway line
3 Royal Birkdale Golf Club
   (direction)
7 Seafront/Beach (direction)

Streets
4 Trafalgar Road
5 Grosvenor Road
6 Harrod Drive

Above Right: Topping the county's first-class batting averages last season, John Crawley hit a career best 281 not out versus Somerset at Southport and was rewarded with an England tour place to Australia last winter.

centre and seafront.

From north: A565 follow signs Southport, then Birkdale and Royal Birkdale Golf Club and County Cricket for Trafalgar Road.

From east: M6 Junction 26, then M58 and A570 to Southport, then as north.

From south: A565 to Birkdale or as from east, then as from north.

WHERE TO STAY AND OTHER INFORMATION

Tourist Information: 01704 533333.

Weather: 0898 500461.

Local Hotels: Prince of Wales Hotel (01704 36688), Royal Clifton Hotel (01704 33771), plus many small hotels and guesthouses.

Local Radio Stations: BBC Radio Merseyside (95.8 MHz FM/1485 KHz MW), Red Rose Radio (97.3 MHz FM/999 KHz MW), BBC Radio Lancashire (104.5 MHz FM/1557 KHz MW).

Local Newspapers: Daily Post, Liverpool Echo, Southport Visitor.

Address: County Cricket Ground, Grace Road, Leicester, Leicestershire LE2 8AD.

Telephone Number for Prospects of Play: 0116 283 6236.

Entrances: Park Hill Drive (Members), Curzon Road (Members, Public, Vehicles), Milligan Road (Players, Officials, Members, Public).

Members' Enclosures: Defined area situated between 'The Meet' and the George Geary Stand in front of the Pavilion and including the top of the Pavilion in the Butler Stand, Fernie Suite, Quorn Suite.

Public Enclosure: Rest of the ground.

Covered Stands: 'The Meet', Pavilion, George Geary Stand.

Open Stands: Permanent seating surrounding the playing area.

Disabled Areas: No special area, request suitable position. A limited amount of space is set aside for cars at the Bennett End.

Car Parking Facilities: Car park at the Bennett End, entered from Curzon Road, can accommodate 500 cars. Otherwise street parking close to ground.

Ground Dimensions: 151m x 133m.

Ground Capacity: 12,000.

Best Crowd: First-Class Match: 16,000 v Australians 1948. Limited-Overs Match: 8,000 v Northamptonshire (NWBT) 1987.

HOW TO GET THERE

Rail: Leicester Midland (BR) 2 miles, South Wigston (BR) 2.25 miles.

Bus: Midland Fox 68, 73 from Belvoir Street, 0.25 mile from Leicester BR Station, (0116 251 1411); also Leicester Corporation 23 from city centre.

Car: The ground is located 1.5 miles south of the city centre, south of the B582 which links the A426 and A50.

From north: M1 Junction 22 or A46, A607 into

↑ North direction (approx.)

Entrances
E1 Park Hill Drive
E2 Curzon Road
E3 Milligan Road

P Pavilion
SB Scoreboard
CP Car Parking
T Toilets
CO Leicestershire CCC Club
   Office
M Leicestershire Museum
CS Club Shop
N1 Pavilion End
N2 Bennett End
R BR Leicester Midland
   (direction)
C City Centre (direction)

Stands
S1 Butler Stand
S2 Fernie Suite
S3 Quorn Suite
S4 George Geary Stand
S5 New Stand
S6 'The Meet'

1 Leicestershire CCC Indoor
   Cricket School

Streets
2 Park Hill Drive
3 Milligan Road
4 Curzon Road
5 Grace Road
6 A426 Aylestone Road

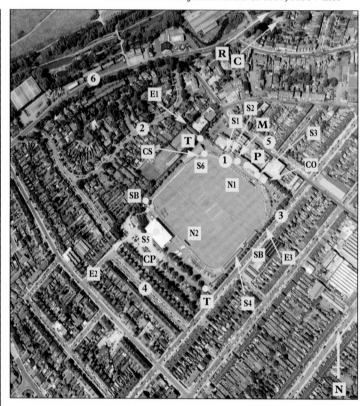

Above Right: South African captain and top order batsman from the Orange Free State, Hansie Cronje, seen batting against Northamptonshire in the 1994 Tetley Bitter Challenge at Northampton, will be a welcome addition to the ranks at Grace Road in 1995.

city centre, follow signs to Rugby into Almond Road, then into Aylestone Road and follow signs County Cricket to Park Hill Drive for County Ground.

From east: A47 into city centre, then as north.
From west: M69 to junction with M1 or A50 to city centre, then as north or south.
From south: M1 Junction 21 or M69, then A46 signposted Leicester City Centre, A426 then Park Hill Drive for County Ground signposted County Cricket.

WHERE TO STAY
AND OTHER INFORMATION
Tourist Information: 0116 254 9922.
Weather: 0898 500412.
Local Hotels: Grand Hotel (0116 255 5599), Post House (0116 289 6688), Holiday Inn (0116 253 1161), The Belmont House (0116 254 4773).
Local Radio Stations: BBC Radio Leicester (95.1 MHz FM/837 KHz MW), Leicester Sound (103.2 MHz FM/1260 KHz MW), Radio Trent (96.2 MHz 999 KHz MW).
Local Newspapers: Leicester Mercury, Leicester Mail, Leicester Trader and Saturday Sports Mercury.

LONDON (LORD'S)

Address: Lord's Cricket Ground, St John's Wood Road, St John's Wood, London NW8 8QN.
Telephone Number for Prospects of Play: 0171 286 8011/0171 266 3825.
Entrances: St John's Wood Road – via Grace Gates (Players, Officials, Members, Vehicles), St John's Wood Road – via Bicentenary Gate (Employees), St John's Wood Road – via East Gate (Public), Wellington Road – via North Gate (Members, Vehicles), Wellington Road (Members, Public), Grove End Road (Players, Officials, Vehicles, Employees).
Members' Enclosure: Pavilion (Members Only), Sir George Allen Stand (MCC Members Only, upper level and exclusive use for Middlesex Members on Middlesex match days only), Warner Stand, Mound Stand (Upper – Debenture Holders Only), Tavern Stand.
Public Enclosure: Grandstand, Compton Stand (Upper, Lower), Edrich Stand (Upper, Lower), Mound Stand (Lower).

Covered Stand: All Members' and Public enclosures part covered.
Open Stands: All Members' and Public Enclosures part open.
Disabled Areas: Special sections in front of Warner Stand and between Sir George Allen Stand and Pavilion.
Car Parking Facilities: No street parking, though limited areas available on meters and on Sundays. Car parking available for Members Only, entrance from Cavendish Road and Wellington Road. During major matches local car parking is arranged by MCC for Members on local school grounds. Public car parking in central London car parks or near Regent's Park Zoo which is now metered.
Ground Dimensions: 166m x 133m.
Ground Capacity: 28,000.
Best Crowd: First-Class Match: 15,000 v Derbyshire 1947. Limited-Overs Match: 15,000 v Somerset (NWBT) 1983.

↑ North direction (approx.)

Entrances
E1 Grace Gates St John's Wood Road
E2 Bicentenary Gate
E3 East Gate
E4 Wellington Gate
E5 North Gate

P Pavilion
SB Scoreboard
CP Car Parking
T Toilets
CS MCC Club Shops
M MCC Cricket Museum
CO MCC Club Office
N1 Nursery End
N2 Pavilion End
T St John's Wood Underground
   (direction)
C Central London/West End (direction)

Stands
S1 Warner Stand
S2 Grand Stand
S3 Compton Stand
S4 Edrich Stand
S5 Mound Stand
S6 Tavern Stand
S7 Sir George Allen Stand (including
   Middlesex Room)

1 Memorial Garden
2 Harris Garden
3 MCC Indoor Cricket School
4 Nursery Ground
5 ICC Office
6 Middlesex CCC Office/Shop
7 TCCB/NCA Offices

Streets
8 A41 Finchley Road
9 St John's Wood Road
10 Grove End Road

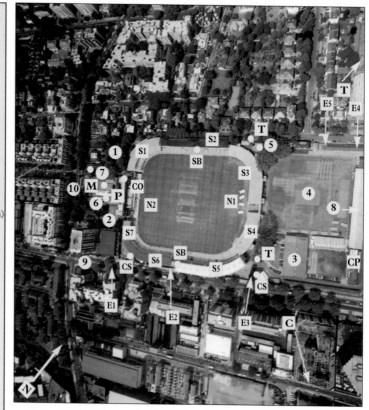

Above Right: Kiwi Dion Nash seen bowling versus the England Amateur XI at Southgate, took 11 wickets and hit 56 runs on his Test début at Lord's versus England in 1994.

HOW TO GET THERE

Rail: St John's Wood Underground (Jubilee Line) 0.5 mile.

Bus: LRT 6, 8, 13, 16, 16A, 46, 74, 82, 113, 159, 274 pass the ground. Also London Country Coaches 719, 757, 768, 797 from Home Counties pass near ground. (0171 222 1234).

Car: The ground is situated opposite St John's Wood Church bounded by Wellington Road, Wellington Place, St John's Wood Road and Grove End Road. *From north:* M1 to motorway terminal roundabout at Brent Cross, then follow A406 North Circular Road, East, then branch left and follow signs West End, take A41 signposted Swiss Cottage and follow Finchley Road to St John's Wood, follow signs Lord's Cricket Ground and A5205 for St John's Wood Road and Grace Gates entrance.

From east: From Holloway district follow signs A503 West End, then at Camden Town follow signs A4201 Regent's Park, enter Regent's Park at Gloucester Gate and use outer circle signposted London Zoo. After passing London Regent's Park Mosque, take immediate right into Hanover Gate and at T-junction take right into A41 Park Road for St John's Wood, keep left for A5205 St John's Wood Road at roundabout for Lord's Cricket Ground.

From west: A40(M) or M41 follow signs Central London, then follow signs A4206 Paddington in Bishop's Bridge Road, enter one-way system signposted Euston and join A5 Edgware Road, then take right into A5205 St John's Wood Road.

From south: From Hyde Park Corner follow signs Ring Road, Oxford into Park Lane A4202, then at Marble Arch follow signs Oxford Circus into Oxford Street A40, then at second traffic lights take A41 Portman Street, follow through Portman Square and Gloucester Place, follow signs A41 Aylesbury and the North, at St John's Wood roundabout take left into A5205 St John's Wood Road for Lord's Cricket Ground.

WHERE TO STAY AND OTHER INFORMATION

Tourist Information: 0181 760 5630.

Weather: 0898 500401.

Local Hotels: The Hilton International Regent's Park Hotel (0171 722 7722) opposite ground, plus many other hotels in central or north-west London.

Local Radio Stations: Greater London Radio (94.9 MHz FM/1488 KHz MW), Capital Radio/Capital Gold (95.8 MHz FM/1548 KHz MW), LBC (97.3 MHz FM/1152 KHz MW).

Local Newspaper: Evening Standard.

UXBRIDGE

Address: Uxbridge Cricket Club, The Pavilion, Gatting Way, Park Road, Uxbridge, Middlesex.
Telephone Number for Prospects of Play: 01895 237571.
Members' Enclosure: Pavilion and defined Members' area in front of the Pavilion and Clubhouse.
Public Enclosure: Rest of the ground.
Covered Stands: Pavilion, Clubhouse.
Open Stands: Temporary raised and ground level seating surrounding the playing area.
Disabled Areas: Space available for vehicles in car park. No special area in ground, request suitable position.
Car Parking Facilities: Car parking available adjoining the ground off Gatting Way for Members only and off Park Road for Public and Sponsors. Street parking in the streets close to Uxbridge Common opposite ground.
Ground Dimensions: 124m x 122m.

Ground Capacity: 6,500.
Best Crowd: First-Class Match: 3,500 v Gloucestershire 1986. Limited-Overs Match: 5,750 v Nottinghamshire (NWBT) 1987.

HOW TO GET THERE
Rail: Uxbridge Underground (Metropolitan/Piccadilly lines) 0.75 mile.
Bus: LRT 223 from Uxbridge and West Ruislip Underground pass ground or 128 and 129 from surrounding areas. (0171 222 1234).
Car: Ground and car parks are situated off A412 Park Road and in Gatting Way 1 mile north of the town centre opposite Uxbridge Common.
From north: M25 Junction 16, then M40 to Junction 2, then follow A412 signposted Uxbridge and County Cricket.
From east: A40 Western Avenue from Central London to Junction 2, then A412 signposted Uxbridge and County Cricket and as above.

↑ North direction (approx.)

Entrances
E1 Park Road via Car Park
E2 Gatting Way
E3 Car Park

P Pavilion
SB Scoreboard
CP Car Parking
T Toilets
CS Club Shop
N1 Town End
N2 Pavilion End
T Uxbridge Underground
   (direction)
C Town Centre (direction)

1 Swimming Pool
2 Dry Ski Slope
3 Bowling Green
4 Uxbridge Moor
5 Brearley Close
6 Gatting Way

Streets
7 A412 Park Road
8 M40 Junction 1/A40 Western
   Avenue (direction)

Above Right: Old Reptonian John Carr topped the first-class batting averages last season with 1,542 runs (av 90.70) which included six hundreds and a career best 261 not out versus Gloucestershire at Lord's.

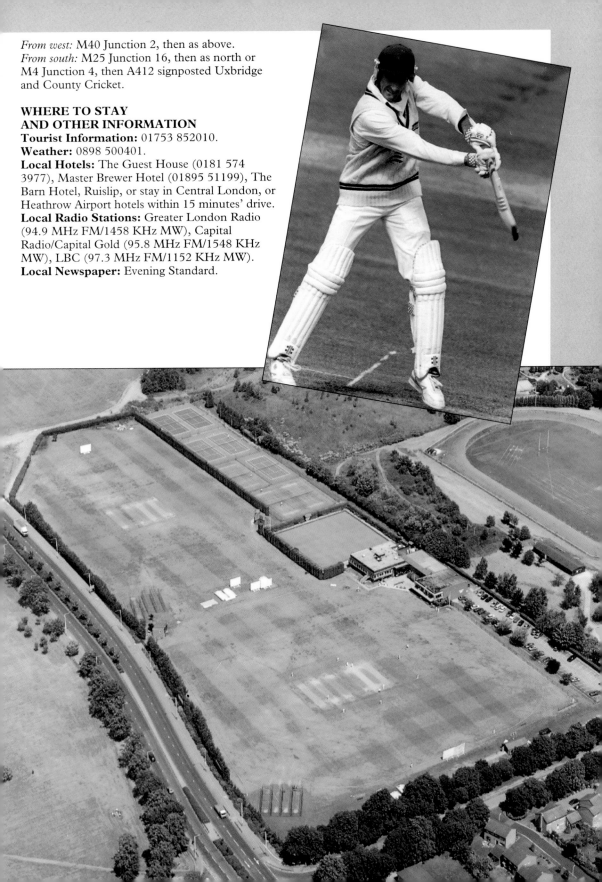

From west: M40 Junction 2, then as above.
From south: M25 Junction 16, then as north or
M4 Junction 4, then A412 signposted Uxbridge
and County Cricket.

WHERE TO STAY
AND OTHER INFORMATION
Tourist Information: 01753 852010.
Weather: 0898 500401.
Local Hotels: The Guest House (0181 574
3977), Master Brewer Hotel (01895 51199), The
Barn Hotel, Ruislip, or stay in Central London, or
Heathrow Airport hotels within 15 minutes' drive.
Local Radio Stations: Greater London Radio
(94.9 MHz FM/1458 KHz MW), Capital
Radio/Capital Gold (95.8 MHz FM/1548 KHz
MW), LBC (97.3 MHz FM/1152 KHz MW).
Local Newspaper: Evening Standard.

NORTHAMPTON

Address: County Cricket Ground, Wantage Road, Northampton, Northamptonshire NN1 4NJ.
Telephone Number for Prospects of Play: 01604 237040.
Entrances: Wantage Road (Players, Officials, Members, Public, Vehicles), Abingdon Avenue (Members, Public).
Members' Enclosure: Spencer Pavilion and enclosure, together with upper part of Main Stand and Ladies Pavilion.
Public Enclosure: Rest of the ground.
Covered Stands: Spencer Pavilion, Main Stand (Upper), Football Stand (part), West Stand, Ladies Pavilion.
Open Stands: Permanent tiered seating/benches and ground level seating surrounding the playing area.
Disabled Areas: None specified, but advise a position on the hardstanding at the Pavilion End.
Car Parking Facilities: Car parking within the ground is limited to the former football field and the area between the Spencer Pavilion and main scoreboard for 12 to 15 vehicles. Car parking is available to the rear of the main stand and there is also ample street parking nearby.
Ground Dimensions: 133m x 132m.
Ground Capacity: 6,500.
Best Crowd: First-Class Match: 21,770 v Australians 1953. Limited-Overs Match: 7,000 v Lancashire (NWBT) 1981.
Anticipated Developments: Club presently considering construction of new stands at former Football Ground End.

HOW TO GET THERE
Rail: Northampton (BR) 2 miles.
Bus: Northampton Transport 1 from Northampton BR to within 200m of ground, (01604 51431); also Northampton Transport 6, 8, 15 from town centre to within 200m of ground.
Car: *From north:* M1 Junction 16, then A45 follow signs Northampton and town centre, then follow A43 signposted Kettering, then follow signs County

↑ North direction (approx.)

Entrances
E1 Wantage Road
E2 Abingdon Avenue

P Players Pavilion
SB Scoreboard
CP Car Parking
T Toilets
CO Northamptonshire CCC Club Office
N1 Abingdon Avenue End (formerly Football Ground End)
N2 Wantage Road End
R BR Northampton Castle (direction)
C Town Centre (direction)

Stands
S1 Main Stand/Club Shop
S2 Executive Box
S3 Pavilion Terrace
S4 West Stand
S5 Football Stand (now demolished)
S6 East Terrace
S7 Ladies Pavilion
S8 Spencer (Old) Pavilion

1 Northamptonshire CCC Indoor Cricket School
2 Bowling Green

Streets
3 Abingdon Avenue
4 Wantage Road
5 Park Avenue South
6 A45 Wellingborough Road
7 A5101 Park Avenue North

Above Right: ' Kumbled': Robin Smith dismissed lbw by Indian spin wizard Anil Kumble during the Second Test in Madras on England's last Tour to India in 1992/93. Anil Kumble is Northamptonshire's new overseas recruit this season.

Ground for county cricket in Abingdon Road and main entrance in Wantage Road.
From east: A45, A4500 or A428 signposted Northampton, then follow signs County Ground as north.
From west: A45 or A43 to town centre, then as north.
From south: M1 Junction 15, then follow signs A508 Northampton, then A43 for Wellingborough Road and Wantage Road following signs County Cricket.

WHERE TO STAY
AND OTHER INFORMATION
Tourist Information: 01604 22677.
Weather: 0898 500413.
Local Hotels: Westone Moat House (01604 406262), Northampton Moat House Hotel (01604 22441), Grand Hotel (01604 34416), Stakis Country Court Hotel (01604 700666).
Local Radio Stations: BBC Radio Northampton (104.2 MHz FM/1107 KHz MW), Hereward Radio (96.6 MHz FM/1557 KHz MW), Northants 96 (96.6 MHz FM/1557 KHz MW), Chiltern Radio (96.9 MHz FM/792 KHz MW).
Local Newspapers: Chronicle and Echo, Northampton Post, Sports Pink (Saturday only), Mercury & Herald, Northamptonshire Image.

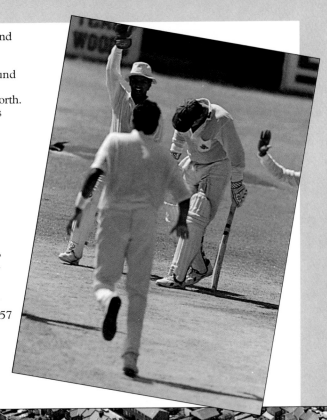

LUTON

Address: Luton Town Cricket Club, Wardown Park, Old Bedford Road, Luton, Bedfordshire.
Telephone Number for Prospects of Play: 01582 27855.
Entrance: Wardown Park via Old Bedford Road (Players, Officials, Vehicles), New Bedford Road (Members, Public, Vehicles).
Members' Enclosure: Defined area situated between Main Scoreboard and Main Entrance to the ground.
Public Enclosure: Rest of the ground.
Covered Stands: Pavilion.
Open Stands: Temporary raised seating together with ground level seating surrounding the playing area.
Disabled Areas: Within the Members' Enclosure and close to sightscreen at Pavilion End.
Ground Capacity: 5,000.
Car Parking Facilities: Extensive car parking in Wardown Park entered from New Bedford Road

and some street parking in surrounding area.
Ground Dimensions: 131m x 132m.
Best Crowd: First-Class Match: 3,500 v Yorkshire 1986. Limited-Overs Match: 4,000 v Middlesex (RAL) 1988.

HOW TO GET THERE

Rail: Luton Midland (BR and Thameslink) 1 mile.
Bus: Luton & District 26 from Mill Street (200m from Luton BR) to ground, (01582 404074); and 6 from town centre to ground.
Car: The ground is situated 0.5 mile from the town centre.
From north: M1 Junction 11, then follow signs A505 Luton into Dunstable Road for town centre, follow signs A6 from town centre to New Bedford Road for Wardown Park and main car park.
From east: A505 signposted Luton, from town

↑ North direction (approx.)

Entrances
E1 Old Bedford Road

P Pavilion
SB Scoreboard
CP Car Parking
T Toilets
CS Club Shop
N1 Stockingstone End
N2 Pavilion End
R BR Luton (direction)
C Town Centre (direction)

1 Wardown Park
2 Luton Museum

Streets
3 A6 New Bedford Road
4 Old Bedford Road
5 Stockingstone Road

Above Right: Northamptonshire top order batsman Robert Bailey on his way to 82 not out, digs out a slow delivery in the Tetley Bitter match versus the Australians at Northampton in 1993.

centre follow New Bedford Road for Wardown Park.

From west: A505 signposted Luton, then as north.

From south: M1 Junction 10/10a, then follow signs Luton and town centre, then signs A6 from town centre as north.

WHERE TO STAY AND OTHER INFORMATION

Tourist Information: 01525 402051/406464.

Weather: 0898 500407.

Local Hotels: Chiltern Hotel (01582 575911), Strathmore Thistle Hotel (01582 34199).

Local Radio Stations: Chiltern Radio (96.9 MHz FM/792 KHz MW), BBC Radio Bedfordshire (95.5 MHz FM/1161 KHz MW), LBC (97.3 MHz/1152 KHz MW), GLR (94.9 MHz FM/1458 KHz MW).

Local Newspapers: Luton News, The Luton Herald, Sports Pink (Saturdays only).

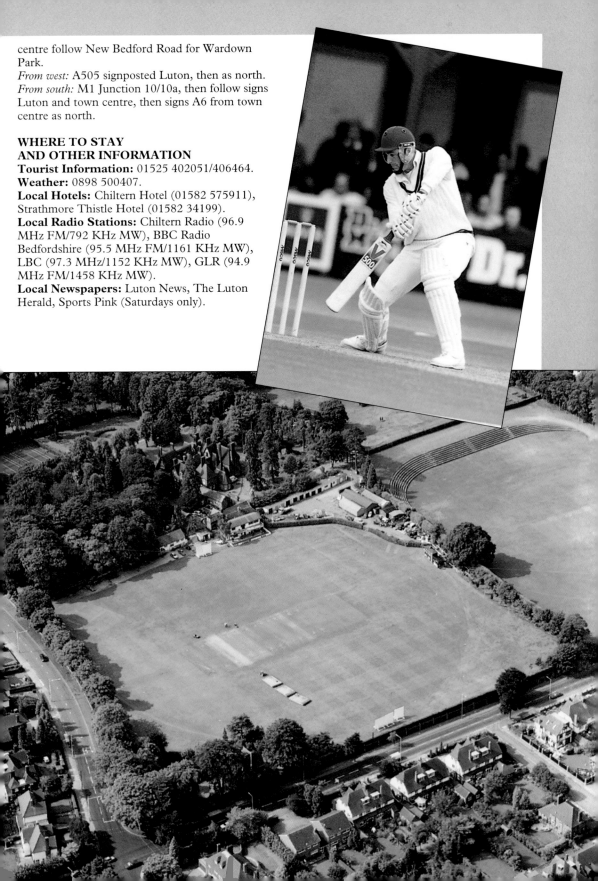

NOTTINGHAM (TRENT BRIDGE)

Address: County Cricket Ground, Trent Bridge, Bridgford Road, Nottingham, Nottinghamshire NG2 6AG.

Telephone Number for Prospects of Play: 0115 982 2753.

Entrances: Dixon Gates (Players, Officials, Vehicles), Bridgford Road (Members, Public, Vehicles), Radcliffe Road (Public), Fox Road (Members, Public, Vehicles), Hound Road (Players, Officials, Members, Vehicles).

Members' Enclosure: Pavilion, West Wing Lower (part), Larwood & Voce Tavern, Tavern Terrace seating.

Public Enclosure: West Wing Lower (part), West Wing Upper, Parr Stand, William Clarke Stand, Radcliffe Road Stand, Scoreboard Stand, Fox Road Stands, New Hound Road Stand.

Covered Stands: Pavilion (part), West Wing Lower, Parr Stand Lower, William Clarke Stand (part), Radcliffe Road Stand Lower, Larwood & Voce Tavern, New Hound Road Stand Lower (part).

Open Stands: Pavilion (part), West Wing Upper, Parr Stand Upper, William Clarke Stand (part), Radcliffe Road Stand Upper, Scoreboard Stand, Fox Road Stands, Tavern Terrace seating, New Hound Road Stand Upper and Lower (part).

Disabled Areas: Ample room on boundary edge, request suitable position. Car parking off Fox Road.

Car Parking Facilities: Some car parking is available within the ground on the Fox Road side on normal county match days. For Test Matches this space is allocated for temporary seating and hospitality facilities. Car parking is available in the park off Bridgford Road, Nottingham Forest FC car park and in adjoining streets.

Ground Dimensions: 160m x 150m (restricted on match days to approximately 141m x 144m).

Ground Capacity: 13,500.

Best Crowd: First-Class Match: 35,000 v Surrey 1948. Limited-Overs Match: 8,500 v Somerset (JPL) 1979.

↑ North direction (approx.)

Entrances
E1 Bridgford Road via Dixon Gates
E2 Bridgford Road
E3 Radcliffe Road
E4 Fox Road
E5 Hound Round

P Pavilion
SB Scoreboard
CP Car Parking
T Toilets
CO Nottinghamshire CCC Club Office
M Nottinghamshire Museum/Library
CS Club Shop
N1 Radcliffe Road End
N2 Hound Road End
R BR Nottingham Midland (direction)
C City Centre (direction)

Stands
S1 Pavilion Terrace
S2 West Wing
S3 Parr Stand
S4 William Clarke Stand
S5 Press Box
S6 Radcliffe Road Executive Suites
S7 Radcliffe Road Stand
S8 Scoreboard Stand
S9 Fox Road Stands
S10 Larwood & Voce Terrace
S11 Larwood & Voce Tavern
S12 New Hound Road Stand

1 Nottinghamshire CCC Indoor Cricket School
2 Trent Bridge Inn
3 Trent Bridge House (Council Offices)
4 Squash Club
5 Nottingham Forest FC Ground
6 Notts County FC Ground (direction)
7 River Trent
8 Trent Bridge
13 County Hall Offices

Streets
9 A606 Radcliffe Road
10 Fox Road
11 A52 Bridgford Road
12 Hound Road

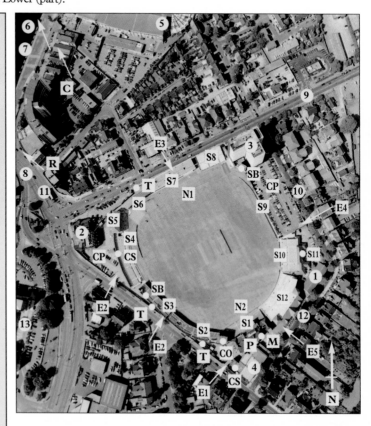

Above Right: All-rounder Chris Lewis celebrates the wicket of West Indian batsman Keith Arthurton during the Third Cable & Wireless Test at the Queen's Park Oval, Trinidad in 1994.

HOW TO GET THERE
Rail: Nottingham Midland (BR) 1 mile.
Bus: Nottingham City 12, 69, 85, 90, 91, 92, 93, 94, 95, 96, 97 and Trent Buses link BR Nottingham with ground and city centre. (0115 950 3665).
Car: *From north:* M1 Junction 26, follow signs A610 Nottingham, then signs to Melton Mowbray, A606 Trent Bridge, cross River Trent and the ground is ahead of you behind 'TBI'.
From east: A52 signposted Nottingham, into West Bridgford, then follow Bridgford Road for ground.
From south: M1 Junction 24, then follow signs Nottingham (South) for Trent Bridge, then right into Bridgford Road for Trent Bridge.
From west: A52 follow signs Nottingham, then follow signs Melton Mowbray, then Trent Bridge, then as north.

WHERE TO STAY
AND OTHER INFORMATION
Tourist Information: 0115 947 0661.
Weather: 0898 500412.
Local Hotels: Albany Hotel (0115 947 0131), Victoria Hotel (0115 941 9561), Royal Moat House International Hotel (0115 941 4444), The Gallery (0115 981 3651), Talbot House Hotel (0115 981 1123).
Local Radio Stations: BBC Radio Nottingham (95.5 MHz FM/1584 KHz MW), Radio Trent (96.2 MHz FM/999 KHz MW).

Local Newspapers: Nottingham Evening Post, Nottingham Trader, Football Post (Saturdays only).

CLEETHORPES

Address: Cleethorpes Cricket Club, The Pavilion and Squash Club, Chichester Road, Cleethorpes, South Humberside.

Telephone Number for Prospects of Play: 01472 691271.

Entrances: Chichester Road (Players, Officials, Member, Public, Vehicles), Daggett Road (Members, Public, Vehicles).

Members' Enclosure: Pavilion and Squash Club together with defined Members' Enclosure which extends from the sightscreen at the Chichester Road End, in front of the Pavilion, at least a third of the way towards the scoreboard.

Public Enclosure: Rest of the ground.

Covered Stands: Pavilion and Squash Club.

Open Stands: Temporary ground level seating surrounding the playing area together with several areas of raised seating and some benches.

Disabled Areas: There are no special facilities for disabled spectators although cars can be parked in a position to watch play.

Car Parking Facilities: Parking is available to the rear of the Pavilion and to the south of the playing area for approximately 300 cars. Additional car parking at the nearby Sports Centre and in adjoining streets.

Ground Dimensions: 128m x 118m.

Ground Capacity: 5,000.

Best Crowd: First-Class Match: 5,000 v Worcestershire 1980. Limited-Overs Match: 2,500 v Middlesex (JPL) 1983.

HOW TO GET THERE

Rail: Cleethorpes (BR) 1.5 miles.

Bus: From BR Cleethorpes take Grimsby-Cleethorpes Transport Company Hopper 8, 8X or 9X for Chichester Road or Daggett Road, passing Chichester Road ground entrance. (01472 358646).

Car: Ground is close to Cleethorpes seafront at southern end.

↑ North direction (approx.)

Entrances
E1 Chichester Road
E2 Daggett Road

P Pavilion
SB Scoreboard
CP Car Parking
T Toilets
CS Club Shop
N1 Daggett Road End
N2 Chichester Road End
R BR Cleethorpes (direction)
C Town Centre (direction)

Stands
S1 Pavilion Terrace

Streets
1 Daggett Road
2 Chichester Road
3 Seafront (direction)

Above Right: Former England opening batsman and Nottinghamshire captain Tim Robinson drives into the covers during his innings of 99 against Glamorgan at Worksop last season.

From north: Use A1 then follow A16 Grimsby, then A1098 Cleethorpes and seafront, then follow signs Old Cleethorpes and County Cricket for Chichester Road.
From west: As north.
From south: Use A1, then follow A16 signposted Cleethorpes and seafront, then as north.

WHERE TO STAY
AND OTHER INFORMATION
Tourist Information: 01472 342422.
Weather: 0898 500454.
Local Hotels: Hotel Kingsway (01472 601122), The Grimsby Crest Hotel (01472 359771), plus many other small hotels and guesthouses.
Local Radio Stations: BBC Radio Humberside (95.9 MHz FM/1485 KHz MW), Viking Radio (96.9 MHz FM/1161 KHz MW).
Local Newspapers: Grimsby Evening Telegraph, Grimsby Gazette, Grimsby Target.

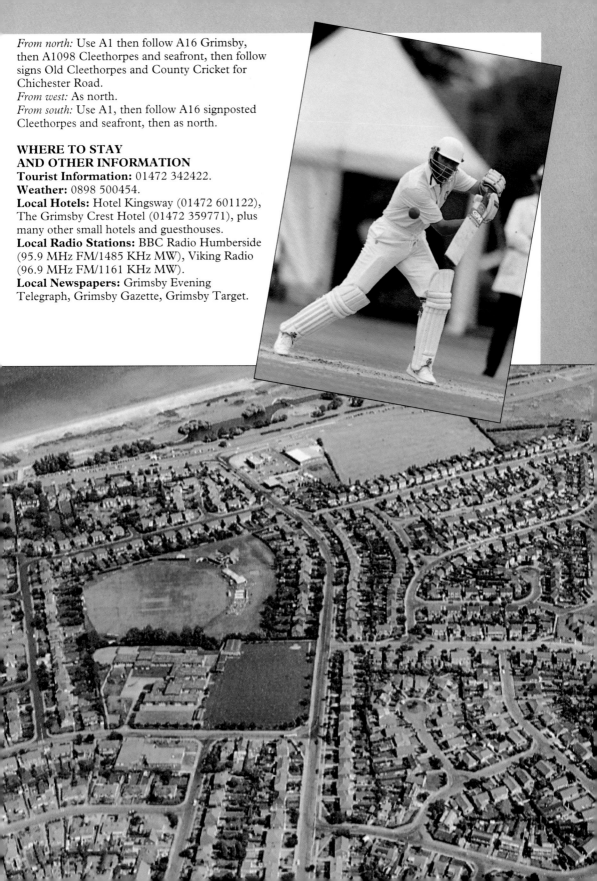

WORKSOP

Address: Worksop Town Cricket Club, The Pavilion, Central Avenue, Worksop, Nottinghamshire.

Telephone Number for Prospects of Play: 01909 472681.

Entrances: Central Avenue (Players, Officials, Members, Public, Vehicles), Netherholme Centre Car Park (Members, Public).

Members' Enclosure: Pavilion, Clubhouse and defined area on the north side of the ground.

Public Enclosure: Rest of the ground.

Covered Stands: Pavilion, Clubhouse, Football Stand.

Open Stands: Temporary ground level seating surrounding the playing area.

Disabled Areas: No special area, request suitable position.

Car Parking Facilities: Parking is available within the ground to the rear of the Pavilion for 100 cars and ample additional space can be found in nearby car parks close to the town centre shopping area.

Ground Dimensions: 126m x 123m.

Ground Capacity: 7,000.

Best Crowd: First-Class Match: 7,000 v Yorkshire 1966. Limited-Overs Match: 3,000 v Derbyshire (JPL) 1970.

HOW TO GET THERE

Rail: Worksop (BR) 0.75 mile.

Bus: Numerous local bus services link BR Worksop and surrounding areas with town centre shopping area close to ground.

Car: Ground is situated close to town centre off Central Avenue.

From north: M1 Junction 31, then follow A57 Worksop, then as above.

From east: A57 or B6089 from A1 signposted Worksop, then as above.

↑ North direction (approx.)

Entrances
E1 Central Avenue
E2 Netherholme Centre Car Park

P Pavilion
SB Scoreboard
CP Car Parking
T Toilets
CS Club Shop
N1 Canal End
N2 Central Avenue End
R BR Worksop (direction)
C Town Centre (direction)

1 Bowling Green
2 Chesterfield Canal

Streets
3 Central Avenue

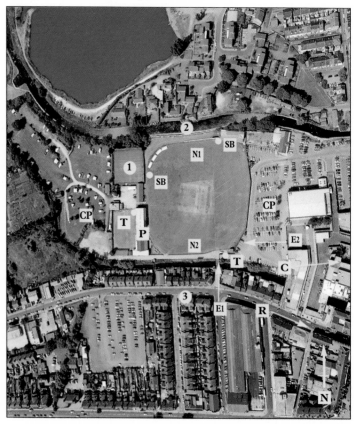

Above Right: Nottingham's Paul Johnson on his way to his top score last season of 132 versus Northamptonshire at Trent Bridge.

From west: A619 follow signs Worksop, then as above.
From south: M1 Junction 30, then follow A619 Worksop, then as above.

**WHERE TO STAY
AND OTHER INFORMATION**
Tourist Information: 01742 569392.
Weather: 0898 500411.
Local Hotels: The Lion Hotel (01909 2179),
Ye Olde Bell, Barnby Moor/Retford,
(01777 705121).
Local Radio Stations: BBC Radio Nottingham
(95.5 MHz FM/1584 KHz MW), Radio Trent
(96.2 MHz FM/999 KHz MW).
Local Newspapers: Nottingham Evening Post,
Worksop Guardian, Sheffield Star.

Address: County Cricket Ground, St James's Street, Taunton, Somerset TA1 1JT.

Telephone Number for Prospects of Play: 01823 272946.

Entrances: Priory Bridge Road (Players, Officials, Members, Vehicles), Priory Bridge Tow Path (Members, Public), Coal Orchard Car Park (Members, Public), St James's Street (Members, Public, Vehicles).

Members' Enclosure: Colin Atkinson Pavilion, Old Pavilion, Ridley Stand (Upper) and defined area between the New Pavilion and the Old Pavilion.

Public Enclosure: River Stand, West Side enclosure, East Side enclosure (part).

Covered Stands: Colin Atkinson Pavilion (part), Executive Boxes, Old Pavilion (Upper), Ridley Stand, Stragglers Pavilion (part), Taunton CC Pavilion (part), River Stand.

Open Stands: Colin Atkinson Pavilion (part), East Side Enclosure, Old Pavilion (lower), Stragglers Pavilion (part), Taunton CC Pavilion (part), West Side Enclosure.

Disabled Areas: Special enclosure in front of the Old Pavilion.

Car Parking Facilities: Limited car parking available within the ground for Players, Officials, Members only. Town centre car parks a short walk away.

Ground Dimensions: 127m x 140m.

Ground Capacity: 8,000.

Best Crowd: First-Class Match: 10,000 v Australians 1948. Limited-Overs Match: 8,500 v Kent (GC) 1979.

Anticipated Developments: New stand, executive boxes, club shop and Somerset Cricket Academy to the east of the playing area under construction winter 1994/95.

HOW TO GET THERE

Rail: Taunton (BR) 0.5 mile.

Bus: From surrounding areas to Bus Station

⬆ North direction (approx.)

Entrances
E1 Priory Bridge Road
E2 St James's Street via J.C. White Gates
E3 Orchard Car Park
E4 Priory Bridge Tow Path

P Colin Atkinson Pavilion
SB Scoreboard
CP Car Parking
T Toilets
CO Somerset CCC Club Office
M Somerset Cricket Museum
CS Club Shop/New Development Stand
N1 River End
N2 Old Pavilion End
R BR Taunton (direction)
C Town Centre (direction)

Stands
S1 Colin Atkinson Pavilion Terrace
S2 Executive Suites
S3 Old Pavilion
S4 Ridley Stand
S5 Stragglers Pavilion
S6 Taunton CC Pavilion
S7 River Stand

1 Somerset CCC Indoor Cricket School
2 River Tone
3 St James's Church

Streets
4 St James's Street
5 A358 Priory Bridge Road

Above Right: Somerset and England quick bowler Andy Caddick is seen appealing for the wicket of Desmond Haynes during the Third Cable & Wireless Test against the West Indies at the Queen's Park Oval, Trinidad in 1994.

thence 500m, also shuttle from town centre 5 min.
Car: County Ground is situated close to main shopping street in St James's Street and Priory Bridge Road.
From north and east: M5 Junction 25, then follow A358 from Creech Castle roundabout to town centre, at next roundabout take exit signposted County Ground.
From west: M5 Junction 26, then follow A38 Taunton and town centre, then follow signs County Ground.
From south: A358 or B3170, then as north.

WHERE TO STAY
AND OTHER INFORMATION
Tourist Information: 01823 274785.
Weather: 0898 500405.
Local Hotel: Castle Hotel (01823 72671).
Local Radio Stations: BBC Radio Bristol (95.5 MHz FM/1548 KHz MW), BBC Radio Devon (103.4 MHz FM/801 KHz MW), GWR (96.5 MHz FM/1260 KHz MW).
Local Newspapers: Somerset County Gazette, West Somerset Free Press, Western Daily Press.

BATH

Somerset

Address: The Pavilion, The Recreation Ground, William Street, off Great Pulteney Street, Bath, Avon.

Telephone Number for Prospects of Play: 01225 424970.

Entrances: William Street (Players, Officials, Members, Public, Vehicles), Spring Gardens Road via River Path (Members, Public).

Members' Enclosure: Pavilion and defined area between Bath Rugby Clubhouse and temporary Members' seating to the east of the Pavilion at the Great Pulteney Street End.

Public Enclosure: Rest of the ground.

Covered Stands: Pavilion and Bath Rugby Clubhouse (upper level) and Rugby Stand – although the first two are some distance from the playing area.

Open Stands: Temporary raised and ground level seating surrounding the playing area.

Disabled Areas: Special area in front of Members' Enclosure. Car parking on rugby field.

Car Parking Facilities: Available on the rugby ground for Players, Officials, Members only. City centre car parks a short distance from the ground.

Ground Dimensions: 133m x 131m.

Ground Capacity: 8,000.

Best Crowd: First-Class Match: 6,500 v Australians 1905. Limited-Overs Match: 5,000 v Lancashire (JPL) 1978.

HOW TO GET THERE

Rail: Bath Spa (BR) 0.5 mile.

Bus: Badgerline 4, 18 link Bath Spa BR with ground (01225 64446) also from surrounding areas to Bus Station, thence 0.5 mile.

Car: The ground is situated off A36 Great Pulteney Street to the east of the city centre by the River Avon and adjoining Bath RFC.

From north: M4 Junction 18, then follow A46 signposted Bath, then as above.

↑ North direction (approx.)

Entrances
E1 William Street
E2 Spring Gardens via River Tow Path

P Pavilion
SB Scoreboard
CP Car Parking
T Toilets
CS Club Shop
CO Club Office
N1 Great Pulteney Street End
N2 North Parade Road End
R BR Bath Spa (direction)
C City Centre (direction)

1 Bath RFC Ground
2 Bath RFC Clubhouse
3 River Avon
4 Bath Sports Centre
8 Bath Abbey (direction)
9 Bath CC Ground

Streets
5 A36 Great Pulteney Street
6 William Street
7 North Parade Road

Above Right: Somerset skipper Andy Hayhurst seen stretching to hit the ball through the covers during the Tetley Bitter Tour Match versus the New Zealanders at Taunton in 1994.

From east: M4 Junction 18, then as north, or M4 Junction 17 then A429 and A4 to Bath, then as above.

From west: A4, A431, A36 to Bath, then as above.

From south: A367 or A36 to Bath, then as above.

WHERE TO STAY
AND OTHER INFORMATION
Tourist Information: 01225 462831.

Weather: 0898 500405 or 500409.

Local Hotels: Royal Crescent Hotel (01225 319090), Fernley Hotel (01225 61603), The Francis Hotel (01225 24257).

Local Radio Stations: BBC Radio Bristol (95.5 MHz FM/1548 KHz MW), GWR Radio (96.3 MHz FM/1260 KHz MW).

Local Newspapers: Bath Chronicle, Western Daily Press, Evening Post and Echo.

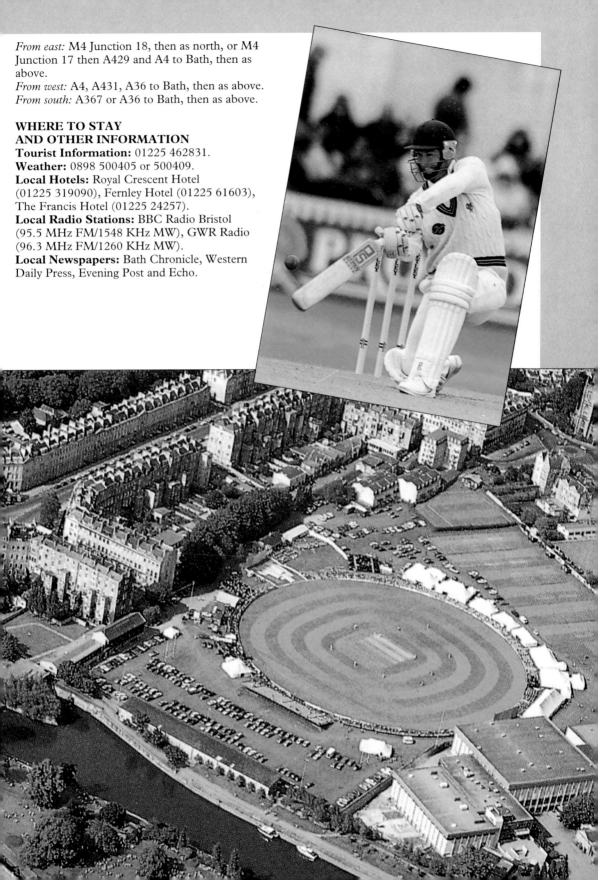

WESTON-SUPER-MARE

Address: The Pavilion, Clarence Park East, Walliscote Road, Weston-Super-Mare, Somerset.

Telephone Number for Prospects of Play: 01934 642345.

Entrances: Clarence Road North (Players, Officials, Vehicles), Walliscote Road (Members), Clarence Road South (Members, Public), Clarence Road East and North (East).

Members' Enclosure: Defined area in front of the Pavilion together with the temporary raised and ground level seating sited between the sightscreen at the Clarence Road North End and Walliscote Road Members' entrance.

Public Enclosure: Temporary raised and ground level seating sited between the sightscreen at the Clarence Road North End and the sightscreen at the Clarence Road South End of the ground.

Covered Stands: Pavilion (Players, Officials only).

Open Stands: Temporary seats form the rest of the ground.

Disabled Areas: Special area in south-west corner of ground with hardstanding for vehicles.

Car Parking Facilities: Within the ground for Players, Officials only. Street parking locally, on the beach front, or in the town centre a short walk away.

Ground Dimensions: 118m x 134m.

Ground Capacity: 6,000.

Best Crowd: First-Class Match: 6,000 v Hampshire 1947. Limited-Overs Match: 5,000 v Warwickshire (RAL) 1990.

HOW TO GET THERE

Rail: Weston-Super-Mare (BR) 0.5 mile.

Bus: From surrounding areas to town centre, thence 0.5 mile. Badgerline 5 links BR Weston-Super-Mare with ground. (01934 621201).

Car: Ground situated at Clarence Park East in

↑ North direction (approx.)

Entrances
E1 Clarence Road North
E2 Walliscote Road
E3 Clarence Road South
E4 Clarence Road East
E5 Clarence Road North (East)

P Pavilion
SB Scoreboard
CP Car Parking
T Toilets
CS Club Shop
CO Club Office
N1 Clarence Road North End
N2 Clarence Road South End
R BR Weston-Super-Mare
    (direction)
C Town Centre (direction)

Streets
1 Clarence Road North
2 Clarence Road South
3 Walliscote Road

4 Seafront

Above Right: Somerset and Pakistan leg-spinner bowler Mushtaq Ahmed seen weaving his magical spell during the National Westminster Bank Trophy Match against Yorkshire at Headingley last season.

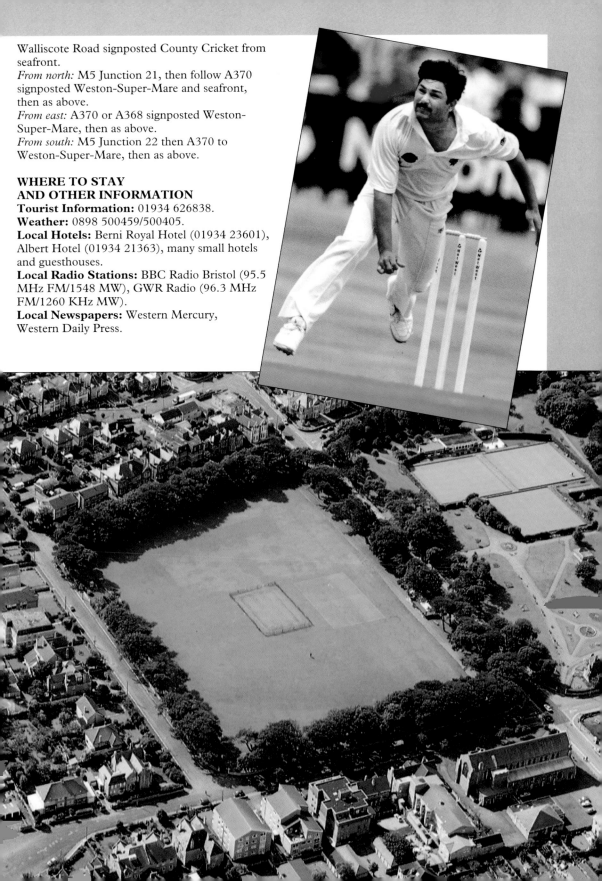

Walliscote Road signposted County Cricket from seafront.
From north: M5 Junction 21, then follow A370 signposted Weston-Super-Mare and seafront, then as above.
From east: A370 or A368 signposted Weston-Super-Mare, then as above.
From south: M5 Junction 22 then A370 to Weston-Super-Mare, then as above.

**WHERE TO STAY
AND OTHER INFORMATION**
Tourist Information: 01934 626838.
Weather: 0898 500459/500405.
Local Hotels: Berni Royal Hotel (01934 23601), Albert Hotel (01934 21363), many small hotels and guesthouses.
Local Radio Stations: BBC Radio Bristol (95.5 MHz FM/1548 MW), GWR Radio (96.3 MHz FM/1260 KHz MW).
Local Newspapers: Western Mercury, Western Daily Press.

LONDON (THE FOSTER'S OVAL)

Address: The Foster's Oval, Kennington, London SE11 5SS.

Telephone Number for Prospects of Play: 0171 582 6660.

Entrances: Hobbs Gates (Players, Officials, Vehicles), Kennington Oval including turnstiles 1-30 in Harleyford Road (Members, Public, Public, Sponsors), Vauxhall End – via West Gate (Public, Vehicles).

Members' Enclosure: Pavilion including areas A, B, C.

Public Enclosure: Rest of the ground including areas CC, D, E, F, G, H, J, K, L, M, N, P, Q, R, S, T, V, W, X, Y, Z.

Covered Stands: Pavilion (part), Fender Stand (part), Lock Stand (part), Laker Stand (part).

Open Stands: Pavilion (part), Fender Stand (part), Peter May Enclosure, Lock Stand (part), Laker Stand (part), Surridge Enclosure, Gover Stand, Stuart Surridge Enclosure, Bedser Stand.

Disabled Areas: Pavilion area for Members or in two special areas for the Public. Car parking by arrangement in advance.

Car Parking Facilities: Limited to Players, Officials only. Street car parking in area surrounding ground or car parks in central London a short distance away.

Ground Dimensions: 170m x 150m (but is usually set at 137m x 140m).

Ground Capacity: 16,500.

Best Crowd: First-Class Match: 80,000 v Yorkshire 1906. Limited-Overs Match: 12,000 v Lancashire (NWBT) 1988.

Anticipated Developments: Completion of Pavilion works including top floor balcony, executive boxes, Members' bar and library/museum.

HOW TO GET THERE

Rail: Oval Underground (Northern Line) 200m, Vauxhall BR and Underground (Victoria Line) 600m.

↑ North direction (approx.)

Entrances
E1 Kennington Oval
E2 Hobbs Gates
E3 Queen's Gate
E4 West Gate
E5 North Gate
E6 Scorebox Gate
E7 Clayton Street Gate

P Pavilion
SB Scoreboard
CP Car Parking
T Toilets
CO Surrey CCC Club Office
M Surrey Cricket Museum/Library
CS The Oval Shop
N1 Pavilion End
N2 Vauxhall End
R Vauxhall BR/Underground (direction)
TT Oval Underground (direction)
C Central London/West End (direction)

Stands
S1 Pavilion Terrace
S2 Bedser Stand
S3 Surridge Enclosure
S4 Gover Stand
S5 Fender Stand
S6 Jardine Stand
S7 Peter May Enclosure
S8 Lock Stand
S9 Laker Stand

1 Ken Barrington Cricket Centre
2 Gas Holders
3 The Cricketers Public House
4 Oval Forecourt
5 Ticket Office
6 Surrey Tavern Public House

Streets
7 Kennington Oval
8 A202 Harleyford Road
9 Clayton Street
10 A3 (direction)
11 A23 (direction)

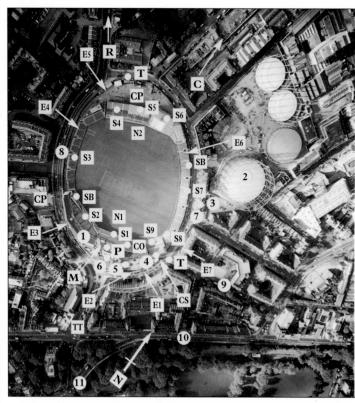

Above Right: Surrey's left-handed top order batsman Graham Thorpe takes evasive action on his way to 114 not out against Australia at Trent Bridge in 1993 when he became only the third England player to score a century on his Test début against the old enemy.

Bus: LRT 3, 36, 36A, 36B, 59, 95, 109, 133, 155, 156, 157, 158, 159, 185, 196. (0171 222 1234).
Car: The ground is located south of the River Thames at Kennington close to the A3, A23 and A202 trunk roads to/from Central London.
From north: From A5 Edgware Road follow signs Marble Arch, then take A202 Park Lane to Grosvenor Place, then follow signs Vauxhall Bridge using Vauxhall Bridge Road, after passing over the River Thames go under the railway bridge and turn right down Harleyford Road for Kennington and The Foster's Oval.
From east: Follow A202 to Kennington district, take Harleyford Road and follow signs for The Oval and county cricket.
From west: M4/M3 or A23, A24 follow signs Central London, then signs Kennington, or as north.
From south: M25 Junctions 6, 7, 8 or 9, then take A22, A23, A24 or A243 signposted London, then follow signs Kennington for county cricket.

WHERE TO STAY
AND OTHER INFORMATION
Tourist Information: 0181 760 5630.
Weather: 0898 500401.
Local Hotels: London Park Hotel (0171 735 9191), or any Central London hotel.
Local Radio Stations: Greater London Radio (94.9 MHz FM/1458 KHz MW), Capital Radio (95.8 MHz FM/1548 KHz MW), LBC (97.3 MHz FM/1152 KHz MW).
Local Newspapers: The Evening Standard, South London Press, Surrey Advertiser.

GUILDFORD

Address: Guildford Cricket Club, The Pavilion, Woodbridge Road, Guildford, Surrey.
Telephone Number for Prospects of Play: 01483 572181.
Entrances: Wharf Road (Players, Officials, Members, Vehicles), Woodbridge Road (Members, Public, Vehicles).
Members' Enclosure: Pavilion, Pavilion terrace, together with defined area between the Pavilion and Woodbridge Road.
Public Enclosure: Rest of the ground.
Covered Stands: Pavilion (part).
Open Stands: Temporary raised seating together with ground level seating surrounding the playing area.
Disabled Areas: No special area, request suitable position.
Car Parking Facilities: Limited car parking available at Railway End of the ground entered from Woodbridge Road for Members only.

Otherwise use multi-storey car park in the city centre a short walk away.
Ground Dimensions: 113m x 119m.
Ground Capacity: 7,500.
Best Crowd: First-Class Match: 7,000 v Hampshire 1938. Limited-Overs Match: 6,000 v Warwickshire (AELL) 1994.

HOW TO GET THERE
Rail: Guildford (BR) or Guildford London Road (BR) both 0.75 mile.
Bus: Green Line buses from surrounding areas to Bus Station thence 0.5 mile.
Car: Ground situated north of city centre off A320 Woodbridge Road.
From north: A320 follow signs Guildford and city centre, then as above.
From east: M25 Junction 10, then follow A3 signposted Guildford and city centre, then as above.
From south: A281 or A3100 follow signs

↑ North direction (approx.)

Entrances
E1 Wharf Road
E2/3 Woodbridge Road

P Pavilion
SB Scoreboard
CP Car Parking
T Toilets
CS The Oval Shop
N1 Railway End
N2 Pavilion End
R BR Guildford (direction)
C City Centre (direction)

Stands
S1 Pavilion Terrace
S2 Members Terraces

1 Railway line

Streets
2 A320 Woodbridge Road

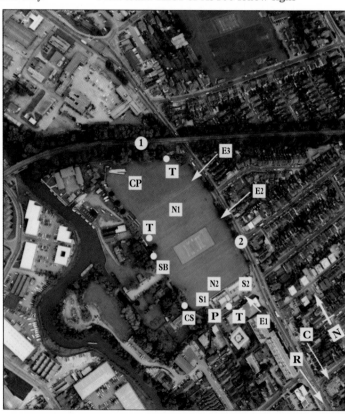

Above Right: Alec Stewart, on his way to 67, is seen stroking the ball through the covers during England's match with St Kitts and Nevis at Warner Park, Basseterre, St Kitts, during England's tour of the Caribbean in 1994.

Guildford and city centre, then as above.
From west: A3 or A31 follow signs Guildford and city centre, then as above.

WHERE TO STAY
AND OTHER INFORMATION
Tourist Information: 01483 444007.
Weather: 0898 500402/500403.
Local Hotels: Angel Hotel (01483 64555), White Horse Hotel (01483 64511).
Local Radio Stations: County Sound (96.4 MHz FM/1476 KHz MW), Radio 210 (102.9 MHz FM/1431 KHz MW).
Local Newspapers: Surrey Advertiser, Surrey Times.

HOVE

Address: County Cricket Ground, Eaton Road, Hove, East Sussex BN3 3AN.
Telephone Number for Prospects of Play: 01273 772766.
Entrances: Eaton Road – via Tate Gates (Players, Officials, Members, Public, Vehicles), Palmeira Avenue (Members, Public, Vehicles).
Members' Enclosure: Pavilion, Pavilion terrace, Wilbury Stand and defined area under trees to Cromwell Road End sightscreen.
Public Enclosure: Rest of the ground.
Covered Stands: Pavilion (part) Wilbury Stand, East Stand.
Open Stands: Pavilion (part), Arthur Gilligan Stand together with permanent and temporary raised and ground level seating including deck chairs surrounding the playing area.
Disabled Areas: Special area plus car parking spaces opposite main Pavilion, north of main scoreboard with entrance from Palmeira Avenue.
Car Parking Facilities: Car parking is available within the ground for Players, Officials, Members only. Public car parking can be found in neighbouring streets and city centre car parks a short walk away.
Ground Dimensions: 130m x 150m.
Ground Capacity: 6,500.
Best Crowd: First-Class Match: 14,500 v Australians 1948. Limited-Overs Match: 6,000 v Middlesex (GC) 1980.
Anticipated Developments: Development approved for four-storey Pavilion, multi-purpose sports hall to north of playing area and hospitality boxes and reconstruction of east side of the ground – commencing in 1995.

HOW TO GET THERE
Rail: Hove (BR) 0.5 mile, Brighton (BR) Thameslink 1 mile.
Bus: Brighton & Hove 7 from either BR station to Cromwell Road for ground. (01273 206666).

↑ North direction (approx.)

Entrances
E1 Eaton Road via Tate Gates
E2 Palmeira Avenue

P Pavilion
SB Scoreboard
CP Car Parking
T Toilets
CO Sussex CCC Club Office
CS Club Shop
N1 Cromwell Road End
N2 Sea End
R BR Hove (direction)
C Town Centre (direction)

Stands
S1 Pavilion Terrace
S2 East Stand
S3 Arthur Gilligan Stand

1 Sussex CCC Indoor Cricket School
2 Cox Memorial Gardens
3 Sussex Squash Rackets Club
4 Sussex Cricketer Public House

Streets
5 Cromwell Road
6 Palmeira Avenue
7 Eaton Road
8 Seafront/Beach (direction)

Above Right: Sussex skipper Alan Wells drives through the covers during his innings for Lavinia Duchess of Norfolk's XI versus the New Zealanders at Arundel last season.

Services 1, 2, 3, 5, 5B, 6, 19, 26, 33, 37, 43, 43A, 46, 49, 59 also pass close to the ground.
Car: *From north:* M25 Junction 7, then join M23 and A23 signposted Brighton, follow signs Pyecombe and Hove after entering Brighton, then follow signs County Ground for county cricket.
From east: A27 follow signs Brighton and town centre, then Worthing, for Hove and County Ground, or take seafront (Kingsway) to Second Avenue, Hove, then cross the A277 into Wilbury Road. Eaton Road is then the first turning on the right for County Ground.
From west: A27 follow signs Hove for County Ground or A259 seafront (Kingsway) to Second Avenue, then as east.

WHERE TO STAY
AND OTHER INFORMATION
Tourist Information: 01273 723755.
Weather: 0898 500456/500457.
Local Hotels: Alexandra Hotel (01273 202722), Imperial Hotel (01273 731121), The Dudley Hotel (01273 736266), many other small hotels and guesthouses.
Local Radio Stations: BBC Radio Sussex (104.5 MHz FM/1161 KHz MW), Southern Sound (103.4 MHz FM/1332 KHz MW).
Local Newspapers: Evening Argus, Brighton & Hove Leader.

Address: Friends of Arundel Castle Cricket Club, The Cricket Office, Arundel Park, Arundel, West Sussex BN18 9LH.

Telephone Number for Prospects of Play: 01903 882462.

Entrances: London Road – via Stables (Players, Officials, Members, Vehicles), London Road – via Arundel Park (Members, Public, Vehicles).

Members' Enclosure: Pavilion and defined Members' Enclosure between main scoreboard and Members' refreshment tent.

Public Enclosure: Rest of the ground. Spectators are advised to bring their own seats to popular matches.

Covered Stands: Pavilion.

Open Stands: Temporary seating surrounding the playing area.

Disabled Areas: No special area, request suitable position, path near pavilion advised.

Car Parking Facilities: Ample parking available in Arundel Park to the north of the ground together with parking close to the entrance and to the south of the ground where some cars can be positioned close to the playing area if space is available.

Ground Dimensions: 152m x 140m.

Ground Capacity: 12,000.

Best Crowd: First-Class Match: 8,000 v Surrey 1993. Limited-Overs Match: 6,500 v Middlesex (AELL) 1994.

HOW TO GET THERE

Rail: BR Arundel, 1 mile.

Bus: Southdown 212, 230 Worthing–Arundel Castle. (01903 37661).

Car: Entrance to Arundel Park is off Arundel bypass in London Road, north of town centre, enter park through stables and parkland, follow signs 'Cricket'.

From north: A29 and A284 signposted Arundel,

⬆ North direction (approx.)

Entrances
E1 London Road via Stable Area
E2 London Road via Arundel Park
   (Car Park)

P Pavilion
SB Scoreboard
CP Car Parking
T Toilets
CO Friends of Arundel Castle
   Club Office
CS Club Shop
N1 Park End
N2 Castle End
R BR Arundel (direction)
C Town Centre (direction)

1 Indoor Cricket School
2 Arundel Castle
3 Arundel Cathedral

Streets
4 A284 London Road

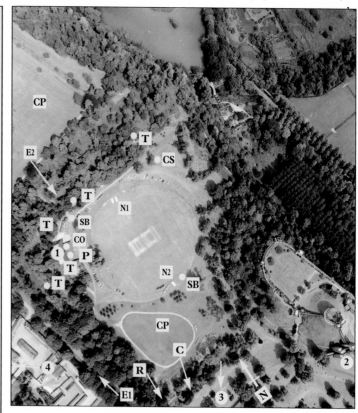

Above Right: Leg-spin bowler Ian Salisbury in action for England against Antigua at the Recreation Ground during England's tour of the West Indies in 1994, when he took 4 for 10.

then follow signs Arundel Park.

From east: A27 signposted Arundel and town centre, then as above

From west: A27 signposted Arundel and town centre, then as above.

From south: A284 signposted Arundel and town centre, then as above.

WHERE TO STAY
AND OTHER INFORMATION

Tourist Information: 01243 823140.
Weather: 0898 500402/500403.
Local Hotels: Norfolk Arms (01903 882101), Bridge Hotel (01903 882242).
Local Radio Stations: BBC Radio Sussex (104.5 MHz FM/1161 KHz MW), Southern Sound (103.5 MHz FM/1323 KHz MW).
Local Newspaper: West Sussex Gazette.

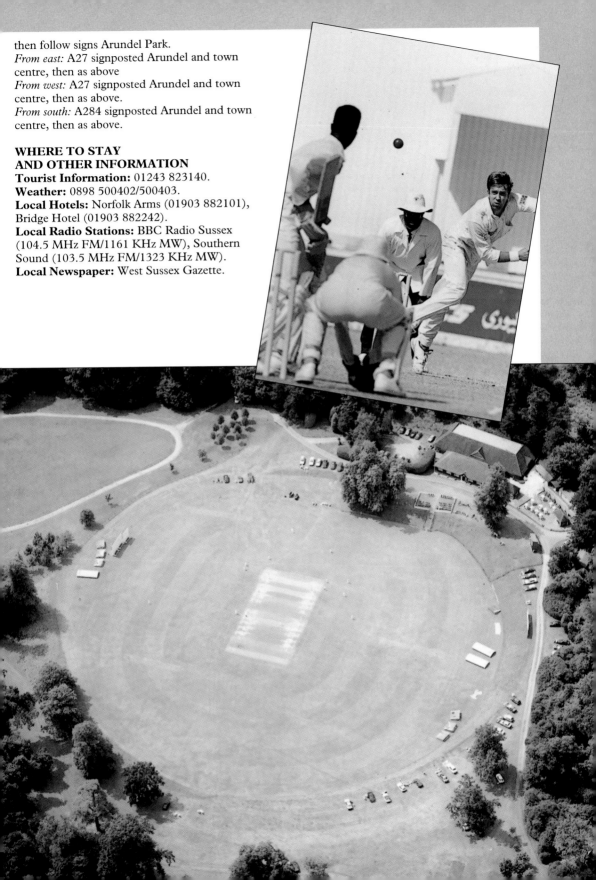

EASTBOURNE

Address: Eastbourne Cricket Club, Eastbourne Saffrons Sports Club, The Saffrons, Compton Place Road, Eastbourne, East Sussex.

Telephone Number for Prospects of Play: 01323 724328.

Entrances: Compton Place Road (Players, Officials, Members, Vehicles), Meads Road (Members, Public), Old Orchard Road/Saffrons Road (Members, Public, Vehicles).

Members' Enclosure: Pavilion and temporary Members' stand of raised and ground level seating.

Public Enclosure: Rest of the ground.

Covered Stands: Pavilion, Football Stand (part), War Memorial Pavilion, Harry Bartlett Pavilion.

Open Stands: Temporary raised and ground level seating including deck chairs surrounding the playing area.

Disabled Areas: Special area available on football ground side.

Car Parking Facilities: There is a large car park available at the rear of the football stand at the Saffrons End of the ground which is entered off Old Orchard Road/Saffrons Road. Alternative car parking can be found in neighbouring streets and town centre car parks.

Ground Dimensions: 120m x 130m.

Ground Capacity: 8,000.

Best Crowd: First-Class Match: 5,000 v Somerset 1948. Limited-Overs Match: 8,000 v Kent (JPL) 1978.

HOW TO GET THERE

Rail: Eastbourne (BR) 0.5 mile.

Bus: From surrounding areas to town centre, within 0.5 mile of ground. Eastbourne Bus 8B from town centre passes ground.

Car: The ground is situated 0.5 mile from the town centre and town hall.

↑ North direction (approx.)

Entrances
E1 Compton Place Road
E2 Meads Road
E3 Old Orchard Road/Saffrons
    Road via Car Park

P Pavilion
SB Scoreboard
CP Car Parking
T Toilets
CS Club Shop
N1 Saffrons End
N2 Meads Road End
R BR Eastbourne (direction)
C Town Centre (direction)

1 Bowling Green
2 War Memorial Pavilion
3 Harry Bartlett Pavilion
4 Eastbourne Town F.C. Ground
5 Eastbourne Town Hall

Streets
6 Compton Place Road
7 Meads Road
8 A259 Grove Road

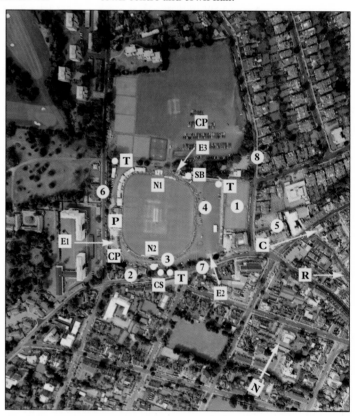

Above Right: Former Yorkshire, Gloucestershire and England batsman Bill Athey was Sussex's leading run scorer last season with 1,022 first-class runs (av 30.96) which included 169 not out against Kent at Tunbridge Wells.

From north: A22 follow signs Eastbourne and town centre, then take A259 to Grove Road and then Saffrons Road. Meads Road is then the first turning on the right for the Saffrons Ground.
From east: A259 follow signs Eastbourne and town centre, then as north.
From west: A259 follow signs Eastbourne and town centre, then as north.

WHERE TO STAY AND OTHER INFORMATION
Tourist Information: 01323 411400.
Weather: 0898 500456/500457.
Local Hotels: Grand Hotel (01323 722611), Chatsworth Hotel (01323 730327), The Wish Tower (01323 722676), many other small hotels and guesthouses.
Local Radio Stations: BBC Radio Sussex (104.5 MHz FM/1161 KHz MW), Southern Sound (103.5 MHz FM/1323 KHz MW).
Local Newspapers: Eastbourne News, Eastbourne Gazette and Herald.

Sussex

Address: Horsham Cricket Club, The Pavilion, Cricket Field Lane, Worthing Road, Horsham, West Sussex.

Telephone Number for Prospects of Play: 01403 254628.

Entrances: Cricket Field Road – via Worthing Road (Players, Officials, Members, Public, Vehicles), Barrackfield Walk – via St Mary's Churchyard (Members, Public).

Members' Enclosure: Pavilion and defined Members' Enclosure in front of the Pavilion.

Public Enclosure: Rest of the ground.

Covered Stands: Pavilion/Clubhouse.

Open Stands: Temporary raised and ground level seating surrounding the playing area.

Disabled Areas: No special area, request suitable position.

Car Parking Facilities: There is a large area for car parking to the south and east of the ground, together with nearby street parking and car parks in the town centre a short walk away.

Ground Dimensions: 126m x 122m.

Ground Capacity: 5,500.

Best Crowd: First-Class Match: 6,000 v Northamptonshire 1948. Limited-Overs Match: 6,500 v Worcestershire (JPL) 1980.

HOW TO GET THERE

Rail: Horsham (BR) 1 mile.

Bus: London Country (SW) H1, H2, H5 link BR Horsham Station with ground. (0181 668 7261).

Car: Take Worthing Road from town centre and turn into Cricketfield Road for Horsham CC. The ground is a short walk from the town centre.

From north: M25 Junction 9, then follow A24 signposted Horsham and town centre, then as above.

From east: A264 follow signs Horsham and town centre, then as above.

From west: A281 or A264 follow signs Horsham

↑ North direction (approx.)

Entrances
E1 Cricket Field Lane
E2 Barrackfield Walk

P Pavilion
SB Scoreboard
CP Car Parking
T Toilets
CS Club Shop
N1 Town End
N2 Railway End
R BR Horsham (direction)
C Town Centre (direction)

1 Tennis Courts
2 Railway line
3 River Arun
4 St Mary's Church

Streets
5 Cricket Field Lane
6 A24 Worthing Road

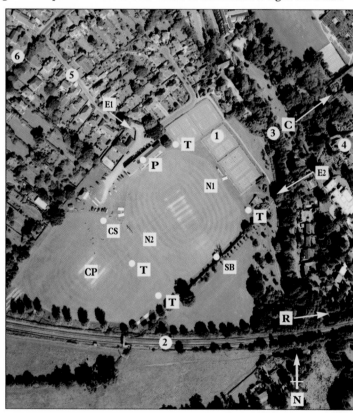

Above Right: Former Nottinghamshire and West Indies all-rounder Franklyn Stephenson was again a key performer for Sussex last season with 752 runs (av 27.85) and 67 wickets (av 20.27).

and town centre, then as above.
From south: A24 or A281 follow signs Horsham and town centre, then as above.

**WHERE TO STAY
AND OTHER INFORMATION**
Tourist Information: 01273 723755.
Weather: 0898 500402/500403.
Local Hotel: Ye Olde King's Head (01403 53126).
Local Radio Stations: BBC Radio Sussex (104.5 MHz FM/1161 KHz MW), Radio Mercury (102.7 MHz FM/1521 KHz MW).
Local Newspapers: West Sussex County Times, Crawley Observer, West Sussex Gazette.

BIRMINGHAM (EDGBASTON)

Address: County Cricket Ground, Edgbaston Road, Edgbaston, Birmingham, West Midlands B5 7QU.

Telephone Number for Prospects of Play: 0121 440 3624.

Entrances: Edgbaston Road (Players, Officials, Members, Public, Vehicles), Constance Road (Members, Public, Vehicles), Pershore Road (Members, Public, Vehicles).

Members' Enclosure: Defined area between William Ansell Stand and Leslie Deakins Stand including R.V. Ryder Stand and Centre Pavilion area.

Public Enclosure: Rest of the ground. For important matches all seats are reserved and numbered except in some parts of the Members' Enclosure.

Covered Stands: Centre Pavilion (part), William Ansell Stand (part) including Tom Dollery Lounge and Cyril Goodway Suite, Priory Stand (part), Aylesford Executive Suites, Raglan Stand (part),

Bob Wyatt Executive Suites, Hill Bank Stand (part), Press Box Stand (part), Calthorpe Suite, Eric Hollies Stand, Leslie Deakins Stand (part).

Open Stands: Pavilion (part), William Ansell Stand (part), Priory Stand (part), Raglan Stand (part), Bob Wyatt Stand (part), Press Box Stand (part), Stanley Barnes Stand, Leslie Deakins Stand (part).

Disabled Areas: In front of Thwaite Scoreboard and by special prior arrangement in other areas.

Car Parking Facilities: Substantial areas for car parking adjoining the ground, mainly for Members' cars. For important matches overflow car parking is available south of Edgbaston Road in Edgbaston Park, in surrounding streets and in multi-storey car parks closer to the city centre.

Ground Dimensions: 148m x 145m.

Ground Capacity: 17,500.

Best Crowd: First-Class Match: 28,000 v Lancashire 1951. Limited-Overs Match: 12,000 v Yorkshire (NWBT) 1982.

↑ North direction (approx.)

Entrances
E1 Edgbaston Road
E2 Edgbaston Road via Thwaite Gates
E3 Constance Road
E4 Pershore Road

P Pavilion
SB Scoreboard
CP Car Parking
T Toilets
CO Warwickshire CCC Club Office
M Warwickshire Cricket Museum
CS Club Shop
N1 City End
N2 Pavilion End
R BR Birmingham New Street (direction)
C City Centre (direction)

Stands
S1 Pavilion Terrace
S2 R.V. Ryder Stand
S3 William Ansell Stand (including Cyril Goodway Suite and Tom Dollery Lounge)
S4 Priory Stand (including Aylesford Executive Suites)
S5 Raglan Stand (including Aylesford Executive Suites)
S6 Bob Wyatt Bank Stand (including Executive Boxes)
S7 Press Box Stand
S8 Stanley Barnes Stand
S9 Eric Hollies Stand
S10 Leslie Deakins Stand (including Calthorpe Suite)

1 Warwickshire CCC Indoor Cricket School
2 River Rea
3 Practice Ground
4 Edgbaston Park

Streets
5 Edgbaston Road
6 Constance Road
7 Pershore Road

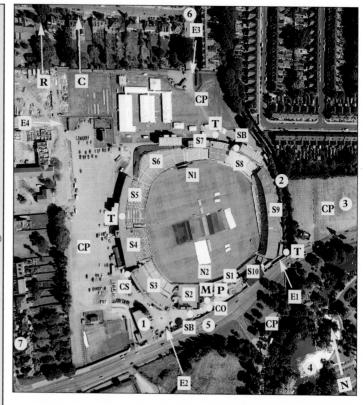

Above Right: Called upon to captain the triple champions, while skipper Dermot Reeve was injured, county stalwart Tim Munton had a breathtaking season taking 81 wickets (av 21.58) which included 7 for 52 versus Derbyshire at Chesterfield.

Anticipated Developments: Construction of new Bob Wyatt Executive Boxes and Bob Wyatt Stand together with a new press box, ready for 1995 season.

HOW TO GET THERE
Rail: Birmingham New Street (BR) 1.75 miles.
Bus: West Midlands Travel 45, 46, 47 link BR Birmingham New Street with ground. Also 1, 52, 61, 63 from City Centre to Edgbaston Road. (0121 200 2601).
Car: *From north:* M6 Junction 6, follow A38 City Centre and pass through city centre and tunnels, 1.5 miles south, take left at traffic lights into Priory Road, across Pershore Road traffic lights and the entrance to the ground is then on the left off Edgbaston Road. Follow signs Edgbaston and County Cricket once south of city centre area for ground.
From east: A45, A41 or A34 follow signs Birmingham and city centre, then Edgbaston for County Cricket, or as north.
From west: M5 Junction 4, follow A38 Birmingham and city centre, pass through Selly Oak and then follow signs Edgbaston and County Cricket.
From south: A441, A435, A34, M40, A41 or A45 follow signs Birmingham and city centre, then follow signs Edgbaston and County Cricket.

WHERE TO STAY
AND OTHER INFORMATION
Tourist Information: 0121 643 2514.
Weather: 0898 500411.
Local Hotels: Beech House Hotel (0121 373 0620), Wentsbury Hotel, Selly Oak (0121 472 1258), The Albany (0121 631 2528), Forte Post House Hotel (0121 357 7444), The Grand Hotel (0121 236 7951), Strathallan Hotel (0121 455 9777).

Local Radio
Stations: BBC Radio WM (95.6 MHz FM/1468 KHz MW), BRMB (96.4 MHz FM/1152 KHz MW), Mercia Sound (97.0 MHz FM/1359 KHz MW), Beacon Radio (97.2 MHz FM/990 KHz MW).
Local Newspapers: Birmingham Post, Birmingham Evening Mail, Birmingham Despatch, Daily News, Sports Argus, (weekends only).

WORCESTER

Address: County Cricket Ground, New Road, Worcester, Worcestershire WR2 4QQ.
Telephone Number for Prospects of Play: 01905 748474.
Entrances: New Road (Players, Officials, Members, Public, Vehicles).
Members' Enclosure: Defined area between New Road Stand (upper) and Diglis End sightscreen including Pavilion and Ladies Pavilion.
Public Enclosure: Rest of the ground.
Covered Stands: Pavilion (part), Ladies Pavilion (part), New Road Stand (part), East Stand.
Open Stands: Pavilion (part), Ladies Pavilion (part), New Road Stand (part), East Stand, Diglis End, Severn Side Seats.
Disabled Areas: Two viewing points on the ground accessible to wheelchairs. Toilet facilities for disabled. Owing to possibility of flooding most buildings are 6–8ft above ground and unfortunately accessible only by steps.
Car Parking Facilities: Car parking is available in the ground and in the field adjoining the Diglis End close to the river and cricket nets. Street parking and nearby car parks are within a short walk over the bridge and into the city centre or in the park opposite the entrance in New Road.
Ground Dimensions: 145m x 136m.
Ground Capacity: 8,500.
Best Crowd: First-Class Match: 14,000 v Australians 1948. Limited-Overs Match: 8,500 v Lancashire (NWBT) 1989.
Anticipated Developments: Proposed new Indoor Cricket School to be commenced in 1995.

HOW TO GET THERE
Rail: Worcester (BR) Foregate Street 0.5 mile, Worcester (BR) Shrub Hill 1 mile. **Bus:** Midland Red West 23, 24, 25, 26, 33 link Angel Place (200m from BR Foregate Street) with ground. (01345 212555).
Car: Ground is situated south of the city centre and south of the River Severn close to Bridge Street.

↑ North direction (approx.)

Entrances
E1 New Road
E2 New Road

P Pavilion
SB Scoreboard
CP Car Parking
T Toilets
CO Worcestershire CCC Club Office
CS Club Shop
N1 New Road End
N2 Diglis End
R BR Worcester Foregate Street (direction)
C City Centre (direction)

Stands
S1 Pavilion Terrace
S2 Ladies Pavilion/Terrace
S3 New Road Stand
S4 New Road Executive Suites
S5 Severn Side Seats

1 River Severn

Streets
2 A44 New Road

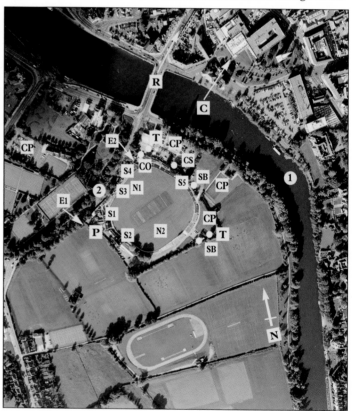

Above Right: Western Australian Tom Moody was in prolific form in 1994 for the midlands county and helped Worcestershire to their first National Westminster Bank Trophy when they beat arch rivals Warwickshire.

From north: M5 Junction 5, then follow A38 signposted Worcester and city centre, then take A44 for New Road and County Cricket, or A443, A449 to city centre, then as above.
From east: A422 or A44 follow signs Worcester and city centre, then as above.
From west: A44, A4103 or A419 follow signs Worcester and city centre, then as above.
From south: M5 Junction 7, follow A44 signposted Worcester and city centre, then as above.

WHERE TO STAY
AND OTHER INFORMATION
Tourist Information: 01905 726311.
Weather: 0898 500411.
Local Hotels: Giffard Hotel (01905 27155), Star Hotel (01905 24308), Bredon Manor Hotel (01684 72293), Fownes Resort Hotel (01905 613151).
Local Radio Stations: Radio Wyvern (102 MHz FM/1530 KHz MW), BBC Radio WM (95.6 MHz FM/1468 KHz MW).
Local Newspapers: Worcester Evening News, Birmingham Post, Birmingham Mail, Express and Star, Berrow's Worcester Journal.

KIDDERMINSTER

Address: Kidderminster Cricket Club, Chester Road Sports Club, Offmore Lane, Chester Road, Kidderminster, Worcestershire DY10 1TH.

Telephone Number for Prospects of Play: 01562 824175.

Entrances: Off Moor Lane (Players, Officials, Members, Vehicles), Chester Road (Members, Public).

Members' Enclosure: Defined area between Pavilion, Long Room and Old Pavilion.

Public Enclosure: Rest of the ground.

Covered Stands: Pavilion, Long Room, Old Pavilion.

Open Stands: Temporary raised seating together with ground level seating surrounding the playing area.

Disabled Areas: No special area, request suitable position.

Car Parking Facilities: Players, Officials, Members in defined area off Moor Lane.

Otherwise street parking in surrounding area or car parks within the town centre.

Ground Dimensions: 131m x 121m.

Ground Capacity: 5,500.

Best Crowd: First-Class Match: 7,000 v Yorkshire 1956. Limited-Overs Match: 3,500 v Middlesex (JPL) 1969.

HOW TO GET THERE

Rail: Kidderminster (BR) 0.5 mile.

Bus: Midland Red from surrounding areas to Bus Station, thence 0.75 mile, Midland Red No 7 passes ground.

Car:

From north: M5 Junction 3, then follow A456 signposted Kidderminster, then take A449 bypass for Offmore Lane and County Cricket close to railway line, or A449, A442 to Kidderminster, then as above.

From east: A456 or A448 signposted

↑ North direction (approx.)

Entrances
E1 Chester Road
E2 Off Moor Lane

P Pavilion
SB Scoreboard
CP Car Parking
T Toilets
CO Club Office
CS Club Shop
N1 Railway End
N2 Pavilion End
R BR Kidderminster (direction)
C Town Centre (direction)

Stands
S1 Pavilion Terrace
S2 Long Room
S3 Old Pavilion

Streets
1 A456 Chester Road
2 Off Moor Lane

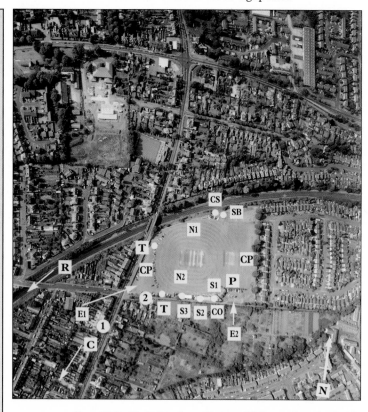

Above Right: Zimbabwe-born Graham Hick, seen here batting for Worcestershire against Warwickshire during the 1994 Benson & Hedges Cup Final, was England's leading run scorer with 304 runs (av 60.80) during the 1994 Cornhill Test Series with South Africa.

Kidderminster, then as north.
From west: A456 or A451 signposted
Kidderminster, then as north.
From south: M5 Junction 6, then follow A449
signposted Kidderminster, then as north.

WHERE TO STAY
AND OTHER INFORMATION
Tourist Information: 01562 829400.
Weather: 0898 500411.
Local Hotels: Gainsborough House Hotel
(01562 754041), Cedars Hotel (01562 745869).
Local Radio Stations: BBC Radio WM
(95.6 MHz FM/1468 KHz MW), Beacon Radio
(97.2 MHz FM/990 KHz MW), Radio Wyvern
(102 MHz FM/1530 KHz MW), BRMB
(96.4 MHz FM/1152 KHz MW).
Local Newspapers: Berrow's Worcester
Journal, Kidderminster Shuttle, Kidderminster
Chronicle.

LEEDS (BASS HEADINGLEY)

Address: The Club Office, Bass Headingley Cricket Ground, St Michael's Lane, Leeds, West Yorkshire LS6 3BR.

Telephone Number for Prospects of Play: 0113 278 7394.

Entrances: St Michael's Lane – via Sutcliffe Gates (Players, Officials, Members, Vehicles), St Michael's Lane – via Main Gates (Members, Public), Kirkstall Lane (Members, Public).

Members' Enclosure: Leeds Pavilion, Bowling Green Stand.

Public Enclosure: North Enclosure seating A, B, C, D, Wintershed Stand Upper, West Terrace Enclosure seating A, B, C, D, E, F, G, H, I, Main Stand Upper (including Grandstand Bar) and Lower.

Covered Stands: Leeds Pavilion, Wintershed Stand Lower, Main Stand Upper and Lower (part).

Open Stands: Leeds Pavilion (part), Bowling Green Stand, North Enclosure seating A, B, C,

D, Wintershed Stand Upper, West Terrace Enclosure seating A, B, C, D, E, F, G, H, I, Main Stand Lower.

Disabled Areas: In designated areas or by arrangement in advance.

Car Parking Facilities: Some car parking is available in the Leeds Rugby South Stand car park, but this is limited on international match days and car parking must be found in neighbouring streets or local parking areas at Beckett Park and Woodhouse Moor. Members' car parking is available off St Michael's Lane on the practice area of the Leeds Rugby Club and main ground although for international matches tickets have to be obtained in advance to gain entry.

Ground Dimensions: 137m x 140m (although for matches the playing area is limited to 130m x 134m).

Ground Capacity: 14,000.

Best Crowd: First-Class Match: 44,507 v

⬆ North direction (approx.)

Entrances
E1 St Michael's Lane via Sutcliffe Gates
E2 St Michael's Lane via Main Gate
E3 St Michael's Lane via Rugby Ground
E4 Kirkstall Lane

P Pavilion (Members)
SB Scoreboard
CP Car Parking
T Toilets
CO Yorkshire CCC Club Office
CS The White Rose Club Shop
N1 Kirkstall Lane End
N2 Football Stand End
R BR Headingley (direction)
C City Centre (direction)

Stands
S1 Leeds Pavilion Terrace
S2 Main Stand
S3 West Terrace
S4 North Enclosure
S5 Wintershed
S6 Executive Suites
S7 Bowling Green Stand

1 Ticket Office
2 Leeds Rugby League Ground
3 Leeds Rugby Offices/Club Shop
4 Yorkshire CCC Indoor Cricket School

Streets
5 St Michael's Lane
6 Kirkstall Lane
7 Cardigan Road
8 A660 Headingley High Street (direction)

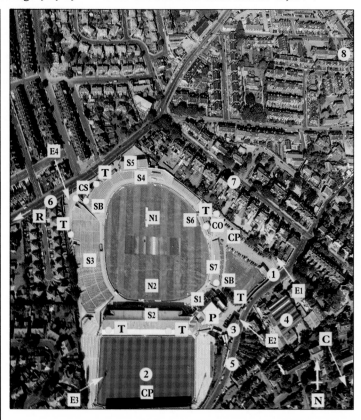

Above Right: Yorkshire and England quickie Darren Gough seen in action during the Texaco Trophy One-Day International between England and South Africa at Old Trafford in 1994.

Lancashire 1948. Limited-Overs Match: 9,500 v Warwickshire (BHC) 1987.

HOW TO GET THERE
Rail: Headingley (BR) 0.5 mile, Leeds Central (BR) 2.5 miles.
Bus: Yorkshire Rider 74–77 link BR Leeds with ground; 1, 4, 56, 93, 96 from city centre pass ground; 38, 39, 93, 96 from city suburbs pass ground. (0113 245 7676).
Car: The ground is situated about 1.5 miles north-west of the city centre and west of the A660.
From north: A660, A61 or A58 follow signs Leeds and city centre, then follow signs Kirkstall district and Headingley for Headingley Cricket Ground turning off A660.
From east: A64, A63 or M62 and M1 follow signs Leeds and city centre, then follow signs Kirkstall district and Headingley on A660 as above.
From west: A58, A62, A647 or M62 and M621 follow signs Leeds and city centre, then follow signs Kirkstall district and Headingley on A660 as above.
From south: A653, A61 or M1 to Junction 43, then follow A61 Leeds and city centre, then follow signs Kirkstall district and Headingley on A660 as above.

WHERE TO STAY
AND OTHER INFORMATION
Tourist Information: 0113 247 8301.
Weather: 0898 500417.
Local Hotels: Queen's Hotel (0113 243 1323), Golden Lion Hotel (0113 243 6454), Forte Post House Leeds/Bramhope (0113 284 2911), The Metropole (0113 24 5081).

**Local
Radio Stations:**
BBC Radio Leeds (95.3 MHz FM/774 KHz MW), Radio Aire (96.3 MHz FM/828 KHz MW).
Local Newspapers: Yorkshire Post, Yorkshire Evening Press, Leeds Weekly News, Bradford Telegraph & News.

BRADFORD

Address: The Yorkshire Academy of Cricket, Bradford Park Avenue Cricket Ground, Canterbury Avenue, Bradford, West Yorkshire.
Telephone Number for Prospects of Play: 01274 391564.
Entrances: Canterbury Avenue (Players, Officials, Members, Vehicles), Horton Park Avenue (Members, Public).
Members' Enclosure: East Terrace including bar beneath and defined Members' Enclosure on terraced area.
Public Enclosure: Rest of the ground.
Covered Stands: None available.
Open Stands: Permanent terrace surrounding the playing area with free-standing temporary seating.
Disabled Areas: No special area, request suitable position at City End adjoining scoreboard.
Car Parking Facilities: Car parking is available at the southern end of the ground for Players, Officials, Members and in the car park of the Speedball Indoor Cricket Centre adjoining the ground off Canterbury Avenue. Alternatively street parking is available locally.
Ground Dimensions: 124m x 130m.
Ground Capacity: 8,000.
Best Crowd: First-Class Match: 30,790 v Gloucestershire 1947. Limited-Overs Match: 8,000 v Nottinghamshire (GC) 1969.

HOW TO GET THERE
Rail: Bradford (BR) 1.25 miles.
Bus: Yorkshire Rider Buses from surrounding areas to Bradford Bus Station thence approximately 0.75 mile from ground. (0113 245 7676).
Car: The ground is situated to the south-west of the city centre and is located off A647 Great Horton Road to Halifax.
From north: A650, A6038 or A658 signposted Bradford and city centre, then follow signs for Halifax as above.

⬆ North direction (approx.)

Entrances
E1/2 Canterbury Avenue
E3/4 Horton Park Avenue

SB Scoreboard
CP Car Parking
T Toilets
CS Club Shop
N1 City End
N2 Southern End
R BR Bradford (direction)
C City Centre (direction)

Stands
S1 East Terrace
S2 South Terrace
S3 West Terrace

1 Speedball Indoor Cricket Centre
2 Yorkshire CCC Cricket
  Academy Centre
3 Site of former Bradford Park
  Avenue Football Ground
4 Site of former Pavilion

Streets
5 A647 Great Horton Road
6 Horton Park Road
7 Canterbury Avenue

Above Right: Mark Robinson, formerly of Northamptonshire, appeals for the wicket of New Zealand skipper Ken Rutherford during the Tetley Bitter Challenge Match at Headingley last season.

From west: A647, B6145, A6025 or M62 Junction 26 then M606, then follow signs Bradford and city centre, then A647 for ground.
From east: A647, A650, A6120 or M62 Junction 26 then M606, then follow signs Bradford and city centre, then as above.
From south: M1 Junction 42, then follow M62 to Junction 26, then M606, then follow signs Bradford and city centre, then as above.

WHERE TO STAY
AND OTHER INFORMATION
Tourist Information: 01274 753678.
Weather: 0898 500417.
Local Hotels: Norfolk Gardens Hotel (01274 734734), Victoria Hotel (01274 728706).
Local Radio Stations: BBC Radio Leeds (95.3 MHz FM/774 KHz MW), Radio Aire (96.3 MHz FM/828 KHz MW).
Local Newspapers: Yorkshire Post, Yorkshire Evening Press, Bradford Telegraph and Argus.

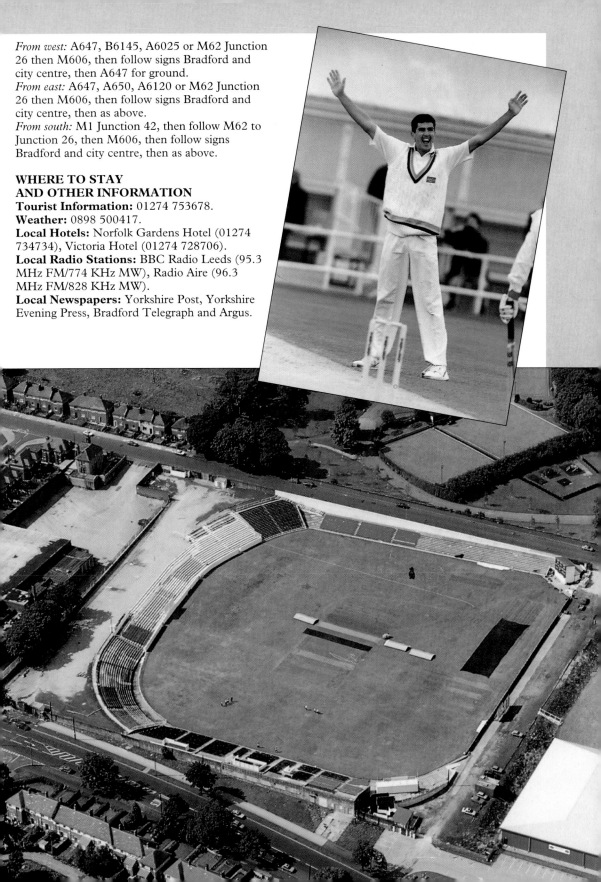

Address: Harrogate Cricket Club, The Pavilion, St George's Cricket Ground, St George's Road, Harrogate, North Yorkshire.

Telephone Number for Prospects of Play: 01423 561301.

Entrances: St George's Road – via Centenary Gates (Players, Officials, Members, Public, Vehicles), St Marks Avenue – via Leyland Gates (Members, Public).

Members' Enclosure: Pavilion, Tavern and defined Members' Enclosure.

Public Enclosure: Rest of the ground.

Covered Stands: Pavilion, Tavern, West Stand.

Open Stands: Pavilion terrace, Tavern terrace, East Side terrace, Scoreboard Mound, permanent and temporary raised and ground level seating surrounding the playing area.

Disabled Areas: No special area, request suitable position on walkway at northern end of ground.

Car Parking Facilities: Car parking is limited to Players, Officials within the ground but there is ample Members' car parking to the rear of the Pavilion and for the Public in neighbouring streets.

Ground Dimensions: 118m x 140m.

Ground Capacity: 8,000.

Best Crowd: First-Class Match: 13,630 v Glamorgan 1962. Limited-Overs Match: 15,000 India v Pakistan (Help the Aged Charity Match) 1986.

HOW TO GET THERE

Rail: Harrogate (BR) 1.25 miles.

Bus: Harrogate & District 36, 653 from BR Harrogate–Leeds/Bradford pass end of St George's Road. (01423 66061).

Car: Ground is situated about 0.5 mile south of the town centre, off the A61 to Leeds.

From north: A1 and A6055 signposted Harrogate

⬆ North direction (approx.)

Entrances
E1 St George's Road via Centenary Gates
E2 St Marks Avenue via Leyland Gates
E3 Rear of Pavilion via Car Park

P Pavilion
SB Scoreboard
CP Car Parking
T Toilets
CO Harrogate CC Office
CS Club Shop
N1 St George's Road End
N2 Pavilion End
R BR Harrogate (direction)
C Town Centre (direction)

Stands
S1 Pavilion Terrace
S2 Tavern/Tavern Terrace
S3 West Stand
S4 Scoreboard Mound
S5 East Enclosure

Streets
1 St George's Road
2 St Mark's Avenue
3 A61 Leeds Road

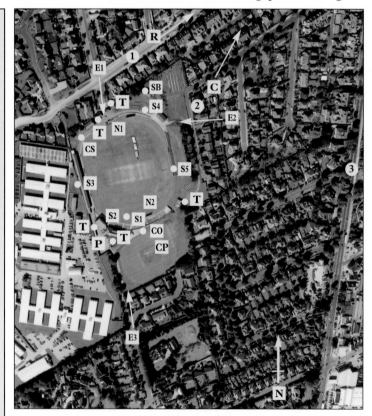

Above Right: Called into the England squad during last summer, although he is yet to make his Test début, the former Worcestershire left-arm spinner, Richard Stemp, took 49 wickets (av 30.46) for Yorkshire in 1994.

or A61 to town centre, then as above.
From east: A59 follow signs Harrogate and town centre, then as above.
From west: A59 or B6162 follow signs Harrogate and town centre, then as above.
From south: A1 and A661 signposted Harrogate or A61, then as above.

WHERE TO STAY AND OTHER INFORMATION
Tourist Information: 01423 525666.
Weather: 0898 500417.
Local Hotels: Crown Hotel (01423 67755), Prospect Hotel (01423 65071), Majestic (01423 68972).
Local Radio Station: BBC Radio York (95.5 MHz FM/1260 KHz MW).
Local Newspapers: Yorkshire Post, Yorkshire Evening Press, Harrogate Herald.

MIDDLESBROUGH

Address: Middlesbrough Cricket Club, The Clubhouse, Acklam Park, Green Lane, Acklam, Middlesbrough, Cleveland.

Telephone Number for Prospects of Play: 01642 818567.

Entrances: Green Lane (Players, Officials, Members, Public, Vehicles).

Members' Enclosure: Pavilion, Clubhouse, East Terrace, defined Members' Enclosure from Pavilion to Rugby Ground End sightscreen.

Public Enclosure: Rest of the ground.

Covered Stands: Pavilion, Clubhouse.

Open Stands: Permanent tiered seating surrounding the playing area on the West, North, East Terraces.

Disabled Areas: Special railed-off area provided at Rugby Ground End adjoining sightscreen.

Car Parking Facilities: Ample car parking for Players, Officials, Members, Public on Middlesbrough Rugby Club pitches to the south of the playing area entered off Green Lane.

Alternatively street parking is available locally.

Ground Dimensions: 144m x 124m.

Ground Capacity: 8,000.

Best Crowd: First-Class Match: 13,100 v Warwickshire 1967. Limited-Overs Match: 6,000 v Nottinghamshire (GC) 1963.

HOW TO GET THERE

Rail: Middlesbrough (BR) 1.25 mile.

Bus: Bus Station is 400m from BR Middlesbrough. Cleveland Transit 14, 15, 16, 24 from Bus Station pass ground. (01642 607124).

Car: Ground is situated south of the town centre in the Acklam district in Green Lane.

From north: A1(M), then follow A177 signposted Middlesbrough or take A19 or A178 to town centre, then as above.

From west: A66 follow signs Middlesbrough and town centre, then A19 to Acklam turn-off using A174 or A1130.

↑ North direction (approx.)

Entrances
E1 Green Lane

P Pavilion
SB Scoreboard
CP Car Parking
T Toilets
CS Club Shop
N1 Green Lane End
N2 Rugby Ground End
R BR Middlesbrough (direction)
C Town Centre (direction)

Stands
S1 Pavilion Terrace
S2 Middlesbrough Rugby
   Clubhouse
S3 Green Lane Terrace
S4 West Terrace
S5 East Terrace

1 Middlesbrough RFC Ground

Streets
2 Green Lane

Above Right: Australian-born Craig White seen bowling for England in his first Test Match versus New Zealand at Trent Bridge in 1994. He will be hoping to avoid injury this season and cement his place in the England side.

From south: A1, then follow A168 and A19 signposted Middlesbrough, follow signs Acklam for Green Lane.

**WHERE TO STAY
AND OTHER INFORMATION**
Tourist Information: 01642 243425.
Weather: 0898 500418.
Local Hotels: Blue Bell Hotel (01642 593939), Dragonara Hotel (01642 248133).
Local Radio Stations: BBC Radio Cleveland (95.0 MHz FM/1548 KHz MW), TFM (96.6 MHz/1170 KHz MW).
Local Newspapers: Northern Echo, Evening Gazette, Hartlepool Mail, Yorkshire Post, Journal, Sunday Sun.

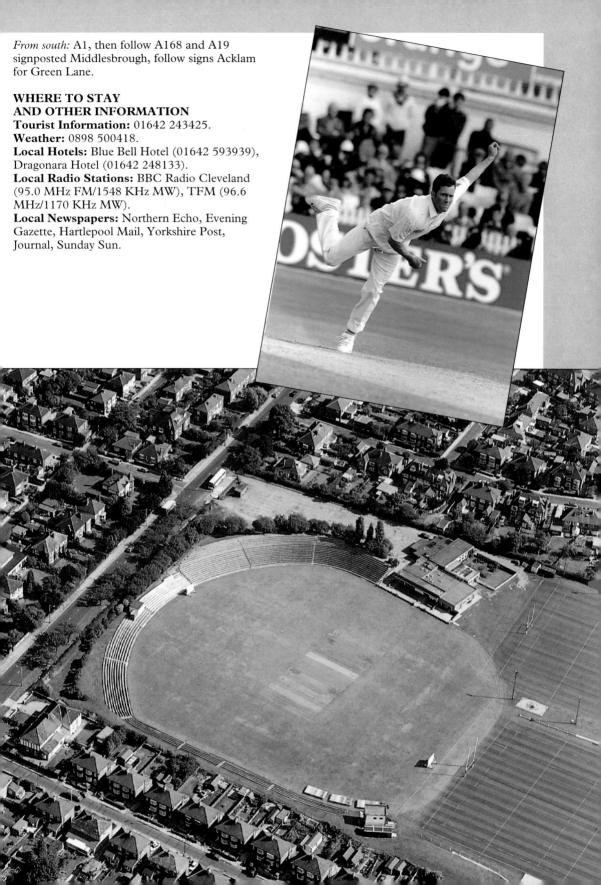

SCARBOROUGH

Address: Scarborough Cricket Club, The Pavilion, North Marine Road, Scarborough, North Yorkshire YO12 7TJ.

Telephone Number for Prospects of Play: 01723 365625.

Entrances: North Marine Road (Players, Officials, Members, Public, Vehicles), Trafalgar Square (Members, Public), Woodhall Avenue (Vehicles).

Members' Enclosure: Pavilion, Pavilion terrace, North Stand enclosure, Trafalgar Square Stand, Enclosure (part).

Public Enclosure: Popular Bank, West Stand Upper (including 'Dropped Catch' Bar beneath), Trafalgar Square Stand, Enclosure (part).

Covered Stands: Pavilion (part), Trafalgar Square Stand including Tea Room Bar.

Open Stands: Pavilion terrace (part), North Stand Enclosure, West Stand Upper, Trafalgar Square Enclosure, Popular Bank.

Disabled Areas: Special area within the Trafalgar Square enclosure.

Car Parking Facilities: No car parking is available within the ground so Members, Public are advised to use one of the town centre car parks or neighbouring streets, some of which are metered.

Ground Dimensions: 132m x 128m.

Ground Capacity: 15,000.

Best Crowd: First-Class Match: 22,946 v Derbyshire 1947. Limited-Overs Match: 12,000 v Worcestershire (RAL) 1989.

HOW TO GET THERE

Rail: Scarborough Central (BR) 0.75 mile.

Bus: United Automobile Services from Whitby and Middlesbrough, East Yorkshire Motor Services from Bridlington and Hull, West Yorkshire Road Car Company from Malton, York and Leeds to town centre Bus Station.

Car: Ground is situated north of the town centre

↑ North direction (approx.)

Entrances
E1 North Marine Road
E2 Trafalgar Square
E3 Woodall Avenue

P Pavilion
SB Scoreboard
CP Car Parking
T Toilets
CO Scarborough CC Office
CS Club Shop
N1 Pavilion End
N2 Trafalgar Square End
R BR Scarborough (direction)
C Town Centre (direction)

Stands
S1 Pavilion Terrace
S2 Popular Bank
S3 Tea Room
S4 Trafalgar Square Stand/Terrace
S5 West Stand
S6 North Stand

Streets
1 Woodall Avenue
2 North Marine Road
3 Trafalgar Square
4 Seafront/Beach

Above Right: New South Wales and Australia left-handed middle order batsman and left-arm bowler Michael Bevan will be Yorkshire's new overseas player this season. He follows Sachin Tendulkar and Richie Richardson into the records for the White Rose county.

off the B1364 North Marine Road adjoining Trafalgar Square.

From north: A171 or A165 follow signs Scarborough and seafront to B1364.
From west: A170 follow signs Scarborough and seafront, then A165 and B1364.
From south: A64 or A165 follow signs Scarborough and seafront, then as above.

WHERE TO STAY
AND OTHER INFORMATION
Tourist Information: 01723 373333.
Weather: 0898 500454.
Local Hotels: Crown Hotel (01723 373491), Reads Hotel (01723 361071), Holbeck Hall (01723 374374), many other small hotels and guesthouses.
Local Radio Station: BBC Radio York (95.5 MHz FM/1260 KHz MW).
Local Newspapers: Scarborough Evening News, The Mercury, Whitby Gazette, Ryedale Shopper, Yorkshire Post, Northern Echo.

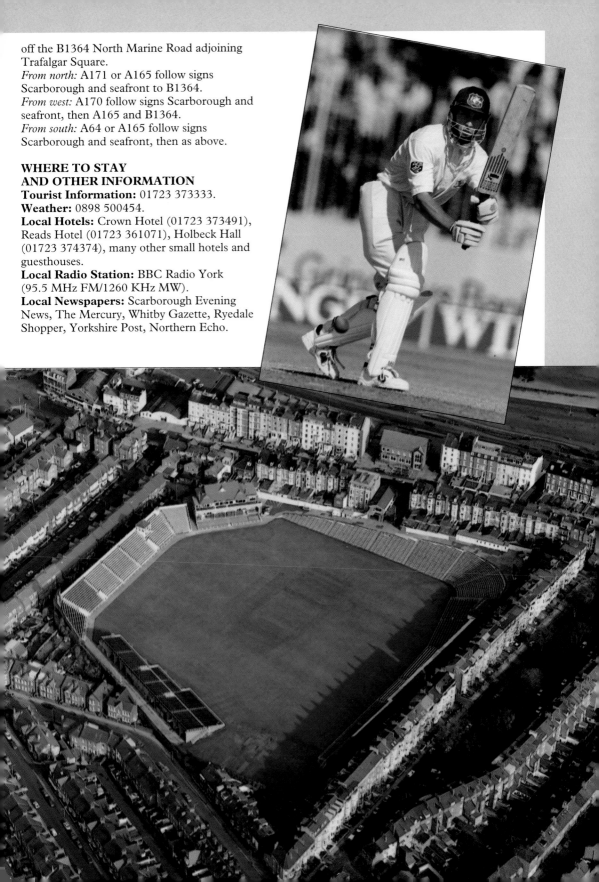

SHEFFIELD

Address: Sheffield Amateur Sports Club, The Pavilion, Abbeydale Park, Abbeydale Park Road South, Dore, Sheffield, South Yorkshire S17 3LJ.
Telephone Number for Prospects of Play: 0114 236 7011.
Entrances: Abbeydale Road South (Players, Officials, Members, Public, Vehicles), Water Lane (Members, Public).
Members' Enclosure: Pavilion, Pavilion terrace and defined Members' Enclosure.
Public Enclosure: Rest of the ground.
Covered Stands: Pavilion, Rugby Stand.
Open Stands: Temporary raised and ground level seating surrounding the playing area.
Disabled Areas: No special area, request suitable position. A disabled toilet is available in the Pavilion.
Car Parking Facilities: Ample car parking is available within the ground for Players, Officials, Members, Public on adjoining sports fields which form part of the SASC complex.

Ground Dimensions: 150m x 148m.
Ground Capacity: 7,500.
Best Crowd: First-Class Match: 8,000 v West Indians 1976. Limited-Overs Match: 4,500 v Essex (JPL) 1986.

HOW TO GET THERE
Rail: Dore and Totley (BR) 100m (link from Sheffield Midland BR).
Bus: South Yorkshire Traction 17, 24 from Pinstone Street 700m from BR Sheffield Midland Station to Abbeydale Park Road South. (0114 275 5655).
Car: Abbeydale Park is situated off the A621 at Dore adjoining Totley off Abbeydale Park Road South 6.5 miles south-west of Sheffield city centre.
From north: M1 Junction 34, follow signs Sheffield and city centre, then A621 signposted Bakewell and Baslow, then as above, or A6102, A61, A6135 or A618 signposted Sheffield and city

⬆ North direction (approx.)

Entrances
E1 Abbeydale Road South
E2 Water Lane

P Pavilion
SB Scoreboard
CP Car Parking
T Toilets
CO Sheffield Amateur Sports Club Office
CS Club Shop
N1 Water Lane End
N2 Pavilion End
R BR Dore & Totley (direction)
C City Centre (direction)

Stands
S1 Pavilion Terrace
S2 Rugby Stand
S3 Sheffield Amateur Sports Club

1 Sheffield RFC Ground
2 Tennis Courts
3 Hockey Pitches
4 Groundsman's House

Streets
5 A621 Abbeydale Road South

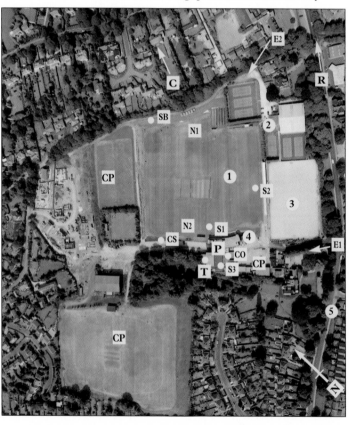

Above Right: Yorkshire's Barnsley-born captain, Martin Moxon, drives through the covers during his innings of 122 versus Kent at Maidstone.

centre, then A621 to Dore, as above.

From east: M1 Junction 33, follow A630 signposted Sheffield and city centre, then as above.

From west: A625 or A621 follow signs Dore and Totley for Abbeydale Park.

From south: M1 Junction 29, follow A617 Chesterfield, then A61 Sheffield; after passing Dronfield, take Greenhill roundabout on southern outskirts of Sheffield and follow signs Dore and Totley on B6054 for Abbeydale Park Road South and SASC ground.

WHERE TO STAY
AND OTHER INFORMATION

Tourist Information: 0114 256 9392.
Weather: 01898 500411.
Local Hotels: Grosvenor House Hotel (0114 22 0041), Hallam Tower Forte Post House (0114 268 6031), Hotel St George (0114 258 3811).
Local Radio Stations: BBC Radio Sheffield (104.1 MHz FM/1035 KHz MW), Radio Hallam (103.4 MHz FM/1548 KHz MW).
Local Newspapers Sheffield Star, Yorkshire Post, The Morning Telegraph.

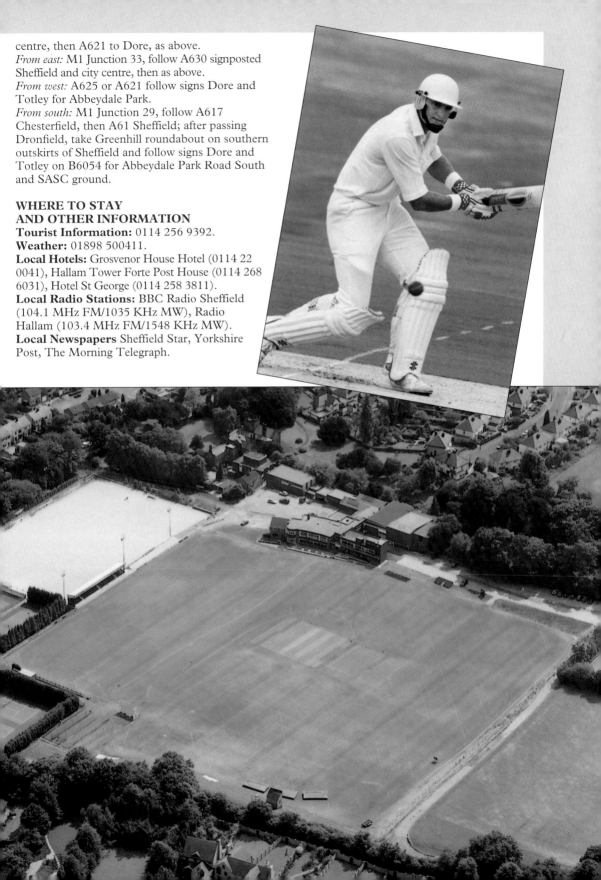

CAMBRIDGE

Address: Cambridge University Cricket Club, Fenner's University Cricket Ground, Wollaston Road, off Mortimer Road, Cambridge, Cambridgeshire.

Telephone Number for Prospects of Play: 01223 353552.

Entrances: Mortimer Road (Players, Officials, Members, Public, Vehicles), Gresham Road – via alleyway (Members, Public).

Members' Enclosure: Pavilion and seating area in front of pavilion.

Public Enclosure: Rest of the ground.

Covered Stands: Pavilion, Ladies Stand.

Open Stands: Temporary ground level seating/benches surrounding the playing area.

Disabled Areas: No special area, request suitable position.

Car Parking Facilities: Car parking available within the ground for Players, Officials, Members only. Public multi-storey car park available off Gonville Place adjoining the ground or in one of the city centre car parks a short walk away.

Ground Dimensions: 147m x 148m.

Ground Capacity: 6,500.

Best Crowd: First-Class Match: 9,000 v West Indians 1950. Limited-Overs Match: 4,500 v Australians (Tour) 1985.

HOW TO GET THERE

Rail: Cambridge (BR) 0.75 mile.

Bus: Cambus 142 or 143 from Bus Station to ground.

Car: Ground is situated close to Parker's Piece at rear of multi-storey car park.

From north: A1 and A604 signposted Cambridge and city centre, then A1309 for Mortimer Road and Fenner's University Cricket Ground, or A10 to city centre, then as above.

From east: A1303 or A45 signposted Cambridge and city centre, then as above.

↑ North direction (approx.)

Entrances
E1 Mortimer Road
E2 Gresham Road via path

P Pavilion
SB Scoreboard
CP Car Parking
T Toilets
N1 Pavilion End
N2 Gresham Road End
R BR Cambridge (direction)
C City Centre (direction)

Stands
S1 Pavilion Terrace
S2 Ladies Stand

1 Tennis Courts
2 Sports Centre
3 Parker's Piece
4 Press Box

Streets
5 Mortimer Road
6 Gresham Road

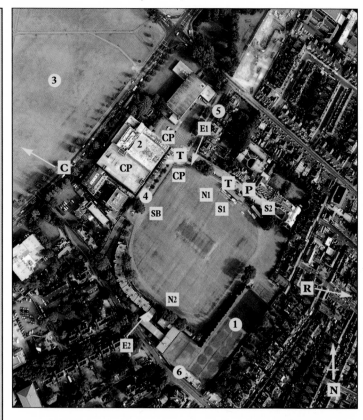

Above Right: James Hodgson and Cambridge University's wicket-keeper Fraser Cooke celebrate a wicket during the friendly match with Middlesex at Fenner's last season.

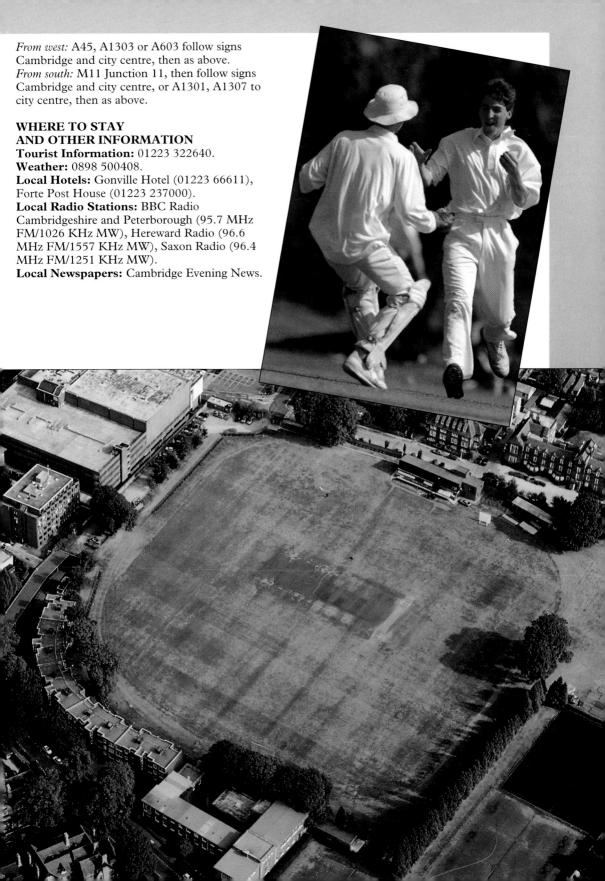

From west: A45, A1303 or A603 follow signs Cambridge and city centre, then as above.
From south: M11 Junction 11, then follow signs Cambridge and city centre, or A1301, A1307 to city centre, then as above.

**WHERE TO STAY
AND OTHER INFORMATION**
Tourist Information: 01223 322640.
Weather: 0898 500408.
Local Hotels: Gonville Hotel (01223 66611), Forte Post House (01223 237000).
Local Radio Stations: BBC Radio Cambridgeshire and Peterborough (95.7 MHz FM/1026 KHz MW), Hereward Radio (96.6 MHz FM/1557 KHz MW), Saxon Radio (96.4 MHz FM/1251 KHz MW).
Local Newspapers: Cambridge Evening News.

OXFORD

Address: Oxford University Cricket Club, The Pavilion, University Parks, Parks Road, Oxford, Oxfordshire.

Telephone Number for Prospects of Play: 01865 57106.

Members' Enclosure: Pavilion and terraced bench seating within Pavilion enclosure.

Public Enclosure: Rest of the ground. Public are advised to bring own seats to matches, as only a few benches are provided.

Covered Stands: Pavilion.

Open Stands: Temporary seating/benches surrounding the playing area.

Disabled Areas: The ground is in a public park and there is ample access, but no car parks. Special arrangements in advance to Assistant Secretary's office.

Car Parking Facilities: Car parking at the rear of the Pavilion for Players, Officials only. There are no car parking facilities for Members or Public except in the city centre car parks or in those streets to the north of the city centre which are free from parking restrictions.

Ground Dimensions: 132m x 140m.

Ground Capacity: Unlimited as sited within University Parks.

Best Crowd: No crowd figures established.

HOW TO GET THERE

Rail: Oxford (BR) 1 mile.

Bus: Oxford 2/A, 10/A from Cornmarket Street, 52 links BR Oxford with Cornmarket Street. (01865 711312).

Car: The University Parks are situated 0.5 mile north-east of city centre, entrance in Parks Road. *From north:* M40/A34, A423 or A43 signposted Oxford and city centre, then follow A4165 for University Parks signposted Parks Road for pedestrian access only to the Parks and cricket ground.

↑ North direction (approx.)

Entrances
E1 Parks Road
E2 Parks Road

P Pavilion
SB Scoreboard
CP Car Parking
T Toilets
CO Oxford University Club Office
N1 Norham Gardens End
N2 Pavilion End
R BR Oxford (direction)
C City Centre (direction)

Stands
S1 Pavilion Terrace

1 The University Parks

Streets
2 Parks Road
3 Norham Gardens

Above Right: Born at Rugby, Oxford University and Northamptonshire right-handed opening batsman Richard Montgomery made a career best 151 for Northamptonshire against Derbyshire at Derby in 1994.

From east: M40/A40 signposted Oxford and city centre, then follow A4165 for University Parks.
From west: A40, A420 or A34 signposted Oxford and city centre, then as east.
From south: M40 Junction 7 then follow A423 to city centre, then as north.

WHERE TO STAY
AND OTHER INFORMATION
Tourist Information: 01865 726871.
Weather: 0898 500406.
Local Hotels: Cotswold Lodge (01865 512121), The Randolph (01865 247481), Eastgate (01865 248244), many other smaller hotels and guesthouses.
Local Radio Stations: BBC Radio Oxford (95.2 MHz FM/1485 KHz MW), Radio 210 (102.9 MHz FM/1431 KHz MW).
Local Newspapers: Oxford Mail, Oxford Times.

Address: Northumberland County Cricket Club, The Pavilion, County Cricket Ground, Osborne Avenue, Jesmond, Newcastle-Upon-Tyne NE2 1JS.
Telephone Number for Prospects of Play: 0191 281 0775.
Entrances: Osborne Avenue (Players, Officials, Members, Public), Lover's Lane – via Clayton Road (Members, Public).
Members' Enclosure: Pavilion and defined Members' Enclosure area 1-3, A, B.
Public Enclosure: Permanent seating areas surrounding the playing area C, D, E, F.
Covered Stands: Pavilion (part), Lambton Arms (part).
Open Stands: Rest of the ground.
Disabled Areas: Special area situated near main scoreboard and groundsman's store at Cemetery End of the ground. No car parking is available within the ground for disabled vehicles.
Car Parking Facilities: No car parking within ground. Use city centre car parks or street parking in Jesmond area.
Ground Dimensions: 117m x 140m.
Ground Capacity: 3,500.
Best Crowd: Best attendance for a Limited-Overs Match: 3,500 Minor Counties (North) v Yorkshire (BHC) 1979.

HOW TO GET THERE
Rail: Newcastle-Upon-Tyne Central (BR) 2 miles; Jesmond (Tyne & Wear Metro), Zone 26 (Green/Red/Yellow Lines) 0.5 mile.
Bus: Nos 4 Heaton–Gosforth and 33 Newcastle–Jesmond from city centre and BR Newcastle Central, OK Travel/Newcastle Busways pass Jesmond via Osborne Avenue. (0191 222 0404).
Car: *From north:* A167, A69, A696 or A1 Great North Road signposted Newcastle and city centre, then follow signs Jesmond and County Cricket, take left into Clayton Road before reaching the

↑ North direction (approx.)

Entrances
E1-E3 Osborne Avenue
E4 Lover's Lane via Clayton Road

P Pavilion
SB Scoreboard
CP Car Parking
T Toilets
CO Northumberland CCC Club Office
CS Club Shop
N1 Osborne Avenue End
N2 Cemetery End
T Jesmond (Tyne & Wear Metro) (direction)
C City Centre (direction)

Stands
S1 Pavilion Terrace
S2 East Terrace (A-B)
S3 South Terrace (C)
S4 West Terrace (D-E)
S5 North Terrace (F)

1 All Saints' Cemetery
2 Lambton Arms & Store

Streets
3 Lover's Lane
4 Clayton Road
5 Osborne Avenue
6 Osborne Road

Above Right: Northamptonshire's captain Allan Lamb holds the record for the highest individual innings, 134, in a limited-overs match on the Jesmond ground for the Callers-Pegasus XI versus the Northumberland/Durham XI in 1982.

North West Radial Road for Osborne Road and
Osborne Avenue.
From east: A1058, B1307, A187 or A186
signposted Newcastle and city centre, then follow
signs Jesmond and County Cricket for Osborne
Road and Osborne Avenue.
From west: A187, A167, A186, B1311 or A695
signposted Newcastle and city centre, then follow
signs Jesmond and County Cricket.
From south: A189, A1(M) then A1, B1307, A167,
A184 or A19(M) signposted Newcastle and city
centre, then follow signs Jesmond and County
Cricket.

WHERE TO STAY
AND OTHER INFORMATION
Tourist Information: 0191 261 0691.
Weather: 0898 500418.
Local Hotels: Cairn Hotel (0191 281 1358),
Hospitality Inn (0191 281 7881), Imperial
Swallow Hotel (0191 281 5511), Northumbria
Hotel (0191 281 4961), Swallow Hotel
(0191 232 5025), various small hotels and
guesthouses.
Local Radio Station: BBC Radio Newcastle
(96.0 MHz FM/1458 KHz MW).
Local Newspapers: Newcastle Journal,
Newcastle Evening Chronicle, Northern
Echo, Sunday Sun.

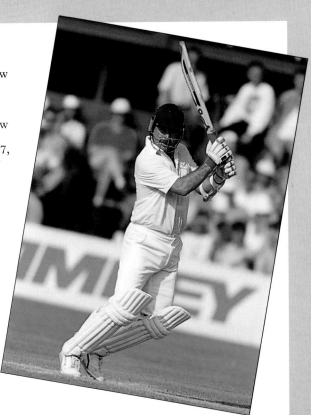

LEEK

Address: Leek Town Cricket Club, The Clubhouse, Highfield Hall, Macclesfield Road, Leek, Staffordshire.

Telephone Number for Prospects of Play: 01583 383693.

Entrances: Macclesfield Road (Players, Officials, Members, Public, Vehicles).

Members' Enclosure: Pavilion and defined Members' Enclosure.

Public Enclosure: Rest of the ground.

Covered Stands: Pavilion and nearby Highfield Hall (Clubhouse).

Open Stands: Temporary seating surrounding the playing area.

Disabled Areas: Special area roped off for major matches, otherwise request suitable position.

Car Parking Facilities: Car parking available adjoining Highfield Hall (Clubhouse).

Ground Dimensions: 140m x 103m.

Ground Capacity: 4,500.

Best Crowd: Limited-Overs Match: 2,500 Derbyshire v Warwickshire (JPL) 1986.

HOW TO GET THERE
Rail: Congleton (BR) 8 miles.

Bus: PMT 218 links BR Stoke-On-Trent with Leek town centre, thence 1 mile to ground. (01782 747000).

Car: *From north:* A523 or A53 to Leek and town centre, ground situated off A523 on northern outskirts of town centre.

From east: A523 and A52, then as north.

From south: A523 or A520, then as north.

From west: A53, then as north.

WHERE TO STAY
AND OTHER INFORMATION
Tourist Information: 01782 284600.

Weather: 0898 500411.

Local Hotels: George Hotel, Burslem (01782 577544), The Jester, (01538 383997), Peak Weaver, Red Lion Hotel.

Local Radio Stations: BBC Radio Stoke-On-Trent (94.6 MHz FM/1053 KHz MW), Radio Signal (102.6 MHz FM/1170 KHz MW), Radio Trent (96.2 MHz FM/999 KHz MW).

Local Newspapers: Derby Evening Telegraph, Leek Post and Times, Evening Sentinel.

Address: Reading Cricket and Hockey Club, The Pavilion, Sonning Lane, off London Road, Sonning-on-Thames, Berkshire RG4 0ST.

Telephone Number for Prospects of Play: 01734 699049.

Entrances: Sonning Lane (Players, Officials, Members, Public, Vehicles).

Members' Enclosure: Pavilion and defined Members' Enclosure.

Public Enclosure: Rest of the ground.

Covered Stands: Pavilion.

Open Stands: Temporary seating surrounding the playing area.

Disabled Areas: No special area, request suitable position.

Car Parking Facilities: Ample car parking is available within the ground and in fields adjoining hockey pitches off Sonning Lane.

Ground Dimensions: 146m x 128m.

Ground Capacity: 4,500.

Best Crowd: Limited-Overs Match: 3,500 Berkshire v Hampshire (NWBT) 1991.

HOW TO GET THERE

Rail: Reading (BR) 2 miles.

Bus: Local buses connect London Road with Reading town centre and BR Reading.

Car: *From north:* A4074, A4155 or A321 signposted Reading and town centre, then follow London Road A4 for Sonning district and Sonning Lane off London Road side of railway bridge for Reading Cricket and Hockey Club.

From east: A4, M4 Junction 10 and A329(M) signposted to Reading town centre, then as north.

From west: A329, A4, M4 Junction 12 signposted Reading town centre, then as north.

From south: A327, A33, M4 Junction 11 signposted Reading and town centre, then as north.

WHERE TO STAY
AND OTHER INFORMATION

Tourist Information: 01734 566226.

Weather: 0898 500406.

Local Hotel: Forte Post House (01734 875485).

Local Radio Station: Radio 210 (97.0 MHz FM/1431 KHz MW).

Local Newspapers: Reading Evening News, Evening Echo.

ARUNDEL

Address: Friends of Arundel Castle Cricket Club, The Cricket Office, Arundel Park, Arundel, West Sussex BN18 9LH.

Telephone Number for Prospects of Play: 01903 882462.

Entrances: London Road – via Stables (Players, Officials, Members, Vehicles), London Road – via Arundel Park (Members, Public, Vehicles).

Members' Enclosure: Pavilion and defined Members' Enclosure between main scoreboard and Members' refreshment tent.

Public Enclosure: Rest of the ground. Spectators are advised to bring their own seats to popular matches.

Covered Stands: Pavilion.

Open Stands: Temporary seating surrounding the playing area.

Disabled Areas: No special area, request suitable position, path near pavilion advised.

Car Parking Facilities: Ample parking available in Arundel Park to the north of the ground together with parking close to the entrance and to the south of the ground where some cars can be positioned close to the playing area if space is available.

Ground Dimensions: 152m x 140m.

Ground Capacity: 12,000.

Best Crowd: 15,000 Lavinia Duchess of Norfolk's XI v Australians 1993.

HOW TO GET THERE

Rail: BR Arundel 1 mile.

Bus: Southdown 212, 230 Worthing–Arundel Castle. (01903 37661).

Car: Entrance to Arundel Park is off Arundel bypass in London Road, north of town centre, enter park through stables and parkland, follow signs Cricket.

From north: A29 and A284 signposted Arundel, then follow signs Arundel Park.

⬆ North direction (approx.)

Entrances
E1 London Road via Stable Area
E2 London Road via Arundel Park (Car Park)

P Pavilion
SB Scoreboard
CP Car Parking
T Toilets
CO Friends of Arundel Castle Club Office
CS Club Shop
N1 Park End
N2 Castle End
R BR Arundel (direction)
C Town Centre (direction)

1 Indoor Cricket School
2 Arundel Castle
3 Arundel Cathedral

Streets
4 A284 London Road

Above Right: Victorian all-rounder and former Sussex player Tony Dodemaide holds the record for the highest individual innings on the ground in a Lavinia Duchess of Norfolk's XI match against a touring team, 131 versus the New Zealanders in 1990.

From east: A27 signposted Arundel and town centre, then as above

From west: A27 signposted Arundel and town centre, then as above.

From south: A284 signposted Arundel and town centre, then as above.

WHERE TO STAY
AND OTHER INFORMATION
Tourist Information: 01243 823140.
Weather: 0898 500402/500403.
Local Hotels: Norfolk Arms (01903 882101), Bridge Hotel (01903 882242).
Local Radio Stations: BBC Radio Sussex (104.5 MHz FM/1161 KHz MW), Southern Sound (103.5 MHz FM/1323 KHz MW).
Local Newspaper: West Sussex Gazette.

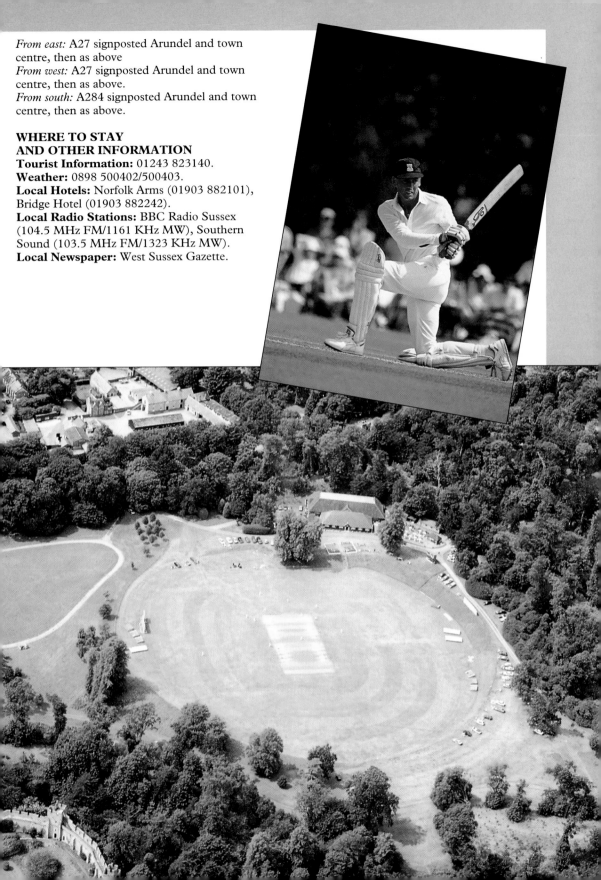

SOUTHGATE

Address: Southgate Cricket Club, The Walker Cricket Ground Trust, The Pavilion, The Waterfall Cricket Ground, Waterfall Road, Southgate, London N14 7JZ.

Telephone Number for Prospects of Play: 0181 886 8381.

Entrances: Waterfall Road (Players, Officials, Members, Public, Vehicles), Mayfield Road – via High Street (Members, Public, Vehicles).

Members' Enclosure: Pavilion and defined Members' Enclosure in front of the pavilion.

Public Enclosure: Rest of the ground.

Covered Stands: Pavilion.

Open Stands: Temporary raised and ground level seating surrounding the playing area.

Disabled Areas: No special area, request suitable position. Parking for disabled vehicles at Church End.

Car Parking Facilities: Car parking in adjoining field to the north of the playing area entered from Mayfield Road for 500 cars together with local school playground and street parking nearby.

Ground Dimensions: 145m x 124m.

Ground Capacity: 7,000.

Best Crowd: Limited-Overs Match: 3,500 England Amateur XI v New Zealand 1994.

HOW TO GET THERE

Rail: Southgate Underground (Piccadilly Line) 0.75 mile; New Southgate and Friern Barnet (BR) 1 mile.

Bus: LRT W9, 121, 125, 298 pass near the ground. (0171 222 1234).

Car: *From north:* M25 Junction 24, then follow A111 signposted Cockfosters, until you reach Southgate Underground at Southgate Circus, then take A1004 High Street to the Green, then take right into A1003 Waterfall Road for cricket ground opposite Christ Church.

↑ North direction (approx.)

Entrances
E1 Waterfall Road
E2 Waterfall Road via car park
E3 Mayfield Road via High Street

P Pavilion
SB Scoreboard
CP Car Parking
T Toilets
N1 Top End
N2 Church End
T Southgate Underground
   (direction)

1 Christ Church
2 Tennis Courts
3 The Walker Cottage
4 Cemetery

Streets
5 Waterfall Road
6 Mayfield Road
7 High Street

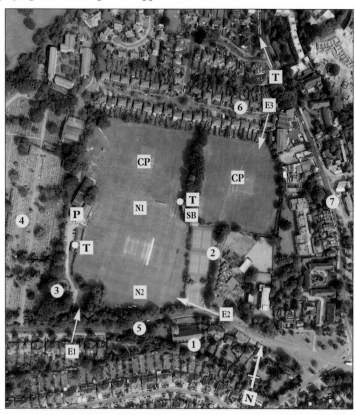

Above Right: Australia 'A' captain during the Benson & Hedges One Day/Night series, Damien Martyn is seen here in action for an Australian XI versus the West Indies at the Bellerive Oval, Hobart, in 1992/93.

From east: M25 Junction 24, then as north; or
A406 North Circular Road to A105 Junction with
Green Lanes, then take right into A105 Green
Lanes, then left into A1004 Alderman's Hill
passing BR Palmer's Green and Southgate, then
right into A1004 Cannon Hill, then left at the
Green followed by first left into A1003 Waterfall
Road for cricket ground opposite Christ Church.
From west: M25 Junction 24, then as north or A406
North Circular Road to New Southgate then take
A110 Bowes Road left, then right at New Southgate
for A1003 Waterfall Road and cricket ground
situated on left opposite Christ Church.
From south: As west or east or A105 from Wood
Green district to Alderman's Hill, Palmer's
Green, then as east.

WHERE TO STAY
AND OTHER INFORMATION
Tourist Information: 0181 760 5630.
Weather: 0898 500401.
Local Hotels: Forte Post House Hampstead
(0171 794 8121), or stay in central or north-
west London.
Local Radio Stations: Greater London
Radio (94.9 MHz FM/1458 KHz MW),
Capital Radio/Capital Gold (95.8 MHz
FM/1548 KHz MW), LBC (97.3 MHz FM/1152
KHz MW).
Local Newspaper: Evening Standard.

TROWBRIDGE

Address: Trowbridge Cricket Club, The Pavilion, County Cricket Ground, Timbrell Street, Trowbridge, Wiltshire.
Telephone Number for Prospects of Play: 01225 752538.
Entrances: Timbrell Street (Players, Officials, Members, Public, Vehicles) Car Park – via British Row (Members, Public, Vehicles), Seymour Road (Members, Public).
Members' Enclosure: Pavilion and defined Members' Enclosure in front of the Pavilion.
Public Enclosure: Rest of the ground.
Covered Stands: Pavilion.
Open Stands: Temporary raised and ground level seating surrounding the playing area.
Disabled Areas: Special area in front of the pavilion, request suitable position. Parking for disabled vehicles at Hospital End.
Car Parking Facilities: Car parking in adjoining field to the south-west of the playing area entered from British Row for 500 cars, together with street parking in surrounding area.
Ground Dimensions: 132m x 115m.
Ground Capacity: 3,500.
Best Crowd: Limited-Overs Match: 3,500 Gloucestershire v Hampshire (RAL) 1989.

HOW TO GET THERE
Rail: Trowbridge (BR) 1 mile.
Bus: Trowbridge Bus Station situated in Market Place 1 mile from the ground; 264, 265 link Trowbridge town centre with Bath and pass close to the ground.
Car: *From north:* A363, signposted Trowbridge, ignore signs to Trowbridge which by-pass Bradford-on-Avon town centre, take right into Stancomb Avenue and left at T-Junction, then second right into Timbrell Street for Trowbridge CC.
From east: B3106, signposted Trowbridge and town centre, then follow signs Staverton/Holt and

↑ North direction (approx.)

Entrances
E1 Timbrell Street
E2 British Row via car park
E3 Seymour Road via High Street

P Pavilion
SB Scoreboard
CP Car Parking
T Toilets
N1 Pond Road End
N2 Hospital End
R BR Trowbridge (direction)
C Town Centre (direction)

Streets
1 Seymour Road
2 Timbrell Street
3 British Row
4 A363 (direction)

Above Right: Queensland batsman Matthew Hayden who had a record breaking summer in 1993, despite not playing in a Test Match, is a member of the Australia 'A' touring party to England this season. He scored 151 in his first match of the 1993 tour versus an England Amateur XI at Radlett.

Canal Road Industrial Estate for ground in Timbrell Street.

From west: A366, signposted Trowbridge and town centre, then as east.

From south: A363, signposted Trowbridge and town centre, then as east.

WHERE TO STAY
AND OTHER INFORMATION
Tourist Information: 01225 707424.

Weather: 0898 500405/500409.

Local Hotels: Gordons Hotel (01225 752072), Hilbury Court Hotel (01225 752949), Polebarn Hotel (01225 777006), or stay in Bath.

Local Radio Station: GWR Radio (97.2 MHz FM/1161 KHz MW).

Local Newspapers: Wiltshire Times, Bath & West Evening Chronicle, Western Daily Press, Bristol Evening Post.

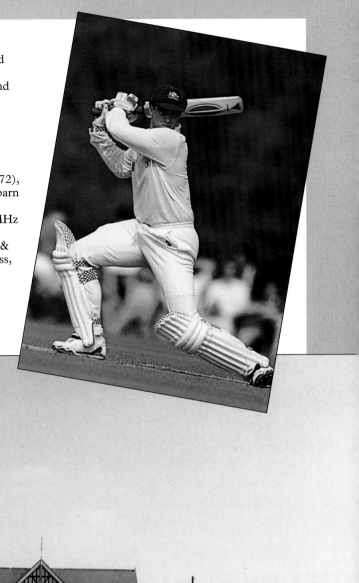

Address: Teacher's Clydesdale Cricket Club, The Pavilion, Titwood Athletic Grounds, Beaton Road, Pollokshields, Glasgow, Scotland G41 4LA.
Telephone Number for Prospects of Play: 0141 423 1463.
Entrances: Beaton Road (Players, Officials, Members), Meldrum Gardens (Players, Officials, Members, Vehicles), Dolphin Road (Members, Public, Vehicles).
Members' Enclosure: Pavilion, Pavilion terrace.
Public Enclosure: North Stand, temporary mobile 200 seat stand, the rest of the ground.
Covered Stands: Pavilion, North Stand.
Open Stands: Temporary raised and ground level seating surrounding the playing area.
Disabled Areas: No special area, request suitable position. Access to the Pavilion is difficult. Car parking is available in Beaton Road to the rear of the Pavilion.
Car Parking Facilities: Car parking is available within the ground for Players, Officials, Members. Ample parking in the adjoining school grounds and local street parking.
Ground Dimensions: 131m x 137m.
Ground Capacity: 5,000.
Best Crowd: First-Class Match: 3,000 v Ireland 1986. Limited-Overs Match: 3,500 v India 1990.

HOW TO GET THERE
Rail: Crossmyloof (BR) 100m, Maxwell Park (BR) 100m, both from Glasgow Central (BR).
Bus: Various buses from city centre to Shawlands Cross, thence 5 min walk to Crossmyloof for Titwood Athletic Grounds.
Car: *From east:* M8 to M77 Spur, take left at roundabout at end of motorway, go straight ahead at first traffic lights and then take left into Dolphin Road at second traffic lights for Titwood Athletic Ground and Clydesdale CC.
From south: M74, then M73 to M8 following

↑ North direction (approx.)

Entrances
E1 Beaton Road
E2 Meldrum Gardens
E3 Dolphin Road

P Pavilion
SB Scoreboard
CP Car Parking
T Toilets
N1 Kirkcaldy Road End
N2 Meldrum Gardens End
R1 BR Crossmyloof (direction)
R2 BR Maxwell Park (direction)
C City Centre (direction)

Stands
S1 Pavilion Terrace
S2 North Stand/Terrace

1 Hutchesons' Grammar School

Streets
2 Kirkcaldy Road
3 Dolphin Road
4 Meldrum Gardens

Above Right: Glasgow Rangers' and Scotland goalkeeper Andy Goram who has represented his country at cricket, combines both games when time is on his side.

signs Glasgow City Centre, stay on motorway and cross River Clyde on M8 Kingston Bridge, then as east.

From north: Cross River Clyde by M8 Kingston Bridge, then as east.

From west: M8 Junction 23 then follow signs A77 Kilmarnock for 0.75 mile to roundabout at end of M77, then as east.

WHERE TO STAY
AND OTHER INFORMATION

Tourist Information: 0141 204 4400.
Weather: 0898 500421.
Local Hotels: Numerous hotels and guesthouses in Glasgow and surrounding areas. For details contact Glasgow Tourist Board, (0141 204 4400).
Local Radio Stations: BBC Radio Scotland (92.5 MHz FM/810 KHz MW), Radio Clyde (102.5 MHz FM/1152 KHz MW).
Local Newspapers: Glasgow Herald, The Scotsman, Scotland on Sunday, Daily Record, Evening Times.

GLASGOW (HAMILTON CRESCENT)

Address: West of Scotland CRGP Cricket Club, The Pavilion, Hamilton Crescent, Peel Street, Partick, Glasgow, Scotland G11 5LU.
Telephone Number for Prospects of Play: 0141 339 0688.
Entrances: Peel Street (Players, Officials, Members, Public, Vehicles).
Members' Enclosure: Pavilion and defined Members' Enclosure.
Public Enclosure: Rest of the ground.
Covered Stands: Pavilion.
Open Stands: Pavilion terrace together with temporary ground level seating surrounding the playing area.
Disabled Areas: An enclosure is available around the perimeter of the ground on the level area near the Tea Room.
Car Parking Facilities: Car parking is available within the ground only for Players, Officials. Street parking is available locally: Peel Street, Fortrose Street, Burgh Hall Street for Members, Public.

Ground Dimensions: 112m x 123m.
Ground Capacity: 4,500.
Best Crowd: First-Class/Limited-Overs Match: 3,500 v Australians 1989.

HOW TO GET THERE
Rail: Partick (BR) 100m, link from Glasgow Queen Street.
Bus: Strathclyde Buses 6, 16, 62, 64, Kelvin Bus 5 link ground with Glasgow city centre and Partick.
Car: Hamilton Crescent is situated in Peel Street off Dumbarton Road to the north-west of central Glasgow.
From north: A81, A879, A803 or A80 follow signs Partick and Partickhill for Hamilton Crescent cricket ground which is entered from Peel Street close to BR Partick.
From east: M8 Junction 17 then follow A82 and Dumbarton for Partick and Peel Street, or A80, A8, A74 or A724 to Glasgow city centre, then follow A82 for Partick.

↑ North direction (approx.)

Entrances
E1 Peel Street
E2 Peel Street/Burgh Hall Street
P Pavilion
SB Scoreboard
CP Car Parking
T Toilets
N1 Pavilion End
N2 Burgh Hall Street End
R BR Partick (direction)
C City Centre (direction)

Stands
S1 Pavilion Terrace
S2 Tea Hut

Streets
1 Peel Street
2 Fortrose Street
3 Burgh Hall Street
4 Dumbarton Road

5 West of Scotland Indoor Cricket School

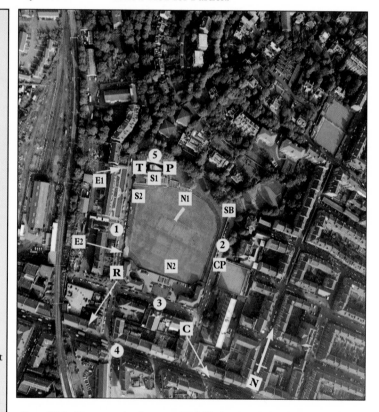

Above Right: Kent opening batsman Neil Taylor, bowled by Phillip De Freitas in 1994, still holds the record for the highest individual innings in a limited-overs match at Hamilton Crescent of 110 for Kent versus Scotland (BHC) in 1991.

From west: M8 Junction 25 then follow A739 signposted Partick for Hamilton Crescent, or A82, A8 or A737 to Glasgow city centre, then follow A82 for Partick.
From south: M74, M73 then M8 Junction 17, then as east, or A749, A726, A77 or A736 to Glasgow city centre, then A82 for Partick.

WHERE TO STAY
AND OTHER INFORMATION
Tourist Information: 0141 204 4400.
Weather: 0898 500421.
Local Hotels: Nearby hotels include The Wickets beside the ground or contact Glasgow Tourist Board (0141 204 4400) for details of many others in Glasgow area.
Local Radio Stations: Radio Clyde (102.5 MHz FM/1152 KHz MW), BBC Radio Scotland (92.5 MHz FM/810 KHz MW).
Local Newspapers: Glasgow Herald, Daily Record, Evening Times, Scotland on Sunday.

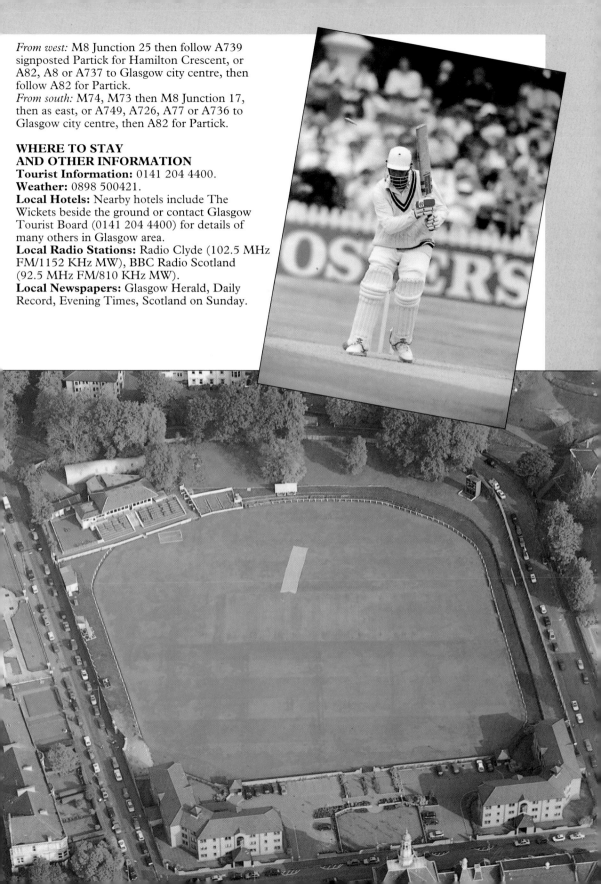

Scottish Cricket Union

Address: Grange Cricket Club, The Pavilion, Raeburn Place, Edinburgh, Scotland EH4 1HQ

Telephone Number for Prospects of Play: 0131 332 2148.

Entrances: Raeburn Place (Players, Officials, Members, Public, Vehicles).

Members' Enclosure: Pavilion and defined Members' Enclosure.

Public Enclosure: Rest of the ground.

Covered Stands: Pavilion.

Open Stands: Temporary ground level seating surrounding the playing area.

Disabled Areas: An enclosure is available on the perimeter of the ground on the level area near the Tea Room.

Car Parking Facilities: Available within ground for Players, Officials, Members only. Street parking in neighbouring streets.

Ground Dimensions: 145m x 135m.

Ground Capacity: 5,000.

Best Crowd: 2,500 v Ireland 1991.

HOW TO GET THERE

Rail: Edinburgh (BR).

Bus: Buses link ground with Edinburgh city centre and railway station.

Car: *From north:* M90 and A90 signposted Edinburgh to city centre, then follow signs B900 for Grange CC in Raeburn Place.

From east: A1, A68 signposted Edinburgh to city centre, then as north.

From west: M9 and A90 or M8 and A80 signposted Edinburgh to city centre, then as north.

From south: A70, A71, A702, A703, A7, A68 signposted Edinburgh to city centre, then as north.

WHERE TO STAY AND OTHER INFORMATION

Tourist Information: 0131 557 1700.

Weather: 0898 500422.

Local Hotels: Many hotels and guesthouses in Edinburgh area. Contact Edinburgh Tourist Board for details, (0131 557 1700).

Local Radio Stations: BBC Radio Scotland (92.5 MHz FM/810 KHz MW), Radio Forth (97.3 MHz FM/1548 KHz MW).

Local Newspapers: The Scotsman, Daily Record, Scotland on Sunday.

↑ North direction (approx.)

Entrances
E1 Raeburn Place
E2 Port Gower Place
E3 Arboretum Avenue

P Pavilion
SB Scoreboard
CP Car Parking
T Toilets
N1 City End
N2 Park End
R BR Edinburgh Waverley (direction)
C City Centre (direction)

Streets
1 Raeburn Place
2 A90 Queensferry Road

FORFAR

Address: Strathmore County Cricket Club, The Pavilion, Lochside Park, Forfar, Scotland.

Telephone Number for Prospects of Play: 01307 64289.

Entrances: Lochview Terrace (Players, Officials, Members, Public, Vehicles).

Members' Enclosure: Pavilion with bar, 500 temporary raised seats, Tea Room verandah.

Public Enclosure: Rest of the ground.

Covered Stands: Pavilion, Tea Room.

Open Stands: Rest of the ground including 200 temporary raised seats.

Disabled Areas: No special area, request suitable position.

Car Parking Facilities: 100 cars can be parked within the ground itself, 200 on the nearby football pitch.

Ground Dimensions: 126m x 134m.

Ground Capacity: 3,750.

Best Crowd: Limited-Overs Match: 2,500 v Lancashire (BHC) 1991.

HOW TO GET THERE

Rail: Dundee (BR) 12 miles.

Bus: City Link buses serve Dundee, then take local buses from Dundee and surrounding areas to Forfar town centre.

Car: *From north:* A94 and B9128 signposted Forfar and town centre, then follow signs for Lochside Park for Strathmore County CC ground.

From east: B9134, B9133 or A932 signposted Forfar and town centre, then as north.

From west: A929 and A932 or A94 or A928 signposted Forfar and town centre, then as north.

From south: A929 and A932 or B9128 signposted Forfar and town centre, then as north.

WHERE TO STAY
AND OTHER INFORMATION

Tourist Information: 01241 72609.

Weather: 0898 500424.

Local Hotels: Royal Hotel, plus smaller guesthouses, or stay in Dundee.

Local Radio Stations: BBC Radio Scotland (92.7 MHz FM/810 KHz MW), Radio Tay (102.8 MHz FM/1161 KHz MW).

Local Newspapers: Dundee Courier and Advertiser, Forfar Dispatch (Weekly), Scotland on Sunday.

↑ North direction (approx.)

Entrances
E1 Lochview Terrace

P Pavilion
SB Scoreboard
CP Car Parking
T Toilets
N1 Loch End
N2 Baronhill End
C Town Centre (direction)

Stands
S1 Tea Pavilion
S2 Store

1 Forfar Loch
2 Forfar RFC Ground

Streets
3 Lochview Terrace

Marylebone Cricket Club

Founded: 1787.
Colours: Red and yellow.
Crest: The letters 'MCC'.
Secretary: R.D.V. Knight.
Assistant Secretary, Administration: J.R. Smith.
Assistant Secretary, Cricket: J.A. Jameson.
Assistant Secretary, Finance: M.R. Blow.
Head Coach: C.T. Radley.
Groundsman: M.J. Hunt.
Scorer/Statistician: E. Solomon.
Newsletter: MCC From Lord's.
Address: Lord's Cricket Ground, St John's Wood Road, London NW8 8QN.
Telephone: 0171 289 1611/5 (Pavilion Switchboard), 0171 289 8979 (Club Office), 0171 289 3649 (Indoor School), 0171 289 1757 (Shop), 0171 289 8011 (Prospects of Play), 0171 266 3825 (Tours Department), 0171 289 5005 (Ticket Office).
Facsimile: 0171 289 9100 (Pavilion), 0171 266 3459 (Club Office).
Rapid Cricketline County Scores: 0891 567500.
Test Match Commentaries Rapid Cricketline: 0891 567567.
Test Match Updates Rapid Cricketline: 0891 567555.
Ground: London (Lord's Cricket Ground, St John's Wood Road).
Other Grounds: No other grounds have been used since 1814.
Second XI (MCC Young Cricketers) Grounds: Southgate CC, The Walker Cricket Ground Trust, The Pavilion, The Waterfall Cricket Ground, Waterfall Road, Southgate, London N14 7JZ, (0181 886 8381). Slough CC, Chalvey Road, Slough, Berks, (01753 520982).

Derbyshire

Founded: 4 November 1870.
Colours: Chocolate, Cambridge blue and amber.
Crest: Rose and imperial crown.
President: G.L. Willatt.
Chairman of Committee: M.A. Horton.
Chairman of Cricket Committee: B. Holling.
General Manager/Secretary: R.G. Taylor TD.
Commercial Manager: M. MacNamee.
County Coach/Cricket Development Officer: A. Hill.
Youth Coaching Officer: J. Brown.
Captain: K.J. Barnett.
Groundsman: S. Birks.
Scorer: S.W. Tacey.
Statistician: F.G. Peach.
Team Sponsor: Birch plc.
Ground Sponsor: Nynex Communications.
Newsletter: *Derbyshire Members News.*
Address: County Cricket Ground, Nottingham Road, Derby, Derbyshire DE2 6DA.
Telephone: 01332 383211.
Facsimile: 01332 290251.
Derbyshire Rapid Cricketline: 0891 567501.
Achievements: County Champions 1936.
Gillette Cup/National Westminster Bank Trophy Winners 1981.

Benson & Hedges Cup Winners 1993.
Sunday League Champions 1990.
Grounds: Derby (County Cricket Ground, Nottingham Road), Chesterfield (Queen's Park, Boythorpe Road) and Ilkeston (Rutland Recreation Ground, West End Drive).
Other Grounds: Heanor (Town Ground, Mayfield Road), Checkley (Uttoxeter Road, Checkley), Knypersley (Victoria and Knypersley Social Welfare Centre, Tunstall Road), Leek (Highfield, Macclesfield Road), Burton-Upon-Trent (Ind-Coope Brewery Ground, Belvedere Road) (Allied Brewery Sports Ground), Long Eaton (Trent College, Derby Road), Cheadle (Tean Road Sports Ground, Tean Road), Repton (Repton School Ground, Repton), Darley Dale (Station Road) and Buxton (The Park, Park Road).
Second XI Grounds: Abbotsholme School, Rocester, Staffs, (01889 590217). Heanor Town CC, Heanor Town Sports & Social Club, Town Ground, Mayfield Avenue, Commonside, Heanor, Derbyshire, (01773 716703). Knypersley CC, Victoria and Knypersley Social Welfare Centre, Tunstall Road, Knypersley, Staffs, (01782 513304). Leek Town CC, The Clubhouse, Highfield Hall, Macclesfield Road, Leek, Staffs, (01583 383693). Belper Meadows CC, The Meadows, opposite Christchurch, Belper, Derbyshire. Shipley Hall CC, Shipley Park, Shipley, Heanor, Derbyshire.

Durham

Founded: 10 May 1882.
Colours: Maroon, Oxford blue and old gold.
Crest: Coat of Arms of County Durham.
Patron: A.W. Austin.
Overseas Patron: Sir D.G. Bradman AC.
President: I.D. Caller.
Chairman/Director: J.D. Robson.
Directors: R.B. Caller, R. Jackson, H.W.M. Milner, I.D. Mills, T. Moffat MBE, N.A. Riddell, M. Roseberry, J. Sherrington, Prof R. Storer.
Chief Executive: G.A. Wright.
Director of Cricket: G. Cook.
Youth Development Officer: M.J. Robinson.
Financial Controller: D. Harker.
Marketing Executive: A.R. Fothergill.
Commercial Manager: Ms D.L. Beaumont.
Captain: M.A. Roseberry.
Head Steward/Ground Administrator: J. Handy.
Groundsman: T. Flintoft.
Scorer/Statistician: B. Hunt.
Club Sponsor: Newcastle Breweries.
Newsletter: *Riverside Review.*
Address: County Cricket Ground, Riverside, Chester-le-Street, Co Durham DH3 3QR.
Telephone: 0191 387 1717.
Facsimile: 0191 387 1616.
Durham Rapid Cricketline: 0891 567502.
Achievements: County Championship 16th 1994.
Benson and Hedges Cup 2nd Round 1993.
Gillette Cup/National Westminster Bank Trophy Quarter-Finalists 1992.
Sunday League 7th 1993.
Grounds: Chester-le-Street (County Ground & Riverside), Darlington (Feethams Cricket Ground, South Terrace), Durham University (Racecourse Ground, Green Lane), Stockton-On-Tees, (Grangefield

Road Ground), Hartlepool (Park Drive), Gateshead Fell (Eastwood Gardens, Low Fell), Chester-Le-Street (Ropery Lane).
Other Grounds: Sunderland (Ashbrooke Cricket Ground), Jesmond (Northumberland CCC Ground, Osborne Avenue, Newcastle-Upon-Tyne), Durham City (Green Lane), South Shields (Westoe Ground, Dean Road), Bishop Auckland (King's Way), Wearmouth (Carley Hill), Consett (Blackfyne Ground).
Second XI Grounds: Norton CC, Station Road, Norton, Stockton-On-Tees, Co Durham, (01642 554031). Sunderland CC, Ashbrooke, Sunderland, Co Durham, (0191 528 4536). Felling CC, Heworth Lane, Heworth, Felling, Co Durham, (0191 469 3645). Philadelphia CC, Bunker Hill, Houghton-le-Spring, Tyne & Wear, (0191 584 1348). Boldon CC, Sunderland Road, East Boldon, Tyne & Wear, (0191 536 4180). Bishop Auckland CC, King's Way, Bishop Auckland, (01388 603371). Shildon Railway CC, Hackworth Street, Shildon, Co Durham, (01388 772068). Durham City CC, The Pavilion, Green Lane, Durham City, (0191 386 9959). Eppleton CC, Church Road, Hetton-le-Hole, Tyne & Wear, (0191 526 1271). Durham School, Quarryhead Lane, Durham City, (0191 386 9959). Seaton Carew CC, The Pavilion, Hornby Park, Elizabeth Way, Seaton Carew, Hartlepool, Cleveland, (01429 260945).

Essex
Founded: 14 January 1876.
Colours: Blue, gold and red.
Crest: Three scimitars with word 'Essex' underneath.
President: D.J. Insole CBE.
Chairman: D.L. Acfield.
Chairman Cricket Committee: G.J. Saville.
Secretary/General Manager: P.J. Edwards.
Marketing Manager: C.A. Blockley.
Assistant Secretary: M.C. Field.
Captain: P.J. Pritchard.
County Coach: A.R. Butcher.
Ground Manager: B. Hughes.
Groundsman: S. Kerrison.
Physiotherapist: J. Davis.
Scorer: C.F. Driver.
Statistician: K. Montgomery.
Sponsor: Air UK.
Newsletter: *Essex News.*
Address: County Cricket Ground, New Writtle Street, Chelmsford, Essex CM2 0PG.
Telephone: 01245 252420.
Facsimile: 01245 491607.
Essex Rapid Cricketline: 0891 567503.
Achievements: County Champions 1979, 1983, 1984, 1986, 1991, 1992.
Gillette Cup/National Westminster Bank Trophy Winners 1985.
Benson & Hedges Cup Winners 1979.
Sunday League Champions 1981, 1984, 1985.
Refuge Assurance Cup Winners 1989.
Grounds: Chelmsford (County Cricket Ground, New Writtle Street), Ilford (Valentine's Park, Cranbrook Road), Southend-On-Sea (Southchurch Park), Colchester (Castle Park, Sportsway off Catchpool Road).
Other Grounds: Colchester (Garrison 'A' Ground, Napier Road), Brentwood (Old County Ground, Shenfield Road), Harlow (Sports Centre, Hammarskjold Road), Leyton (Leyton High Road Youth Sports Ground, High Road), Westcliff-On-Sea (Chalkwell Park) and Purfleet (Thames Board Mills Sports Ground).
Second XI Grounds: Brentwood CC, Old County

Ground, Shenfield Road, Brentwood, Essex, (01277 212580). Newbury Park CC, Newbury Park Sports Ground, Ford Sports & Social Club, Aldborough, Near Ilford, Essex, (0181 590 3797). Wickford CC, Patmore Memorial Ground, Runwell Road, Wickford, Essex, (01268 763023). Orsett & Thurrock CC, School Lane, Orsett, Essex. Leigh-On-Sea CC, Chalkwell Park, London Road, Leigh-On-Sea, Essex, (01702 76603). Maldon CC, The Promenade, Maldon High Street, Maldon, Essex. Aveley CC, Cricket Ground, Aveley, Essex. Romford CC, Gidea Park, Romford, Essex.

Glamorgan
Founded: 6 July 1888.
Colours: Blue and gold.
Crest: Gold daffodil.
Patron: HRH The Prince of Wales.
President: W. Wooller.
Chairman: F.D. Morgan.
Chairman Cricket Committee: H.D. Davies.
Secretary: G.R. Stone.
Cricket Secretary: M.J. Fatkin.
Commercial Manager: A.P. Dilloway.
Accountant: P. Pullin.
Marketing Assistant: Miss V.L. Snook.
Captain: H. Morris.
Coach: J. Derrick.
Director of Coaching: A. Jones MBE.
Assistant Coach: D.J. Shepherd.
Physiotherapist: D. Conway.
Ground Supervisor: L.A. Smith.
Scorer: B.T. Denning.
Hon Statistician: Dr A.K. Hignell.
Hon Librarian: D. Irving.
Sponsors: Acer 7, ASW Holdings Plc, Anderson Consulting and Cardiff Bay Development Corporation.
Newsletter: *Glamorgan Matters.*
Address: Sophia Gardens, Cardiff, Wales CF1 9XR.
Telephone: 01222 343478.
Facsimile: 01222 377044.
Glamorgan Rapid Cricketline: 0891 567504.
Achievements: County Champions 1948, 1969.
Gillette Cup/National Westminster Bank Trophy Finalists 1977.
Benson & Hedges Cup Semi-Finalists 1988.
Sunday League Champions 1993.
Grounds: Cardiff (Sophia Gardens, Cathedral Road), Swansea (St Helen's Ground, Bryn Road), Neath (The Gnoll, Dyfed Road), Ebbw Vale (Eugene Cross Park, Newchurch Road), Abergavenny (Pen-y-Pound, Avenue Road), Pontypridd (Ynysangharad Park, Ynysybwl Road), Colwyn Bay (Penrhyn Avenue, Rhos-On-Sea).
Other Grounds: Newport (Athletic Club Sports Ground, Rodney Parade), Pentyrch CC (Pentyrch CC, Cricket Ground), Aberystwyth (University College of Wales Sports Ground, Llanbadarn Road), Brecon (Christ College Cricket Ground), Llandudno (The Oval, Gloddaeth Avenue), Merthyr Tydfil (Hoover Sports Ground, Merthyr Road), Llanelli (Stradey Park, Denham Avenue) and BP Llandarcy (BP Oil Llandarcy Refinery Ltd Sports Ground, Crymlyn Bog).
Second XI Grounds: Ammanford CC, Ammanford Park, Ammanford, (01269 594988). Bridgend CC, New Bridge Fields, Bridgend, (01656 663075). BP Llandarcy CC, BP Works Ground, Llandarcy, (01792 813232). Panteg CC, Panteg House, Newport Road, Panteg, (01495 756117). Pontarddulais CC, Pontarddulais Park, Pontarddulais, (01792 882556). Pontymister CC, Cricket Ground, Pontymister, (01633 615071). Usk CC, Cricket Ground, Usk, (01291 33754).

Gloucestershire

Founded: 1871.
Colours: Blue, green, gold, brown, sky-blue and red.
Crest: Coat of arms of the City and County of Bristol.
Patron: HRH The Princess of Wales.
President: J.A. Horne JP.
Chairman: R.W. Rossiter.
Chairman Cricket Committee: C.S.J. Coley.
Chief Executive: P.G.M. August.
Hon Treasurer: N.P. Walters.
Finance Manager: R. Hayman.
Senior Coach: A.W. Stovold.
Assistant Coach: P.W. Romaines.
Youth Coach: G.G.M. Wiltshire.
Marketing Manager: A.J. Brassington.
Captain: R.C. Russell.
Groundsman: D. Brindle.
Scorer: B.H. Jenkins.
Statistician: K. Gerrish.
Sponsors: Carlsberg-Tetley.
Newsletter: *Gloucestershire News.*
Address: Sun Alliance County Cricket Ground, Nevil Road, Bishopston, Bristol, BS7 9EJ.
Telephone: 0117 924 5216.
Facsimile: 0117 924 1193.
Gloucestershire Rapid Cricketline: 0891 567505.
Achievements: County Champions 1874, 1876, 1877; Joint Champions 1873.
Gillette Cup/National Westminster Bank Trophy Winners 1973.
Benson & Hedges Cup Winners 1977.
Sunday League 2nd 1988.
Grounds: Bristol (Sun Alliance County Cricket Ground, Nevil Road), Gloucester (King's School, Archdeacon Meadow) and Cheltenham (College Ground, Thirlestaine Road).
Other Grounds: Moreton-in-Marsh (Moreton Cricket Ground, Batsford Road), Stroud (Eriniod Ground), Tewkesbury (Swilgate), Gloucester (Winget Sports Ground, Tuffley Avenue), Cheltenham Town (Victoria Ground, Prince's Street), Cheltenham Dowty Arle Court (Dowty Arle Court CC, Sir George Dowty Plc Sports Ground), Lydney (Recreational Trust Ground, Swan Road), Swindon (County Ground, County Road), Trowbridge (Trowbridge CC County Cricket Ground, Timbrell Street).
Second XI Grounds: Dowty Arle Court CC, Sir George Dowty Plc Sports & Social Club, Memorial Clubhouse, Hatherley Lane, Arle Court, Cheltenham, Gloucestershire, (01242 533231).

Hampshire

Founded: 12 August 1863.
Colours: Blue, gold and white.
Crest: Tudor rose and crown.
President: W.J. Weld.
Chairman: D. Rich FCA.
Chairman Cricket Committee: J.R. Gray.
Chief Executive: A.F. Baker FCA.
County Coach: T.M. Tremlett.
Assistant Coach: R.E. Hayward.
Marketing Manager: M.N.S. Taylor.
Accountant: J.C.D. Newman.
Captain: M.C.J. Nicholas.
Groundsman: N. Gray.
Scorer: V.H. Isaacs.
Statisticians: V.H. and R.V. Isaacs.
Sponsors: Southern Electric Plc.
Newsletter: *Hampshire News.*

Address: County Cricket Ground, Northlands Road, Southampton, Hampshire SO9 2TY.
Telephone: 01703 333788/333789.
Facsimile: 01703 330121.
Hampshire Rapid Cricketline: 0891 567506.
Achievements: County Champions 1961, 1973.
Gillette Cup/National Westminster Bank Trophy Winners 1991.
Benson & Hedges Cup Winners 1988.
Sunday League Champions 1975, 1978, 1986.
Grounds: Southampton (County Cricket Ground, Northlands Road), Basingstoke (May's Bounty, Bounty Road), Portsmouth (United Services Officers' Sports Ground, St Michael's Road).
Other Grounds: Bournemouth (Dean Park, Cavendish Road).
Second XI Grounds: No additional grounds are used for Second XI matches.

Kent

Founded: 6 December 1870.
Colours: Maroon and white.
Crest: White horse on red background.
Patron: HRH The Duke of Kent KG.
President: J.G. Overy.
Chairman: D.S. Kemp MA.
Chairman Cricket Committee: D. Ufton.
Hon Treasurer: A. Levick.
Secretary: Brig S.T.W. Anderson OBE MC.
Indoor Sports Centre Manager: B.W. Luckhurst.
Marketing Manager: Miss C.L. Benson.
Groundsman: B.A. Fitch.
Ground/Match Manager: P.J. Foster.
Coach/Cricket Manager: D.H. Foster.
Director of Youth Coaching: A.G.E. Ealham.
Physiotherapist: F. Errington.
Captain: M.R. Benson.
Scorer: J. Foley.
Hon Curators: E.W. Swanton/C.H. Taylor.
Statistician: H.R. Milton.
Sponsors: Blue Circle.
Newsletter: *Kent Calling.*
Address: St Lawrence Cricket Ground, Old Dover Road, Canterbury, Kent CT1 3NZ.
Telephone: 01227 456886.
Facsimile: 01227 762168.
Kent Rapid Cricketline: 0891 567507.
Achievements: County Champions 1906, 1909, 1910, 1913, 1970, 1978; Joint Champions 1977.
Gillette Cup/National Westminster Bank Trophy Winners 1967, 1974.
Benson & Hedges Cup Winners 1973, 1976, 1978.
Sunday League Champions 1972, 1973, 1976.
Grounds: Canterbury (St Lawrence Cricket Ground, Old Dover Road), Tunbridge Wells (Nevill Cricket Ground, Warwick Park), Folkestone (Folkestone Sports Ground, Cheriton Road) and Maidstone (Mote Park, Willow Way).
Other Grounds: Blackheath (Rectory Field, Charlton Road), Dover (Crabble Athletic Ground, Lewisham Road), Gillingham (Garrison Ground, Marlborough Road), Gravesend (Bat & Ball Ground, Wrotham Road), New Beckenham (Midland Bank Sports Ground, Lennard Road), Dartford (Hesketh Park, Pilgrims Way).
Second XI Grounds: Dover CC, Crabble Athletic Ground, Lewisham Road, Dover, Kent, (01304 204452). Bowaters Sports Ground, Sittingbourne, Kent, (01795 24411 ext 260). Orpington CC, Sports

Ground, Orpington, Kent, (01689 34902). Gore Court CC, Sports Ground, Sittingbourne, Kent, (01795 23813). Gillingham, Garrison Ground, Marlborough Road, Gillingham, Kent, (01634 281317). British Gas Plc, Sports Ground, Eltham, London, (0181 859 1579). Ashford CC, Cricket Ground, Ashford, Kent, (01233 631315). Dartford CC, Hesketh Park, Dartford, Kent, (01322 225152).

Lancashire

Founded: 12 January 1864.
Colours: Red, green and blue.
Crest: Red rose.
Patron: HM The Queen.
President: Sir Bernard Lovell.
Chairman: R. Bennett.
Chief Executive: J.M. Bower.
Secretary: Miss R.B. Fitzgibbon.
Coach/Cricket Manager: D. Lloyd.
Marketing Manager: J. Cumbes.
Captain: M. Watkinson.
Groundsman: P. Marron.
Physiotherapist: L. Brown.
Dressing Room Attendant: R. Spriggs.
Scorers: W. Davies/M. Proctor.
Statistician/Librarian: Rev M.G. Lorimer.
Museum Curator: K.A. Hayhurst.
Sponsors: Nyrex CableComms.
Newsletter: *Red Rose News.*
Address: Old Trafford Cricket Ground, Talbot Road, Old Trafford, Manchester M16 0PX.
Telephone: 0161 848 7021.
Facsimile: 0161 848 9021.
Lancashire Rapid Cricketline: 0891 567508.
Test Match Commentaries Rapid Cricketline: 0891 567567.
Test Match Updates Rapid Cricketline: 0891 567555.
Achievements: County Champions 1881, 1897, 1904, 1926, 1927, 1928, 1930, 1934; Joint Champions 1879, 1882, 1950.
Gillette Cup/National Westminster Bank Trophy Winners 1970, 1971, 1972, 1975, 1990.
Benson & Hedges Cup Winners 1984, 1990.
Sunday League Champions 1969, 1970, 1989.
Refuge Assurance Cup Winners 1988.
Grounds: Manchester (Old Trafford Cricket Ground, Talbot Road), Liverpool (Aigburth Cricket Ground, Aigburth Road), Southport (Trafalgar Road, Birkdale), Lytham (Church Road, Lytham), Blackpool (Stanley Park, West Park Drive).
Other Grounds: No other grounds have been used since 1969.
Second XI Grounds: Lancaster CC, Lune Road, Lancaster, (01524 65087). Northern CC, Moor Park, Great Crosby, Liverpool, (0151 924 1594). Wigan CC, Bull Hey, Parsons Walk, Wigan, (01942 41581).

Leicestershire

Founded: 25 March 1879.
Colours: Dark green and scarlet.
Crest: Gold running fox on green ground.
President: B.A.F. Smith.
Chairman: J.M. Josephs.
Chairman Cricket Committee: P.R. Haywood.
Chief Executive: A.O. Norman.
Hon Secretary: J.J. Stone.
Hon Treasurer: R. Goadby.
Administrative Secretary: K.P. Hill.
Commercial Manager: M.J. Turner.

Marketing Manager: Miss N.S. Holyoake.
Cricket Manager: J. Birkenshaw.
Captain: N.E. Briers.
Physiotherapist: R. Stenner.
Groundsman: L.A. Spence.
Scorer: G. York.
Hon Curator: J. Barlow.
Statistician: D.A. Lambert.
Sponsors: Mercia Health Benefits.
Newsletter: *Inside Edge.*
Address: County Cricket Ground, Grace Road, Leicester, Leicestershire LE2 8AD.
Telephone: 0116 283 1880/283 2128.
Facsimile: 0116 244 0363.
Leicestershire Rapid Cricketline: 0891 567509.
Achievements: County Champions 1975.
Gillette Cup/National Westminster Bank Trophy Finalists 1992.
Benson & Hedges Cup Winners 1972, 1975, 1985.
Sunday League Champions 1974, 1977.
Ground: Leicester (County Cricket Ground, Grace Road).
Other Grounds: Coalville (Snibston Colliery Ground, Owen Street), Loughborough (Park Road, Loughborough), Hinckley (Hinckley CC, Sports Ground, Leicester Road), Hinckley (Coventry Road).
Second XI Grounds: Market Harborough CC, Cricket Ground, Market Harborough. Uppingham School, School Grounds, Uppingham, Rutland, (No Telephone). Lutterworth CC, Church Street, Lutterworth, (No Telephone). Kidworth CC, Cricket Ground, Kidworth, (No Telephone). Oakham CC, Cricket Ground, Oakham. Hinckley Town CC, Leicester Road, Hinckley, (01455 615336). Barwell CC, Cricket Ground, Barwell.

Middlesex

Founded: 2 February 1864.
Colours: Blue.
Crest: Three seaxes.
Patron: HRH The Prince Philip, Duke of Edinburgh KG KT.
President: D.C.S. Compton CBE.
Chairman: R.V.C. Robins.
Chairman Cricket Committee: R.A. Gale.
Secretary: J. Hardstaff MBE.
Accountant: B.T. Hallworth.
Marketing Manager: R. Clarke.
County Coach: D. Bennett.
Assistant Coach: I.J. Gould.
Physiotherapist: S.M. Shephard.
Groundsmen: M.J. Hunt (Lord's)/R. Ayling (Uxbridge).
Captain: M.W. Gatting MBE.
Scorer: M.J. Smith.
Statistician: E. Solomon.
Sponsors: Panasonic.
Newsletter: *Middlesex Matters.*
Address: Lord's Cricket Ground, St John's Wood Road, London NW8 8QN.
Telephone: 0171 289 1300/1310.
Facsimile: 0171 289 5831.
Middlesex Rapid Cricketline: 0891 567510.
Achievements: County Champions 1866, 1903, 1920, 1921, 1947, 1976, 1980, 1982, 1985, 1990, 1993; Joint Champions 1949, 1977.
Gillette Cup/National Westminster Bank Trophy Winners 1977, 1980, 1984, 1988.
Benson & Hedges Cup Winners 1983, 1986.
Sunday League Champions 1992.

Refuge Assurance Cup Winners 1990.
Grounds: London (Lord's Cricket Ground, St John's Wood Road), Uxbridge (Uxbridge CC, Gatting Way, Park Road).
Other Grounds: Enfield (Enfield CC, Lincoln Road, Enfield), Southgate (Southgate CC, The Walker Cricket Ground, Waterfall Road), Watford (Watford Town CC, Woodside, Garston, Watford).
Second XI Grounds: Birkbeck College (University of London), Birkbeck Avenue, Oldfield Lane, Greenford, (0181 578 1930). Ealing CC, Crofton Road, Ealing, London W5, (0181 997 1858). Enfield CC, Lincoln Road, Enfield, Middx, (0181 363 2841). Finchley CC, East End Road, Finchley, London N3 (adjoining Middlesex CCC Indoor Cricket School/Squash Centre), (0181 346 1822). Harefield CC, Breakspear Road, North Harefield, Middx, (01895 822225). Harrow CC, Wood End Road, Harrow, Middx, (0181 422 0932). Lensbury Club, Broom Road, Teddington, Middx, (0181 977 8821). Old Actonians CC, Gunnersbury Drive, Ealing, London W5, (0181 567 4556). Old Merchant Taylors CC, Durrants Sports Ground, Croxley Green, Rickmansworth, (01923 773014). Potters Bar CC, The Walk, Potters Bar, Herts, (01707 54801). RAF Sports Ground, Vine Lane, Uxbridge, Middx, (01895 37144). Richmond CC, Old Deer Park, Kew Road, Richmond, Surrey, (0181 940 2520). Southgate CC, The Walker Cricket Ground, Waterfall Road, Southgate, London N14, (0181 886 8381). South Hampstead CC, Milverton Road, Hampstead, London NW6, (0181 459 2801). St Albans CC, Clarence Park, Clarence Road, St Albans, Herts, (01727 50388). Watford Town CC, Woodside, Garston, Watford, Herts, (01923 679589). Winchmore Hill CC, Ford's Grove, Winchmore Hill, London N21, (0181 360 1271). Shenley Park, Radlett Lane, Shenley, Herts, (01923 859022).

Northamptonshire

Founded: 31 July 1878.
Colours: Maroon.
Crest: Tudor rose.
Patrons: The Earl of Dalkeith/The Earl Spencer.
President: W.R.F. Chamberlain.
Chairman: L.A. Wilson.
Hon Treasurer: T.W. Baughen.
Chairman Cricket Committee: R. Wills.
Chief Executive: S.P. Coverdale MA, LlB.
County Coach: R.M. Carter.
Cricket Development Officer: B.L. Reynolds.
Captain: A.J. Lamb.
Medical Officer: Dr J.A.G.D. Raphael.
Physiotherapist: K. Russell.
Groundsman: R. Bailey.
Scorer: A. Kingston.
Statistician: L.T. Newell.
Sponsors: Carlsberg-Tetley.
Newsletter: *Tudor Rose Clippings.*
Address: County Cricket Ground, Wantage Road, Northampton, Northamptonshire NN1 4NJ.
Telephone: 01604 232917.
Facsimile: 01604 232855.
Northamptonshire Rapid Cricketline: 0891 567511.
Achievements: County Championship 2nd 1912, 1957, 1965, 1976.
Gillette Cup/National Westminster Bank Trophy Winners 1976, 1992.
Benson & Hedges Cup Winners 1980.
Sunday League 3rd 1991.

Grounds: Northampton (County Cricket Ground, Wantage Road), Luton (Wardown Park, Old Bedford Road).
Other Grounds: Peterborough (Baker Perkins Sports Ground), Peterborough Town CC (Bretton Gate, Westwood), Kettering (Kettering CC, Northampton Road), Wellingborough (Wellingborough School, Irthlingborough Road), Brackley (Brackley CC, off Buckingham Road), Bedford (Bedford School, Burnaby Road), Milton Keynes (Bletchley CC, Manor Fields, Bletchley), Tring (Pound Meadow, Station Road), Finedon (Dolben Cricket Ground, Avenue Road) and Horton (Horton House CC, Horton).
Second XI Grounds: Oundle School, School Ground, Oundle, (No Telephone). Bedford School, Burnaby Road, Bedford, (01234 353435 – school hours only). Old Northamptonians CC, Cricket Ground, Northampton. Peterborough Town CC, Bretton Gate, Westwood, Peterborough, Cambs, (01733 262202). Great Oakley CC, Cricket Ground, Great Oakley, (No Telephone). Bedford Modern School, School Grounds, Bedford, (No Telephone). Banbury Twenty Club, Daventry Road, Banbury, Oxon, (01295 263757). Tring Park CC, Station Road, Tring, Herts, (01442 823080). Wellingborough School, Irthlingborough Road, Wellingborough, (01933 222427).

Nottinghamshire

Founded: March/April 1841.
Colours: Green and gold.
Crest: Coat of arms of the City of Nottingham.
President: C.F. Ward CBE.
Chairman: A. Wheelhouse.
Chairman Cricket Committee: R.T. Simpson.
Secretary/General Manager: B. Robson.
Senior Coach: J.A. Ormrod.
Cricket Development Manager: J.H.C. Cope.
PR Executive: C.S. Slater.
Commercial Manager: S.B. Hasson.
Marketing Manager: M.A. Arthur.
Marketing Executive: J.J. Ellison.
Marketing Administrator: Mrs P. Smith.
Captain: R.T. Robinson.
Groundsman: R. Allsopp.
Scorer: G. Stringfellow.
Librarian/Statistician: Peter Wynne-Thomas.
Sponsors: Carling.
Newsletter: *Trent Bridge Monthly.*
Address: County Cricket Ground, Trent Bridge, West Bridgford, Nottingham, Nottinghamshire NG2 6AG.
Telephone: 0115 982 1525.
Facsimile: 0115 945 5730.
Nottinghamshire Rapid Cricketline: 0891 567512.
Test Match Commentaries Rapid Cricketline: 0891 567567.
Test Match Updates Rapid Cricketline: 0891 567500.
Achievements: County Champions 1865, 1868, 1871, 1872, 1875, 1880, 1883, 1885, 1886, 1907, 1929, 1981, 1987; Joint Champions 1869, 1873, 1879, 1882, 1889.
Gillette Cup/National Westminster Bank Trophy Winners 1987.
Benson & Hedges Cup Winners 1989.
Sunday League Champions 1991.
Grounds: Nottingham (Trent Bridge, West Bridgford), Cleethorpes (Cleethorpes CC, Chichester Road), Worksop (Worksop Town CC, Town Ground, Central Avenue).
Other Grounds: Nottingham (John Player & Sons Sports Ground, Aspley Lane), Newark-On-Trent (RHP Limited Sports Ground, Elm Avenue).

Second XI Grounds: Caythorpe CC, Sports Ground, Caythorpe, Nottingham, (0115 966 3132). Farnsfield CC, Station Lane, Farnsfield, Mansfield, Notts, (01623 882986). Steetley Ironworks CC, Sports Ground, Shireoaks, Near Worksop, Notts, (01909 480682). Worksop College, Worksop, Notts, (01909 472286). Worthington Simpson Sports Ground, Lowfield Lane, Balderton, Newark-On-Trent, Notts, (01636 702672). Clipstone Welfare CC, Seventh Avenue, Mansfield, Notts, (01623 636590). Collingham CC, Dale Field, Collingham, Notts, (01636 892921). John Player's Athletic Club, Sports Ground, Aspley Lane, Nottingham, (0115 929 4244). Southwell CC, Brackenhurst Farm College, Southwell, Notts, (No Telephone). Sleaford CC, London Road, Sleaford, Lincs, (01529 303368). Nottingham High School, Valley Road, Nottingham, (0115 960 5605).

Somerset

Founded: 18 August 1875.
Colours: Black, white and maroon.
Crest: Wessex Wyvern.
Chairman: J. Luff.
Chairman Cricket Committee: B.C. Rose..
Chief Executive: P.W. Anderson.
Hon Treasurer: R. O'Donnell.
Marketing Manager: Mrs G. Tesser.
Director of Cricket: R.M.H. Cottam.
Senior Coach: P.J. Robinson.
Schools Coach: J.G. Wyatt.
Captain: A.N. Hayhurst.
Groundsman: P. Frost.
Hon Medical Officer: P.L.B. Squire MB BS.
Scorer: D.A. Oldham.
Statisticians: M.F. Hill/N. Johns.
Sponsors: Taunton Cider.
Newsletter: *Somerset News.*
Address: The County Ground, St James's Street, Taunton, Somerset TA1 1JT.
Telephone: 01823 272946.
Facsimile: 01823 332395.
Somerset Rapid Cricketline: 0891 567513.
Achievements: County Championship 3rd 1892, 1958, 1963, 1966, 1981.
Gillette Cup/National Westminster Bank Trophy Winners 1979, 1983.
Benson & Hedges Cup Winners 1981, 1982.
Sunday League Champions 1979.
Grounds: Taunton (The County Ground, St James's Street), Bath (Recreation Ground, William Street), Weston-Super-Mare (Clarence Park, Walliscote Road).
Other Grounds: Bristol (Imperial Ground, West Town Lane), Yeovil (Westland Sports Ground, Westbourne Close), Yeovil (Johnson Park, Boundary Close), Glastonbury (Morlands Athletic Sports Ground, Street Road), Torquay (Recreation Ground), Weston-Super-Mare (Devonshire Road Park Ground), Brislington (Ironmold Lane), Street (Millfield School), Frome (Agricultural Showgrounds).
Second XI Grounds: North Perrott CC, Cricket Ground, North Perrott, Near Crewkerne, (No Telephone). Glastonbury CC, Tor Leisure Centre, 7 Street Road, Glastonbury, (01458 32393). Clevedon CC, Esmond Grove, Clevedon, (0117 987 7585). Weston-Super-Mare CC, Devonshire Park Road, Weston-Super-Mare, Somerset, (No Telephone). Winscombe CC, Recreation Ground, Winscombe, (0193484 2720). Westland's Sports CC, Westbourne Close, Preston Grove, Yeovil, (01935 703619). Bristol Imperial Ground, West Town Lane, Bristol, (0117 977 6659).

Surrey

Founded: 22 August 1845.
Colours: Chocolate and silver.
Crest: Prince of Wales' Feathers.
Patron: HM The Queen.
President: J.M. Poland.
Chairman: B.G.K. Downing.
Chairman Cricket Committee: J.A. Fulford.
Chief Executive: G.A. Woodman.
Marketing Director: M.S. Newton.
Director of Cricket: M.J. Edwards.
County Coach: G.S. Clinton.
Assistant Coach: G.R. Dilley.
Captain: A.J. Stewart.
Groundsman: P.D. Brind.
Finance Manager: M. Brown.
Stadium Manager: A.J. Green.
Scorer/Statistician: K.R. Booth.
Sponsor: Foster's.
Newsletter: *Around The Foster's Oval.*
Address: The Foster's Oval, Kennington, London SE11 5SS.
Telephone: 0171 582 6660.
Facsimile: 0171 582 7769.
Ticket Office: 0171 582 7764.
Surrey Rapid Cricketline: 0891 567514.
Test Match Commentaries Rapid Cricketline: 0891 567567.
Test Match Updates Rapid Cricketline: 0891 567555.
Achievements: County Champions 1864, 1887, 1888, 1890, 1891, 1892, 1894, 1895, 1899, 1914, 1952, 1953, 1954, 1955, 1956, 1957, 1958, 1971; Joint Champions 1889, 1950.
Gillette Cup/National Westminster Bank Trophy Winners 1982.
Benson & Hedges Cup Winners 1974.
Sunday League 5th 1969, 1980, 1988, 1989.
Grounds: London (The Foster's Oval, Kennington) and Guildford (Guildford CC, Woodbridge Road).
Other Grounds: Byfleet (BAC Ground, Byfleet), Sunbury-On-Thames (Kenton Court Meadow, Lower Hampton Road), Leatherhead (Leatherhead CC, Cricket Ground), Leatherhead (St John's School), Sutton (Cheam Road), Godalming (Charterhouse School), Tolworth (Decca Sports Ground), East Molesey (Metropolitan Police Sports Ground, Imber Court) and Banstead (Banstead CC, Avenue Road).
Second XI Grounds: Banstead CC, Avenue Road, Banstead, Surrey, (01737 358838). National Westminster Bank Sports Ground, Turle Road, Norbury, Surrey, (Pavilion – 0181 764 1170; Office – 0181 679 5638). Oxted CC, Master Park, Oxted, Surrey, (01883 712792). Wimbledon CC, Church Road, Wimbledon, London SW19, (0181 946 7403). Bank of England Sports Ground, Priory Lane, Roehampton, London SW15, (0181 876 8417). Purley CC, The Ridge, off Foxley Lane, Purley, Surrey, (0181 660 0608). Cheam CC, Station Way, Cheam, Surrey, (0181 642 1817).

Sussex

Founded: 1 March 1839.
Colours: Dark blue, light blue and gold.
Crest: County arms of six martlets (in shape of inverted pyramid).
President: The Duke of Richmond and Gordon FCA.
Chairman: A.M. Caffyn.
Secretary: N. Bett.

County Coach: N. Gifford MBE.
Assistant Coaches: C.E. Waller and P. Cale.
Youth Development Officer: I.C. Waring.
Director of Marketing: R. Griffiths.
Marketing Manager: J.M. Parks.
Assistant Marketing: M.J. Charman.
Captain: A.P. Wells.
Groundsman: P.J. Eaton.
Physiotherapist: S. Robertson.
Scorer: L.V. Chandler.
Statistician/Librarian: H.O. Osborne.
Sponsors: Merrydown Wine Plc.
Newsletter: *Hove and Away.*
Address: County Ground, Eaton Road, Hove, East Sussex BN3 3AN.
Telephone: 01273 732161.
Facsimile: 01273 771549.
Sussex Rapid Cricketline: 0891 567515.
Achievements: County Championship 2nd 1902, 1903, 1932, 1933, 1934, 1953, 1981.
Gillette Cup/National Westminster Bank Trophy Winners 1963, 1964, 1978, 1986.
Benson & Hedges Cup Semi-Finalists 1982.
Sunday League Champions 1982.
Grounds: Hove (County Ground, Eaton Road), Horsham (Horsham CC, Cricket Field Road), Eastbourne (Eastbourne Saffrons Sports Club, The Saffrons), Arundel Castle (The Friends of Arundel Castle CC, Arundel Park).
Other Grounds: Pagham (Pagham CC, Nyetimber Lane, Pagham), Hastings (Central Cricket Ground, Priory Meadow).
Second XI Grounds: Hastings and St Leonards Priory CC, Central Cricket and Recreation Ground, Priory Meadow, Queens Road, Hastings, East Sussex, (01424 424546). Hurstpierpoint College, College Grounds, off Malthouse Lane, Hurstpierpoint, (01273 833636). Chichester Priory Park CC, Priory Park, Priory Lane, Chichester, West Sussex. Eastbourne College, College Grounds, Eastbourne, (01323 37411). Brighton College, College Grounds, Brighton, (01273 697136). Lewes Priory CC, The Stanley Turner Ground, Kingston Road, Lewes, (01273 473732). Sidley CC, Cricket Ground, Sidley, (01424 217078). Haywards Heath CC, Perrymount Road, Haywards Heath, (01444 451384).

Warwickshire
Founded: 8 April 1882.
Colours: Blue, gold and silver.
Crest: Bear and ragged staff.
President: The Rt Hon The Earl of Aylesford KStJ JP, Her Majesty's Lord Lieutenant for the County of West Midlands.
Chairman: M.J.K. Smith OBE.
Chief Executive: D.L. Amiss MBE.
Assistant Secretary (Cricket): A.S.M. Oakman.
Hon Treasurer: W.N. Houghton FCA.
Cricket Development Officer: R.M. Cox.
Director of Coaching: P.A. Neale.
Accountant: A. Wilkes.
Marketing Manager: S. Edwards.
Coach/Youth Cricket Organiser: R.N. Abberley.
Captain: D.A. Reeve.
Club Superintendent: M. White.
Physiotherapist: S.J. Nottingham.
Groundsman: S.J. Rouse.
Scorer: A.E. Davis.
Statisticians: R.W. Brooke/T.M.K. Walton.
Museum Curator: K. Kelly.

Team Sponsor: Brew XI.
Club Sponsors: Peugeot.
Newsletter: *Beyond the Boundary.*
Address: County Cricket Ground, Edgbaston, Birmingham, West Midlands B5 7QU.
Telephone: 0121 446 4422.
Facsimile: 0121 446 4544.
Warwickshire Rapid Cricketline: 0891 567516.
Test Match Commentaries Rapid Cricketline: 0891 567567.
Test Match Updates Rapid Cricketline: 0891 567555.
Achievements: County Championship Champions 1911, 1951, 1972, 1994.
Gillette Cup/National Westminster Bank Trophy Winners 1966, 1968, 1989, 1993.
Benson & Hedges Cup Winners 1994.
Sunday League Champions 1980, 1994.
Ground: Birmingham (County Ground, Edgbaston).
Other Grounds: Coventry (Courtaulds Sports Ground, Lockhurst Lane), Coventry (Coventry & North Warwickshire CC, Bulls Head Ground), Nuneaton (Griff & Coton Sports Ground, Heath End Road).
Second XI Grounds: Aston CC, Cricket Ground, Aston, Birmingham, West Midlands, (0121 308 6638). Knowle & Dorridge CC, Knowle, Warwicks, (01564 774338). Leamington Town CC, Arlington Avenue, Leamington Spa, Warwicks, (01926 423854). Mitchells & Butlers CC, Portland Road, Birmingham, West Midlands, (0121 429 2467). Moseley CC, Moseley, Birmingham, West Midlands, (0121 744 5694). Old Edwardians CC, Solihull, Birmingham, West Midlands, (0121 744 6831). Solihull CC, Solihull, West Midlands, (0121 705 5271). Stratford-On-Avon CC, Stratford-On-Avon, Warwicks, (01789 297968). Studley CC, Studley, Warwicks, (01527 853668). Walmley CC, Walmley, West Midlands, (0121 351 1349).

Worcestershire
Founded: 11 March 1865.
Colours: Dark green and black.
Crest: Shield argent bearing fess between three pears sable.
Patron: His Grace The Duke of Westminster.
President: T.W. Graveney OBE.
Chairman: C.D. Fearnley.
Chairman Cricket Committee: M.G. Jones.
Secretary: Rev M.D. Vockins.
Hon Treasurer: P. Seward.
County Coach: D.L. Houghton.
Cricket Development Officer: M.S. Scott.
Public Relations Officer: B.L. D'Oliveira.
Marketing Manager: J. Osborne.
Captain: T.S. Curtis.
Physiotherapist: J. Smith MCSP, SRP.
Groundsman: R. McLaren.
Scorer: J.W. Sewter.
Statistician: L.W. Hatton.
Sponsors: Powerline.
Newsletter: *Worcestershire Members Newsletter.*
Address: County Cricket Ground, New Road, Worcester, Worcestershire WR2 4QQ.
Telephone: 01905 748474.
Facsimile: 01905 748005.
Worcestershire Rapid Cricketline: 0891 567517.
Achievements: County Champions 1964, 1965, 1974, 1988, 1989
Gillette Cup/National Westminster Bank Trophy Winners 1994.
Benson & Hedges Cup Winners 1991.

Sunday League Champions 1971, 1987, 1988
Refuge Assurance Cup Winners 1991.
Grounds: Worcester (County Cricket Ground, New Road), Kidderminster (Offmore Lane, Chester Road).
Other Grounds: Dudley (The County Ground, Tipton Road), Stourbridge (Stourbridge War Memorial Ground, Amblecote), Stourport-On-Seven (Parsons Controls Holdings Limited, The Chainwire Club Sports Ground, Minister Road), Halesowen (Halesowen CC, Sports Ground, Grange Road), Hereford (Racecourse Ground, Grandstand Road).
Second XI Grounds: Halesowen CC, Grange Road/Dog Kennel Lane, Halesowen, West Midlands, (0121 550 2744). Old Hill CC, Haden Hill Park, Cradley Heath, West Midlands, (01384 66827). Ombersley CC, Cricket Ground, Ombersley, Near Kidderminster, (No Telephone). Stourbridge CC, Stourbridge War Memorial Ground, Amblecote, Stourbridge, West Midlands. Royal Grammar School Worcester, Flagge Meadow, Worcester, (No Telephone). Barnt Green CC, Cherry Hill Road, Barnt Green, West Midlands (0121 445 1684).

Yorkshire
Founded: 1863.
Colours: Oxford blue, Cambridge blue and gold.
Crest: White rose of Yorkshire.
Patron: HRH The Duchess of Kent.
President: Sir Lawrence Byford CBE QPM LLD DL.
Chairman: B. Walsh QC.
Chairman Cricket Committee: D.B. Close CBE.
Chief Executive: C.D. Hassell.
Assistant Secretary: D.M. Ryder.
Marketing Executive: Ms D. Betts.
Director of Cricket: S. Oldham.
Club Coach: D.E.V. Padgett.
Academy Coach: M.K. Bore.
Captain: M.D. Moxon.
Physiotherapist: W. Morton.
Groundsman: K. Boyce.
Scorer: J.T. Potter.
Statisticians: R.D. Wilkinson/M. Pope.
Museum Curator/Librarian: A. Woodhouse.
Sponsors: Joshua Tetley & Son.
Newsletter: *The White Rose.*
Address: Bass Headingley Cricket Ground, St Michael's Lane, Headingley, Leeds, West Yorkshire LS6 3BU.
Telephone: 0113 278 7394.
Facsimile: 0113 278 4099.
Yorkshire Rapid Cricketline: 0891 567518.
Test Match Commentaries Rapid Cricketline: 0891 567567.
Test Match Updates Rapid Cricketline: 0891 567555.
Achievements: County Champions 1867, 1870, 1893, 1896, 1898, 1900-02, 1905, 1908, 1912, 1919, 1922-25, 1931-33, 1935, 1937-39, 1946, 1959-60, 1962-63, 1966-68; Joint Champions 1869, 1949.
Gillette Cup/National Westminster Bank Trophy Winners 1965, 1969.
Benson & Hedges Cup Winners 1987.
Sunday League Champions 1983.
Grounds: Leeds (Bass Headingley Cricket Ground, St Michael's Lane), Bradford (Yorkshire Cricket Academy, Park Avenue), Sheffield (Abbeydale Park, Abbeydale Park Road South, Dore), Middlesbrough (Middlesbrough CC, Acklam Park, Green Lane), Harrogate (Harrogate CC, St George's Road), Scarborough (Scarborough CC, North Marine Road).
Other Grounds: Huddersfield (Fartown), Sheffield (Bramall Lane), Hull (The Circle, Anlaby Road), Barnsley (Shaw Lane).
Second XI Grounds: Bingley and Bingley CC, Waggon Lane, Cottingley Bridge, Bingley, (01274 563480). Sheffield United CC, Bawtry Road Ground, Sheffield, (0114 243 1099). Todmorden CC, Centre Vale, Burnley Road, Todmorden, (01706 813140). York CC, Clifton Park, Shipton Road, York, (01904 623602). Marske-By-Sea CC, Windy Hill Lane, Marske-By-Sea, (01642 484361). Elland Cricket Athletic and Bowling Club, Hullen Edge, Elland, Leeds, (01422 372682).

Cambridge University
Founded: 1820.
Colours: Pale blue.
Crest: University crest.
President: Lord Butterfield (Downing).
Hon Secretary: C. Pitcher, Selwyn College, Cambridge CB3 9DQ. (01223 332100).
Fixture Secretary: Dr J. Edwards, Faculty of Economics and Politics, Sidgwick Avenue, Cambridge CB3 9DD. (01223 335220).
Hon Treasurer: Prof K. Siddle, Department of Clinical Biochemistry, Level 4, Laboratory Block, Addenbrooke's Hospital, Hills Road, Cambridge CB2 2QR. (01223 336789).
Cricket Coach: G.J. Saville.
Captain: A.R. Whittall.
Groundsman: A. Pocock.
Scorer/Statistician: A.R. May.
Sponsors: University Arms Hotel, Cambridge.
Address: Cambridge University Cricket Club, Fenner's University Cricket Ground, Wollaston Road, off Mortimer Road, Cambridge, Cambridgeshire.
Telephone: 01223 353552.
County Scores Rapid Cricketline: 0891 567500.
Achievements: Varsity Match: Winners on 53 occasions.
Benson & Hedges Cup Quarter-Finalists 1990 as Combined Universities.
Ground: Cambridge (Fenner's University Cricket Ground).
Other Grounds: No other grounds have been used for matches.

Oxford University
Founded: 1800.
Colours: Dark blue.
Crest: Two crowns above OUCC.
President: M.J.K. Smith OBE (St Edmund Hall).
Senior Treasurer and Fixture Secretary: S.R. Porter MA DPhil, Nuffield College, Oxford, Oxfordshire OX1 1NF. (01865 278500).
Assistant Secretary: P.G.B. James.
Cricket Coach: L.J. Lenham.
Captain: G.I. Macmillan.
Groundsman: R. Sula.
Scorer/Statistician: G.S. Gordon.
Newsletter: *OUCC News.*
Address: Oxford University Cricket Club, The Pavilion, The University Parks, Oxford, Oxfordshire.
Telephone: 01865 57106.
Rapid Cricketline County Scores: 0891 567500.
Achievements: Varsity Match: Winners on 47 occasions.
Benson & Hedges Cup Quarter-Finalists 1990 (as Combined Universities).
Ground: Oxford (The University Parks).
Other Grounds: Christ Church College Cricket Ground,

Iffley Road, Oxford, (01865 243992) – occasionally used in addition to The Parks.

Minor Counties Cricket Association

Founded: 1895.
Colours: Red, silver and black.
Crest: White horse.
President: V.M.E. Holt DL.
Chairman: J.E.O. Smith MBE.
Secretary/Team Secretary/Statistician: D.J.M. Armstrong.
Captain: I. Cockbain.
Scorer: A.J. Pearce.
Address: Thorpe Cottage, Mill Common, Ridlington, North Walsham, Norfolk NR28 9TY.
Telephone: 01692 650563.
Minor Counties Rapid Cricketline: 0891 567519.
Achievements: Benson & Hedges Cup Zonal Group Stage:-
Minor Counties (North) 1972-75, 1979.
Minor Counties (South) 1972-75, 1979.
Minor Counties (East) 1976-78.
Minor Counties (West) 1976-78.
Minor Counties C.A. 1980-1994.
Grounds: Used for staging home matches against touring sides and in the Benson & Hedges Cup Zonal Rounds:- Reading CC (Sonning Lane, off London Road), Leek Town CC (Highfield, Macclesfield Road), Newcastle-Upon-Tyne (Northumberland CCC, Jesmond Cricket Ground).
Other Grounds: Torquay CC, Trowbridge CC, Darlington CC, Finchampstead CC, Old Hill CC (Cradley Heath), Oxford (Christ Church College Cricket Ground), Slough CC, Walsall CC, Shrewsbury CC, Reading Cricket & Hockey Club, Bowdon CC, Wellington CC, Watford Town CC, Chippenham CC, High Wycombe CC, Lincoln CC, Ipswich CC, Chesham CC, Norwich CC (Lakenham), Amersham CC (Shardeloes), Longton CC (Trentham Road, Blurton), Bedford Town CC, Stoke-On-Trent CC (County Ground), Scunthorpe & Appleby Frodingham Works CC, Macclesfield CC, Marlow CC, Stone CC, Swindon CC, Chester-le-Street CC (Ropery Lane), Cheadle CC, Plymouth CC (Peverell Park), Cleethorpes CC, Chester Boughton Hall CC, Oxton CC (Birkenhead).
Second XI Grounds: Walsall CC, Cricket Ground, Walsall, West Midlands, (01922 22094). Sleaford CC, London Road, Sleaford, Lincs, (01529 303368). Northampton Saints CC, Cricket Ground, Northampton. Marlow CC, Pound Lane, Marlow, Bucks, (016284 83638).

Friends of Arundel Castle

Colours: Dark Blue.
Crest: Red Baskerville 'N'.
Secretary: Miss D. Osborne, Friends of Arundel Castle Cricket Club, The Cricket Office, Arundel Park, Arundel, West Sussex BN18 9LH.
Telephone: 01903 882462.
Scorer: Mrs K. Cohen.
Groundsman: P. Eaton.
Rapid Cricketline County Scores: 0891 567500.
Ground: Castle Park, Arundel. No other grounds have been used for matches.

Scottish Cricket Union

Founded: 1909, previous Scottish Cricket Union existed 1880-83.

Colours: Blue and white.
Crest: Thistle.
President: J.R. Laing.
Chairman: C.H. Carruthers.
Secretary: R.W. Barclay.
General Manager: A.J. Ritchie.
Administrator/Captain: J.D. Love.
Scorer/Statistician: N.J. Leitch.
Address: Caledonia House, South Gyle, Edinburgh EH12 9DQ.
Telephone: 0131 317 7247.
Facsimile: 0131 317 7103.
Rapid Cricketline County Scores: 0891 567500.
Achievements: Benson & Hedges Cup Zonal Round/1st Round 1980-94.
National Westminster Bank Trophy 1st Round 1983-94.
Grounds: Glasgow (Teacher's Clydesdale CC, Titwood, Pollokshields), Glasgow (West of Scotland CRGP CC, Hamilton Cresent, Partick), Forfar (Strathmore County CC, Lochside Park), Edinburgh (Grange CC, Raeburn Place).
Other Grounds: Aberdeenshire CC, Mannofield, Morningside Road, Aberdeen AB1 7NB, (01224 317888). Ayr CC, Cambusdoon, Alloway, Ayr, (01292 42296). Drumpellier CC, Langloan, Coatbridge, (01236 23713). Dumfries CC, Nunholm, Nunholm Road, Dumfries DG1 1JW, (01387 52527). Forfarshire CC Forthill, Broughty Ferry, Dundee, (01382 75550). Greenock CC, Glenpark, Brisbane Street, Greenock, (01475 24037). Kelburne CC, Whitehaugh, Paisley, Glasgow, (0141 889 4844). Perth County CC, Gannochy Sports Pavilion, The North Inch, Perth, (01738 23852). Stenhousemuir CC, The Tryst, Stenhousemuir, Larbert, (01324 562448). Watsonians CC, Myreside, Myreside Road, Edinburgh, (0131 447 5200).

Irish Cricket Union

Founded: 1859.
Colours: Green.
Crest: Shamrock.
President: K.F. O'Riordan.
Chairman: F.A. Malin.
Hon Secretary/Statistician: D. Scott.
Manager: J. Boyce.
Director of Coaching: V.F. Savino.
Captain: P.B. Jackson.
Scorer: E.M. Power.
Address: 45 Foxrock Park, Foxrock, Dublin 18, Republic of Ireland.
Telephone: 010 3531 289 3943 (Home/Fax), 010 3531 679 3661 (Office).
Facsimile: 010 3531 679 8837.
Rapid Cricketline County Scores: 0891 567500.
Achievements: Gillette Cup/National Westminster Bank Trophy 1st Round 1980-94.
Grounds: Clontarf Cricket Club, The Pavilion, Castle Avenue, Clontarf, Dublin 3, (010 3531 332 6214). Downpatrick CC, Stangford Road, Downpatrick, (010 3531 612869). Malahide CC, Malahide Cricket Ground, Castle Avenue, Malahide, Co Dublin, (010 3531 450607). Leinster CC, Observatory Lane, Rathmines, Dublin 6, (010 3531 972428). North of Ireland CC, Ormeau Cricket Ground, Ormeau Road, Belfast 7, (01232 221096). Coleraine CC, Lodge Road, Coleraine, Co Derry, (01265 3972). Carlisle CC, Kimmage, Dublin, (010 3531 555490). Eglinton CC, 2 Woodvale Road, Eglinton, Co Derry, (01504 810250). North Down CC, Comber, Co Down, (01247 878306).